The White West

The White West

Fascism, Unreason, and the Paradox of Modernity

Edited by Kader Attia, Anselm Franke & Ana Teixeira Pinto

Sternberg Press

Whose Universal?

War Ecologies

Aesthetic Currencies

Automating Apartheid

Preface

The "White West" project began with a conference organized in May 2018 by Kader Attia, Ana Teixeira Pinto, and Giovanna Zapperi at a forum in Paris for decolonial debate run by Kader Attia, with contributions by Larne Abse Gogarty, Florian Cramer, Angela Dimitrakaki, Quinsy Gario, Ferenc Gróf, Léopold Lambert, Sven Lütticken, Olivier Marboeuf, Pascale Obolo, Natascha Sadr Haghighian, and Marina Vishmidt. We titled the conference "The Resurgence of Fascism as a Cultural Force," since widespread opinion found the current usage of the term fascism "alarmist" and "imprecise." These responses made us aware of how poorly understood the term had become and spurred the urge to reengage it.

In collaboration with La Colonie, Kader Attia and Ana Teixeira Pinto organized a second conference in June 2019. Named after a 2017 essay by Nikhil Pal Singh, "The Afterlife of Fascism," it examined the recurring elements of fascism in contemporary society. For this event, the speakers included Norman Ajari, Denise Ferreira da Silva, Sven Lütticken, Revital Madar, Karine Parrot, Rijin Sahakian, Nikhil Pal Singh, Françoise Vergès, and Louisa Yousfi. A third conference, "Automating Apartheid," took place in January 2020 at the Kunsthalle Wien in Vienna by invitation of the directors What, How & for Whom/WHW (Ivet Ćurlin, Nataša Ilić, and Sabina Sabolović), with contributions by Florian Cramer, Radhika Desai, David Golumbia, Marina Gržinić, Rose-Anne Gush, Zakiyyah Iman Jackson, Nitzan Lebovic, Olivier Marboeuf, Ciraj Rassool, Dorcy Rugamba, Kalpana Seshadri, and Felix Stalder.

Together with Anselm Franke and the Haus der Kulturen der Welt (HKW) in Berlin, a fourth event was programmed. Titled "Whose Universal?," the conference was meant to examine the paradox at the heart of modernity regarding who is included and excluded in systems of justice, but it was unfortunately derailed by the COVID-19 crisis. Instead, we organized a podcast with a range of conversation partners: Norman Ajari, Ramon Amaro, Paola Bacchetta, Florian Cramer, Denise Ferreira da Silva, Priyamvada Gopal, Barnor Hesse, Max Jorge Hinderer Cruz, Donna V. Jones, Rajkamal Kahlon, David Lloyd, Olivier Marboeuf,

A. Dirk Moses, Prabhat Patnaik and Utsa Patnaik, Nikhil Pal Singh, Felix Stalder, and Françoise Vergès. A scaled-down version of the conference, with Norman Ajari, A. Dirk Moses, Nikhil Pal Singh, and Françoise Vergès, took place at HKW in July 2021.

A last event was organized in collaboration with the 12th Berlin Biennale, curated by Kader Attia, and took place in July 2022. Inspired by Siraj Ahmed's book *The Stillbirth of Capital* (2012), the first part of this event looked at the feedback loop between sovereign power and military commerce, and its ties to what the sociologist Andre Gunder Frank calls "the development of underdevelopment": the active process of restricting the periphery's development to benefit the imperial centers. The second part was devoted to removing the sublime, and adjacent categories like the exotic and the grotesque, from their pristine post-Enlightenment lineage—a history of aesthetic ideas that purport to exist without any messy entanglements at sites of imperial extraction or expansion—and to examine the disturbing conflation of embodied and encultured experience that the discourse of philosophical aesthetics engenders. The contributors were Siraj Ahmed, Sladja Blazan, Katrine Dirckinck-Holmfeld, Priyamvada Gopal, Max Jorge Hinderer Cruz, Zakiyyah Iman Jackson, A. Dirk Moses, Prabhat Patnaik and Utsa Patnaik, Rasha Salti, Kerstin Stakemeier, and Françoise Vergès.

The present publication is a result of the conference series, and we are deeply thankful to all who have contributed to it, as well as to all the brilliant speakers who generously contributed to the "White West" events. We would also like to thank Susanne Wagner, Agnes Wegner, June Drevet, Alix Hugonnier, WHW (Ivet Ćurlin, Nataša Ilić, and Sabina Sabolović), and Bernd Scherer for affording us the possibility to realize the conference series, the podcast, and this publication.

—Kader Attia, Anselm Franke, and Ana Teixeira Pinto

Scan this code to access the *White West* podcast series:

Introduction
Unreason and Modernity

Anselm Franke and Ana Teixeira Pinto

> It is on the basis of a distinction between reason and unreason (passion, fantasy) that late-modern criticism has been able to articulate a certain idea of the political [...]. Within this paradigm, reason is the truth of the subject and politics is the exercise of reason in the public sphere. The exercise of reason is tantamount to the exercise of freedom, a key element for individual autonomy. The romance of sovereignty, in this case, rests on the belief that the subject is the master and the controlling author of his or her own meaning.
> —Achille Mbembe, "Necropolitics"

Since the election of far-right leaders like Donald Trump and Jair Bolsonaro, liberals have tried to put a name to what they are defending from these illiberal heads of state. "Reason" is what most commentators often settle for, with our present moment variously called the "post-truth era" or the "age of unreason." But haunting each of these formulations is the specter of a problem that many authors have long identified. As the political scholar Barnor Hesse has written, certain things become "impossible to formulate because the means by which they could be formulated have been excluded from the discursive context." The series of conferences and podcast episodes that led to the current publication has attempted to answer the fundamental question: What must remain unspeakable for Western representations of rationality to "sustain their power of universal reiteration in contemporary political theory"?[1]

Reason's Unreason

Fascism, as a political ideology, is hard to define, and this book does not try to offer a definition. What we propose instead is to look at fascism as a constitutive element of imperial doctrine, not an unhinged, exceptional particularity. White supremacy, the philosopher Charles Mills argues, is the system that "has made

1. Barnor Hesse, "Escaping Liberty: Western Hegemony, Black Fugitivity," *Political Theory* 42, no. 3 (2014): https://doi.org/10.1177/0090591714526208.

the modern world what it is today," yet it is seen as the backdrop against which other systems, like fascism, liberalism, or social democracy, "which we are to see as political," play out.[2] But white supremacy is a political system, not just a cultural setup, and arguably the most important political ideology of modernity—as such, it does not remain siloed, limited to explicitly racist theories like polygenism, craniometry, or eugenics, but bleeds into the entirety of the semantic field, whether this field concerns social, economic, or scientific life. The very conceptualization of "the political" in the modern era, our publication contends, is entwined with the struggle for racial hegemony.

There is a tradition of scholarship that supports the view that fascism is a thing of unreason, a political pathology. From this follows the argument predicating the singularity of the Holocaust on its irrationality, which in turn is demonstrated by the uneconomic nature of the crimes committed. In the immediate aftermath of World War II, as the political scholar Mahmood Mamdani details in *Neither Settler nor Native* (2020), the Allies reconceptualized Nazism as "an accumulation of individual crimes rather than a political project." By focusing on atrocities, the victors could align Nazism "with the crimes of hundreds of thousands, even millions, of individuals," and call for justice for its victims. The denazification process "became a punitive effort rather than a politically transformative one," treating Nazi atrocities as forms of criminal rather than political violence, thereby delinking National Socialism from other modalities of nationalism and their legacies of extrajudicial bloodshed, deportations, differential allocation of resources, racialized citizenship, or activation of murderous mobs.[3]

The same tendency to individualize and pathologize political violence animates *The Authoritarian Personality*, published in 1950 to widespread interest. The team of prominent researchers who authored the book—Theodor W. Adorno, Else Frenkel-Brunswik, Daniel Levinson, and Nevitt Sanford—developed the "F scale" to gauge the psychological predisposition for fascism among democratic citizenry. The F scale charted the devolution of individuated and autonomous liberal subjects into an irrational, frenzied mob.

2. Charles W. Mills, *The Racial Contract* (Ithaca, NY: Cornell University Press, 1997), 1–2.

3. Mahmood Mamdani, *Neither Settler nor Native: The Making and Unmaking of Permanent Minorities* (Cambridge, MA: Harvard University Press, 2020), 102.

In his well-known 1995 essay "Eternal Fascism," Umberto Eco argued that fascism does not have a political philosophy; it only has rhetoric. Its features cannot be organized into a system. It appeals to unreason, not to reason.

The resurgence of fascism under figures such as Bolsonaro, Rodrigo Duterte, and Trump has been narrated along these lines, as a descent into lunacy or an outburst of unfocused anger spilling into the public sphere, running rampant over middle-class civility. However, more recent events like President Joe Biden's nomination of Elliott Abrams, a member of the Reagan administration who oversaw Efraín Ríos Montt's genocide against the Indigenous Maya Ixil people in Guatemala in the 1980s, to join the US Advisory Commission on Public Diplomacy undermine any attempt to narrate Trump's presidency as an aberration from democratic norms. Fascism is not a form of lunacy or descent into mass psychosis. Fascism is not a political anomaly or irrational. Fascism is a structural aspect of modernity. "Such figures of sovereignty are far from a piece of prodigious insanity," as Achille Mbembe writes in "Necropolitics" (2003).[4] The history of modernity is thus "not so much about the progress of reason as it is about *the history of reason's unreason*," whose legacy continues to trouble contemporary society and its public spheres to the present day.[5]

The Paradox of Modernity

The markers of modernity—progress, development, modernization, industrialization, urbanization—suggest a comparative chronology. Backwardness defines the non-European in contrast to the concept of Western civilization, under whose terms the nature of time came to be defined. This "denial of coevalness," as the anthropologist Johannes Fabian has termed it, ultimately consigns colonized subjects to the waiting room of history and the disempowered to the past.[6] And because the non-European is hopelessly "behind

4. Achille Mbembe, "Necropolitics," trans. Libby Meintjes, *Public Culture* 15, no. 1 (2003): 14.

5. Achille Mbembe, in "In Conversation: Achille Mbembe and David Theo Goldberg on 'Critique of Black Reason,'" *Theory, Culture and Society*, July 3, 2008, https://www.theoryculturesociety.org/blog/interviews-achille-mbembe-david-theo-goldberg-critique-black-reason; italics in original.

6. See Johannes Fabian, *Time and the Other: How Anthropology Makes Its Object* (New York: Columbia University Press, 1983).

the times," successive waves of colonial and neocolonial depredation are, to this day, justified by the necessity to assimilate to modernity, to develop, to "catch up." Theft, or that which is taken—via enslavement, land grabs, depredation, or plunder—can thus be codified as a gift, as the dispensation of futurity. From this perspective, geopolitics is a form of chronopolitics. Temporality becomes a biopolitical, and hence necropolitical, instrument: the distribution of time becomes the distribution of territory, and therefore the distribution of life. The Enlightenment, to quote the cultural theorist John Jervis, "transforms civilizing into a project, one in which the state itself is involved in programs of social betterment. Rationalism, Enlightenment, and the potential for imperialism come together here. Enlightenment becomes a mission, intolerant of otherness," which devises a system of justice for the few while erecting a system of *justified* discrimination for the many.[7] Universalism crowds out others.

This is the paradox of modernity: whereas the modern revolutions claim they fought to eliminate distinctions of class, caste, rank, and status, the modern age is also the epoch that instituted the concept of racial difference. The Enlightenment's set of inconsistent claims—all human beings are equal, some human beings can be justly owned—is usually brushed aside as the last gasp of a premodern order, a residue or vestige of medieval savagery that bled into modernity. But race and racism, unlike xenophobia or sectarianism, are "distinctly modern ideas."[8] Immanuel Kant, who is credited with introducing the concept of race into philosophical jargon, indexes a preoccupation with history and progress to differences of skin tone.[9]

The history of imperial expansion is an eschatological tale as well as a form of political economy, offering its own story of human

7. John Jervis, "The Modernity of the Fin de Siècle," in *The Fin-de-Siècle World*, ed. Michael Saler (New York: Routledge, 2015), 60.

8. Andrew Valls, introduction to *Race and Racism in Modern Philosophy*, ed. Andrew Valls (Ithaca, NY: Cornell University Press, 2005), 1.

9. For Kant's take on race, see "Of the Different Races of Human Beings" (1775), "Determination of the Concept of a Human Race" (1785), "On the Use of Teleological Principles in Philosophy" (1788), and "Anthropology from a Pragmatic Point of View" (1798), in *Anthropology, History, and Education*, ed. Günter Zöller, trans. Mary Gregor et al. (Cambridge: Cambridge University Press, 2007); and "Physical Geography" (1802), in *Natural Science*, ed. Eric Watkins, trans. Lewis White Beck et al. (Cambridge: Cambridge University Press, 2012).

fulfillment. The Enlightenment grafts a distinction between bad (insolvent) and good (solvent) desires onto the concepts of history and progress. Addressing his fellow philosopher Johann Gottfried Herder's contention that the good life is a value in itself and not synonymous with a political project whose achievement is the sole prerogative of Europeans, Kant famously quipped that the life of the Indigenous islanders of Tahiti, lived on the edge of history, is neither properly human nor worth living: "Does the author really mean that, if the happy inhabitants of Tahiti, never visited by more civilized nations, were destined to live in their peaceful indolence for thousands of centuries, it would be possible to give a satisfactory answer to the question of why they should exist at all, and of whether it would not have been just as good if this island had been occupied by happy sheep and cattle as by happy human beings who merely enjoy themselves?"[10] Johann Gottlieb Fichte, a disciple of Kant's and a founding figure of the school of German Idealism, agreed, writing that "reason is not there for the sake of existence, but existence for the sake of reason."[11]

Hegel would later develop these opinions into a fully fleshed out philosophy of history. Usually credited with the insight that reason has a history, Hegel claimed, more specifically, that reason does not simply have a history, reason *is* history. This conflation of reason and history is called Spirit. For Hegel, reason does not just order the world, giving it form and meaning; reason gives the world its *orientation*. History is the process by which Spirit realizes its essence—namely, freedom—which is at the same time its telos. In *The Phenomenology of Spirit* (1807), written around half a century before Darwin's theory of evolution gripped the public's imagination, Hegel outlined a developmental schema by which the unity and identity of Spirit reveals itself *in and as history*, thereby arranging all difference and conflict as relay points of a single sequence.[12] Within this system, desire emerges as the driving force of world development. This desire cannot be directed toward

10. Immanuel Kant, "Reviews of Herder's Ideas on the Philosophy of the History of Mankind," in *Kant: Political Writings*, ed. H. S. Reiss (Cambridge: Cambridge University Press, 1991), 219–20.

11. Johann Fichte, *The Vocation of Man*, trans. Peter Preuss (Indianapolis, IN: Hackett, 1987), 91.

12. Walter Arnold Kaufmann, *Hegel: Reinterpretation, Texts, and Commentary* (New York: Doubleday, 1965), 148.

natural objects, however; for if it were, it would be identical to the desires expressed by the islanders, which are, according to Hegel and Kant, the desires of the animal: desire that is uncreative because, by affirming both the present and the world as it is, it does not engender history. For self-consciousness to emerge, desire must be creative—that is, it must orient itself toward that which is not yet in the world, and must be realized as action negating the given.[13] Creative desire entails a temporal dimension; it is a desire for "becoming," a desire in which the *future* takes primacy. And because the content of the subject is a function of its object, as the desires of its islanders are devalued, the islanders themselves, by extension, are devalued too.

To be human, for Hegel, is to free oneself from nature.[14] The function of culture is to undo nature in order to create a (man-made) second world. The failure to free oneself from nature is described as a cultural failure, which Hegel attributes to conceptual inadequacy. From Hegel's perspective, race is an index of this failure. "Negroes," he wrote in *Lectures on the Philosophy of History*, "are enslaved by Europeans and sold to America. Bad as this may be, their lot in their own lands is even worse, since there a slavery quite as absolute exists; for it is the essential principle of slavery, that man has not yet attained a consciousness of his freedom, and consequently sinks down to a mere Thing—an object of no value."[15] Though he seems undecided whether the non-white races are constitutionally unable to articulate their unconscious drives toward a conscious—that is, rational—project, or whether they are just immature and underdeveloped, his writings make room for imperial expansion and military occupation to be codified as a form of emancipation, a way of awaking in the not-yet human the dormant seeds of their own sublation. Colonialism was, as Mbembe puts it, "a fundamentally 'civilizing' and 'humanitarian' enterprise. The violence that was its corollary could only ever be

13. See Alexandre Kojève, *Introduction to the Reading of Hegel: Lectures on the "Phenomenology of Spirit,"* ed. Allan Bloom, trans. James H. Nichols Jr. (Ithaca, NY: Cornell University Press, 1980), 4–5.

14. Teshale Tibebu, *Hegel and the Third World: The Making of Eurocentrism in World History* (Syracuse, NY: Syracuse University Press, 2011), 28.

15. Georg Wilhelm Friedrich Hegel, *Lectures on the Philosophy of History*, trans. John Sibree (Kitchener, CA: Batoche Books, 2001), 113.

moral."[16] Hence another paradox: only by force can most people be freed.

Whose Universal?

Hegel is worthy of closer examination. Not because he is the worst offender, but because he is still the go-to author for political theorizations of anti-fascism—or for all who disagree with the philosopher Isaiah Berlin's mid-twentieth-century attack on Hegel's "positive liberty" and wish to defend collective justice rather than individual self-determination.[17] But also because Hegelian notions anchor Adorno and Max Horkheimer's *Dialectic of Enlightenment* (1944), a book that invokes the modern history of unreason to argue that irrational regress inheres in rational progress's totalizing logic. Fascism is thus a result of Enlightenment thought reverting to mythology, but the authors obfuscate the paradox-ridden history of the bourgeois concept of universal reason by excising its formative ties to sites of colonial extraction and expansion, where the irrational other serves as a foil to the rational settler's meta-narrative.[18] Most importantly, because the fantasies subtending Hegelian notions of openness and freedom invariably shape

16. Achille Mbembe, *Critique of Black Reason*, trans. Laurent Dubois (Johannesburg: Wits University Press, 2017), 12.

17. Berlin attacked Hegel's statism as a dogmatic and dangerous prelude to totalitarianism. He opposed the concept of "positive freedom," the freedom to fully emancipate the individual, with "negative freedom," the absence of coercion or interference by an exterior social body, which Berlin believed is the only form of freedom not open to political abuse. Similar critiques by centrist commentators like Berlin have contributed to the view that Hegel offers resources to the left. Isaiah Berlin, "Two Concepts of Liberty," in *Four Essays on Liberty* (Oxford: Oxford University Press, 1969), 118–72.

18. Adorno and Horkheimer define unreason as the inability to make correct distinctions, thus aligning with Enlightenment tradition. The pre-rational is characterized by confusing reality and imagination or representation, while Enlightenment rationality draws that boundary. Rationality is narrated as a process of converting premodern categories like magic into proper categories like technology or aesthetics. However, the authors do not examine how the causality principle that rules Western rationality maps onto the chronopolitics of race. See also Christopher Bracken, *Magical Criticism: The Recourse of Savage Philosophy* (Chicago: University of Chicago Press, 2008), 22–23. For the process of conversion, see Anselm Franke and Ana Teixeira Pinto, "The Cosmology of Conversion," in *Ceremony: Burial of an Undead World* (Leipzig: Spector Books), 289–90; for Adorno's definition of developed Western consciousness (i.e., rationality), see the 1962 radio interview published as "Elias Canetti: Discussion with Theodor W. Adorno," *Thesis Eleven*, no. 45 (1996): 4.

the progressive logic within which the political itself must be thought. Hegel's contributions to racial capitalism, as the literary scholar Rei Terada argues, "matter particularly much because they continue to characterise the preferences of left political theory," which does not desire "not to be racist" as much as it "desires to minimise the scope of race."[19]

By playing race "against a falsely transparent humanity," Hegel makes the notion of openness "into the measure of authentic development," which he then uses "to generate racist images of Africans" who are defined by its lack.[20] As the philosopher Denise Ferreira da Silva has written, "The very arsenal designed to determine and to ascertain the truth of human difference already assumed Europeanness/whiteness as the universal measure."[21] Hegel's "radical openness to history," to return to Terada's argument, is an Enlightenment technology that produces the particular it claims to be the opposite of in order to "input[e] racism elsewhere to demand colonial access."[22] Overcoming difference—that is, overcoming race—is tantamount to becoming white. While others point to Hegel's distaste for essentialisms to prove his opposition to nativism or the corporatist metaphors that organize fascist doctrine, we would argue for a continuity. The life of the Spirit is nonracial, or even anti-racial. But despite or precisely because of this, it nonetheless takes part in the logic of racialization. Without the will to examine these conceptual frameworks, whose alleged universality elides the experiences of everyone who is not a straight cis white man, contemporary philosophy will continue to help rationalize what Mills calls "the racial contract."

The Afterlife of Fascism

Published in 1950, the same year as *The Authoritarian Personality*, Aimé Césaire's essay "Discourse on Colonialism" insisted that

19. Rei Terada, "Hegel's Racism for Radicals," *Radical Philosophy* 2, no. 5 (Autumn 2019): 12, 11.

20. Terada, 16.

21. Denise Ferreira da Silva, "1 (life) ÷ 0 (blackness) = ∞ − ∞ or ∞ / ∞: On Matter beyond the Equation of Value", *e-flux journal*, no. 79 (February 2017): https://www.e-flux.com/journal/79/94686/1-life-0-blackness-or-on-matter-beyond-the-equation-of-value/.

22. Terada, "Hegel's Racism for Radicals," 16.

what in Europe is called fascism is just colonial violence finding its way back home. He called Nazism "the crowning barbarism" that accrued from the "daily barbarisms" perpetrated against colonized folk, and indicted the Western bourgeoisie for cultivating that same violence up until the Gestapo came knocking at their door.

To this day, rather than forming the polar opposite of totalitarianism, social democracy accommodates a totalitarian dimension. The so-called golden decades of social democracy in the West—from the end of the Second World War until the late 1960s—were coterminous with racial oppression at home and colonial violence abroad. As the economists Utsa Patnaik and Prabhat Patnaik argue, capitalism is characterized by another relationship in addition to the one between capital and wage labor—namely, a structural relationship described by the term "imperialism" and manifest in the domination of the Global South by the Global North.[23]

Césaire's admonitions went unheeded. While the relation between settler colonialism and fascism remained poorly understood, the Cold War reduction of the political to an epic battle between the forces of freedom and unfreedom allowed the West to elide the colonial question and the struggles of the Third World, ultimately conflating fascism and communism under the blanket designation of "despotism" or "totalitarianism." By the late 1950s, fascism had become another generic term denoting an undifferentiated evil, leaving the postwar consensus to conclude that it was a negation or distortion of modernity, not one of its constitutive features. Still dominant today, this tendency to pathologize fascism fails to incorporate the colonial dimension, obscuring the continuities between fascism and the biopolitics of empire, ultimately depoliticizing both.

But colonialism, as the political scholar Nikhil Pal Singh has maintained, is not something that happened in our past; it is an expansionary process that keeps moving forward and outward. Though the United States believes that fascism is not native to its political culture, many of the elements that define it, as Singh notes in his 2017 essay "The Afterlife of Fascism," inhere in the conflicts attendant upon frontier expansion, slavery, and the removal of Indigenous peoples, and keep recurring in a disaggregated form

23. Utsa Patnaik and Prabhat Patnaik, *A Theory of Imperialism* (New York: Columbia University Press, 2016).

today.[24] The logic of white supremacy still presides over the differential distribution of benefits and burdens, structuring forms of formal and informal rule. This is why, according to Singh, "liberal democracy in the United States has always been a very strained and constrained institution, governed by a series of exceptions derived from the legacies of settler colonialism, slavery, and Jim Crow laws."[25] And we can often find the elements that define fascism, like state-sanctioned terror, processes of racial ascription, or extrajudicial killings, in present-day society, which still differentiates between those whom the law protects but does not bind and those whom the law binds but does not protect.

Almost seventy-five years after "Discourse on Colonialism" was published, as the West indulges in fantasies of the subjugation of white people, the process of colonization has been renewed with increased ferocity. The hunger for lithium and cobalt, rare-earth elements used for mobile devices and electric vehicles, and the continuous underdevelopment of countries where these resources are extracted make apparent the structuring force of race in geopolitics and the role of the digital economy in the production and reproduction of a new settler frontier.

To this day, the legacies of colonialism tend to find expression in a language that is familiar and compelling—typically gesturing toward universalism, like "all lives matter," or individual agency, like "not all men"—and hence remain largely unquestioned. Principles like openness, universalism, humanism, freedom, and individualism—saturated with colonial formations—function in lockstep with the development of a globally integrated economy rooted in Western hegemony.

The White West contends that without the will to confront the role of race in the production and reproduction of global wealth differentials, the question of the good life can only be raised in distorted form, under the guise of nativism or the tech industry's promises of magical abundance—weak utopias whose structural inconsistencies open up an ambiguous space in which a critique or

24. Nikhil Pal Singh, "The Afterlife of Fascism," in *Race and America's Long War* (Berkeley: University of California Press, 2017), 98–122.

25. This quotation paraphrases Singh's discussion of "The Afterlife of Fascism" on episode 1 of *The White West: Whose Universal?*, https://soundcloud.com/hkw/sets/the-white-west-whose-universal.

disruption of capitalism can be inflected in the direction of fascism. This book, divided into four sections, with a prose poem in the middle, is an attempt to engage the overlaps between metaphysical predicates and colonial legacies, as well as the undertheorized continuities between fascism and settler colonialism.

Contributions

The first section, "Whose Universal?," begins with the cultural theorist Donna V. Jones's contribution, "Inheritance and Finitude: Toward a Literary Phenomenology of Time," which ties the quest for immortality to the temporal structure of the economy. Surveying the promises of transhumanism, Jones points to the paradox of immortality: only those great men we deem to be immortal can truly die because only greatness is singular, hence irreplaceable. Those whose lives are deemed not worth living can be killed with impunity since they are not singular but just "species life," and species life lives on in "countless others." By leaving unexamined the connotations of the techno-scientific quest for immortality, we leave undisturbed a metaphysical matrix saturated with colonial formations, which bears an oppressive ideological force.

In "Fractal Thinking," the philosopher Denise Ferreira da Silva takes contemporary philosophy to task, arguing that "the racial is the single most important ethico-juridical concept in the global present." Yet it is one that certain prominent philosophers miss because they are unable to grasp how the afterlife of colonialism generates capital outflows that deplete the resources of southern nations and force them into underdevelopment, only for them to reappear in Europe as the alleged threat of immigration. Historical materialism, she argues, would prove the best basis for a critique of capital if historical materialists would understand that coloniality inheres in all forms of capital accumulation.

The genocide scholar A. Dirk Moses's "Imperial Reason, Permanent Security, and the Dawn of Everything" asks: At what point did warfare became a constant of human life? He traces the roots of "permanent security" to the ancient Roman juridical model linking domestic care and military domination, and the crucial role of terror in imperial conquest and colonial governance, to connect present-day policies of pacification and preemptive strikes. Moses's essay aims to help us understand "how security dilemmas came to define and limit our imagination of human freedom."

The book's second section, "War Ecologies," opens with the philosopher Norman Ajari's "Fetishized Repression: Institutional Racism as a European Civil System," which examines the juridical genealogy of *le racisme d'état* by delving into the legacy of Carl Schmitt's *The Nomos of the Earth* (1950), the work in which the Nazi jurist details how the colony and the nation-state are co-constituted. Here, the supremacy of white civilization, Ajari argues, emerges as the essence of modern international law. Arcing back to seventeenth- and eighteenth-century sources, Ajari describes the dichotomy between inter-European wars and wars of colonial conquest—the latter declare their victims to be "savages" in order to rationalize the extreme savagery unleashed upon them—detailing the racist genesis of the Janus-like modern state, which operates as an engine of subjugation to those it racializes either abroad or at home.

In "America and the Cold War Origins of the (White) West," the cultural theorist Nikhil Pal Singh argues that though the end of the Second World War marked the beginning of the dissolution of the Eurocentric world order, it also, paradoxically, strengthened the power of the West over the rest of the world. For developing nations and nations newly formed, any promise of growth "implied acceptance that the past injustices that led to the impoverishment of these areas would not be actively redressed or repaired." For the Western powers, the challenge was to ensure that reforming their method would not compromise their usage of coercive force. What could not be tolerated was the possibility of an otherwise, hence the mobilization of Orientalist tropes to engender a moral (and racial) panic around the alleged threat of communist contagion, in a process in which the zealous safeguarding of "vital interests" swiftly devolved Western liberal democracies into what Reinhold Niebuhr called a "less vicious version of the Nazi creed."

In "Anything You Can Imagine Is Here," the scholar and curator Rijin Sahakian examines the structural force of race in geopolitics by describing the wars waged against Iraq in 1991 and 2003 as a petri dish for the global future: "a space primed for universal subordination under state and non-state actors," composed of increased police militarization, privatized security, proxy battles, and paramilitary forces that have acquired enough power to build their own infrastructures. Detailing the rhetorical devices that allow for the perpetrator to double as victim, Sahakian studies the dehumanization complex and the creation of chaos as a global currency undergirding hegemony machines.

The book's interlude, "Blue Land," by the writer, curator, and film producer Olivier Marboeuf, is a poetic expression of the author's frustration with the unending emotional labor that befalls Black scholars, who are constantly called upon to assuage white racial anxieties and accommodate the sensibilities of those who take solace in associating with Black people. Taking to task the toppling of statues and the erecting of effigies of Black female activists in their stead, films that narrate enslavement as a failure of masculinity and foreground hypermasculine Black heroes as redeemers, and those, like the editors of this volume, who organize seminars about fascism, this prose poem tells us that the ultimate madness is attempting to theorize the madness that was modernity.

The third section, "Aesthetic Currencies," begins with the literary theorist Sladja Blazan's "The Promise of the Nonhuman: An Existentialist Trope in the Anthropocene," a look at how the concept of the nonhuman is used to reconcile calls for humanity to unite with decolonial prompts to leave the human behind, since the history of humanism, laden with harrowing backstories, is something to overcome, not aspire to. However, representations of the nonhuman are continually filtered through Eurocentric frameworks, and Blazan cautions that in most fictional takes of moving beyond the human, the nonhuman appears as a figure of negation against which the human can reconfigure itself, failing to yield any meaningful movement—fictional or otherwise—to signal a departure from the figurations of personhood that undergird settler capitalism.

Against the backdrop of a recent polemic involving a London gallery promoting white-supremacist speech, the art historian Larne Abse Gogarty's essay "The Art Right" examines the fascist-curious trend in the cultural milieu. Appeals to free speech in the narrow sense of hate speech can (and often do) clash with freedom in a broader sense, she writes, contributing to political unfreedom. And the conflict between freedom of speech and identity politics is not a conflict between freedom and unfreedom but a conflict between two divergent conceptions of freedom, namely freedom to harm and freedom from harm.

In "Formless Labor," the art historian Kerstin Stakemeier looks at labor, which Marx locates at the center of his ontology of modern life, to argue that it is not the "variable abstractions of exchange that govern modernity," but rather it is the abstraction of labor, into a form of exchange. She suggests a "cosmological reading of labor," not to abandon it as the nucleus of social formations but to overturn "the modern ontology of its social character," and the violence that inheres in its humanist attributes.

The fourth and final section, "Automating Apartheid," begins with the media theorist Ramon Amaro's "An Analytics of Obligation: On Algorithmically Mediated Labor and the Transference of Racial Value," an analysis of how machine learning rearticulates the ways traditional work is performed. Algorithms now mediate between "human acts, or the act of being human," and the networked imperatives of growth and profitability. Whereas humanism emphasizes the "subjective dimension of labor," narrating work as a relation plagued by alienation or exploitation that needs to be overcome, it fails to account for enslaved labor, which had no subjective relation to labor but acquired a dual financial function as a tool that produces both material value and a storage of value. To say algorithmic economies are systems of enslavement would trivialize the plight of the enslaved, but a system that reorganizes labor by means of obligation, Amaro argues, reiterates servitude, while the current intersection of technology and human labor fails "to account for the realities of race, anti-Blackness, and slavery."

In "Biometrics as White Biopolitics," the historian Nitzan Lebovic surveys the colonial origin of biometric sciences to argue that a genocidal principle inheres in classification systems that both equate biological norms with morals and view deviation as a threat to the order of life, hence devoid of the right to exist. Politicizing the physical traits of the population, the purpose of biometrics, Lebovic maintains, was always to create "a total political weapon that transcends the limitations of space and time, collective ideology and the individual body." Operating under the cloak of darkness, biometric technologies are hardly a form of soft power; instead, from their inception to the present day—as demonstrated by the sale of biometric technology to dictatorial regimes and extreme-right actors—they have served the most illiberal forms of power.

The media theorist Felix Stalder's "Digital Colonialism" looks into the export of European legal codes to colonized countries and their role in the eradication of the communal usage of land and resources by establishing the rule of private property. This is a precedent for the current capture of lifeworlds, rendered into private property by big data. Then as now, Stalder argues, alternative ways of organizing social life are decimated to make room for a top-down way of structuring the social that, at its most benign, promotes an environment that leaves people free to choose their course of action yet erects a "choice architecture" that "favors certain outcomes over others."

In closing, we would like to extend our special thanks to all of our authors, without whose generosity this publication and its adjacent project would not have been possible.

Whose Universal?

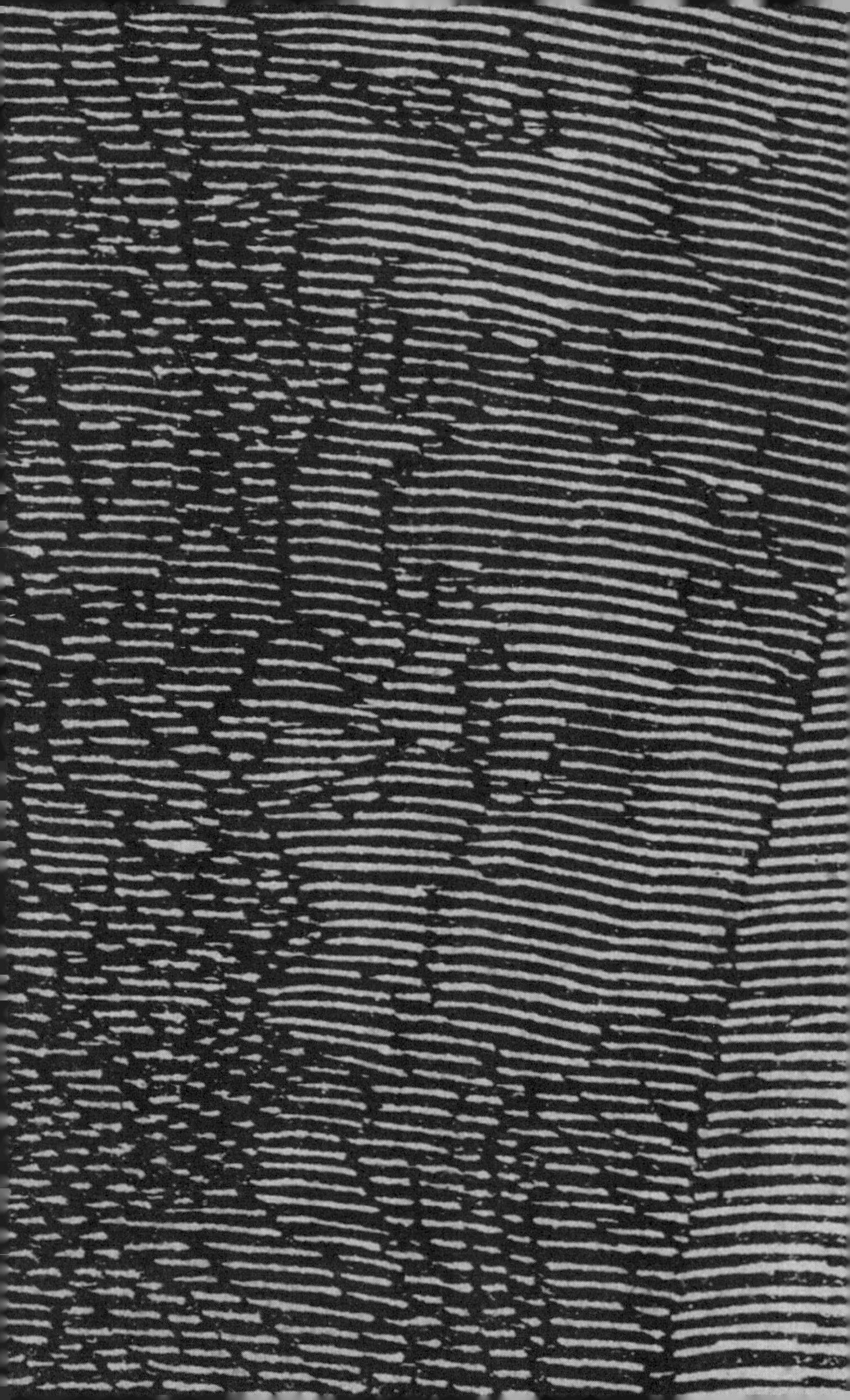

Inheritance and Finitude
Toward a Literary Phenomenology of Time

Donna V. Jones

I shall explore here why lived time—which is a time of a life, and thus a time with a foreseeable end that is not (or at the very least is feared will not be) a beginning—is different from the physicist's working conception of time. In particular, I am interested in the experience of time for subaltern and minority groups. I shall begin with a rapid overview of the Marxist analysis of the work hour, but I want to move beyond it to a time of ends and explore the quest for immortality once again, especially in forms relevant for oppressed groups. Because I am interested less in the sociology than in the phenomenology of time, I shall focus on experiences of hurry, anxiety, hope, longing, waiting, enduring, planning, promising, joyful expectation, grief, and most of all the fear of our death-pervaded lives.[1] Like Justice Potter Stewart on pornography, St. Augustine could not define time; unlike Stewart, he knew it not when he saw it but when he experienced it flowing through him as a self-aware subject.[2] E. P. Thompson laid bare how time has come to be altogether something less subjective and more mechanical.[3] Instead of hours being divided as days and nights, or subject to seasonal variation, the modern hour becomes in his account an abstract, homogenous, standardized unit of a mechanical device.[4] One is like another, no matter how differently it is experienced. Experience is sacrificed to mechanism. Time is what the clock measures. From a Romantic rather than Marxist perspective, Henri Bergson fought against this conflation, though without strictly opposing the subjective to the mechanical. After all, even Bergson recognizes that the new technology of cinema, with its ability to vary frame speed so as to protract and speed up time,

1. See Raymond Tallis, *Of Time and Lamentation: Reflections on Transience* (New York: Columbia University Press, 2017).

2. See Saint Augustine, *Confessions*, trans. Henry Chadwick (Oxford: Oxford University Press, 2009), chap. 10 and 11.

3. See E. P. Thompson, "Time, Work Discipline, and Industrial Capitalism," *Past & Present*, no. 38 (1967): 56–97.

4. See Eviatar Zerubavel, *Hidden Rhythms: Schedules and Calendars in Social Life* (Berkeley: University of California Press, 1985).

and to do jump cuts and edits, not only expresses the subjective experience of time but possibly also deepens it.[5] It has proven a mistake to oppose the time of technology to the time of life; they are interpenetrated in ways that we will always struggle to understand. Martin Heidegger and Gilles Deleuze were right to caution against any such romantic polar opposition.[6]

Thompson's historical-materialist sociology of time tracks the revolutionary devices of clocks and watches, though it is quaint to have him follow the two centuries it took for the revolutionary clock and watch to diffuse through society knowing that smartphones today have reached billions of users in a decade, more or less. In all practical terms, time does speed up. As Benjamin Noys has argued, accelerationism is arguably the signature of our times, rooted in what Karl Marx discovered and called turnover time.[7] That is, the faster capital moves through its moments of money, input commodities, production process, output commodities, and sale, the more value is accumulated over the year. Rest of any kind is a delay, an arresting of turnover time. The world opens up to a 24/7 temporality, as Jonathan Crary has brilliantly argued.[8] Aristotle called the use of money to make money *chrematistics*; Marx specified what for Aristotle was an unnatural use of money as the circuit of capital. Aristotle worried what would happen to the good life if the method of acquiring goods becomes but a moment in the making of money, endlessly.[9] Crary gives us the annihilation of the good life in our 24/7 dystopia, where one is available every waking minute, whether on the job or not, to work on call. Always being on call is a neoliberal conception of time. Leisure time then closes each circuit of capital by becoming a time for consumption, enabled at any moment of the night with one

5. For Henri Bergson on cinema, see Ronald Bogue, *Deleuze on Cinema* (New York: Routledge, 2003), 11–41.

6. See Jimena Canales, *The Physicist and the Philosopher: Einstein, Bergson and the Debate That Changed Our Understanding of Time* (Princeton, NJ: Princeton University Press, 2015).

7. See Benjamin Noys, *Malign Velocities: Accelerationism and Capitalism* (Winchester: Zero Books, 2013); and Karl Marx, *Capital: A Critique of Political Economy*, vol. 2, trans. David Fernbach (London: Penguin Classics, 1993).

8. See Jonathan Crary, *24/7: Late Capitalism and the Ends of Sleep* (London: Verso, 2014).

9. See Aristotle, *Nicomachean Ethics*, trans. David Ross (Oxford: Oxford University Press, 2009), bk. 5.

quick click. The process can begin anew without delay; the pursuit of value not only knows no quantitative limit, it also proceeds without delay. Time becomes continuous, not discrete; analog, not digital. Military experiments with sleepless soldiers presage a future where physical and biological limits to capital give way under the pressure of unyielding time. Capital will even penetrate whatever dream life survives to improve its personalized sales algorithms. The time of capital has no outside. It is always awake; it is a time without shadows. And it is altogether more insidious than a time of calendars and schedules through which we move mechanically, beginnings and endings determined by mechanical devices.

Thompson explores an earlier stage of market society where the creation and standardization of clock time leads to the reorganization of industrial production in its own image, imposing a logic that agriculture, with its obedience to natural cycles, never did. Yet it should be noted that agriculture created the future, which simply did not exist for us as hunter-gatherers who were not preparing and waiting for a harvest yet to come.[10] But the mechanical clock also creates a new world. Work discipline means that in an abstract, standardized, and homogenous unit a certain quantity of work has to be performed. It is now numbers all the way down. Time and quantity are numbers, flip sides of the same coin. A certain quantity of work measured in the number of things produced or the number of actions performed defines what an hour is; if you do less, then you have not done an hour's worth of work as reflected in the wage. You may well have worked more than an abstract hour, and it may well have been felt as even more time than that. But time is measurable. An hour is not only the passing of so much abstract time. It is the performance of so much quantifiable labor in a measurable unit of abstract time.

And here we have what Moishe Postone has called the "treadmill" of modernity.[11] If, with rising productivity, the most efficient producers can produce more measurable output or perform more measurable actions in an abstract hour, then what the more efficient accomplish in an hour now defines what quantity of activity or output defines an hour. Those who are slower and less efficient

10. See Yuval Noah Harari, *Homo Sapiens: A Brief History of Mankind* (New York: HarperCollins, 2015).

11. Moishe Postone, *Time, Labor, and Social Domination: A Reinterpretation of Marx's Critical Theory* (Cambridge: Cambridge University Press, 1996), 291.

don't do as much in an hour; so now their hour of work won't count as an hour of work, at least as far as pay goes, until they catch up and do as much in an hour as the more efficient can. But what is the reward for catching up? Only that their hour of work again counts as an hour of work, and an hour of work has been redefined as more dense. No one gets ahead, no one gets more time; one runs forward to stay in place. Modernity is on a treadmill.

Time is thus not defined simply in abstract or the mechanical terms of hours pure and simple; time becomes a container for activity, but the activity also defines its temporal container. Activity is not simply measured in time; it is also time. That is, an hour becomes a socially valid hour only if it is filled by an ever-changing quantity of work. For this reason, Postone says social time is not abstract and Newtonian. What counts as an hour is always being redefined by what the most efficient can produce in an hour; failure to adjust is thus nothing less than a waste of time. If one takes longer than an hour to do what others can do in an hour, then one has not performed an abstract hour's worth of work and won't be compensated for an hour's worth of labor, or the output won't have the same value, monetarily expressed, as an hour of a more productive laborer. So output per hour increases because an hour is measured by an increasing quantity of output. What counts as an hour does in fact change with rising productivity; time is not simply fixed mechanically and abstractly. This is the deep structure of time, the basic conception of time in terms of measurable output per abstract unit of time. It organizes our activity in a time of technological frenzy. Even in the academy, as Immanuel Kant pointed out, an a priori sense of time organizes our experience.[12]

So we have a whole set of temporal conceptions to make sense of the present: Thompson's work hour, Marx's turnover time, Noys's accelerationism, Crary's 24/7, and Postone's treadmill temporality. And of course we can add here that for youth today, without minimal levels of income, the future is no longer something that can be planned for, much less controlled and conquered,

12. Mark McGurl gives another example of this dynamic: we could say that by quality time with children we try to maximize the moments of parental attention in a given hour. McGurl, "Real/Quality," in *Time: A Vocabulary of the Present*, ed. Joel Burges and Amy J. Elias (New York: New York University Press, 2016), 209–24.

mired as they are in an endless present of debt payments and dead ends. The passage of time is something at best endured, but also illusorily in a state of stasis. There is no present when it can't be distinguished from the past and the future; time proves to be an illusion, though in a different and more subjective way than the time that disappears from the block universe of the physicists' space-time continuum.

I have suggested ways in which our understanding and experience of time is itself temporal, historicist, rooted in time and place, rendering the word *time* applied across time an empty abstraction or generalization. The modern conception of time is not a modernist discovery of what time is, or has always been; it is not a discovery of a Platonic form of time but a bringing into being of a time that is not timeless but rooted in structures of modernity. It may seem that my turn now to lived time as a time of anticipated finitude and the quest for transcendence or immortality returns us to time outside history, and belonging to the human condition as such.

Yet I intend to reveal contradictory meanings immortality has today by contrasting techno-scientific promises and the demands of black lives. It is in these contradictory meanings of immortality, I will argue, that our understanding of time is perhaps most fully disclosed, even more so than through the capitalist work hour. Immortality is of course the promise of beating or cheating time, of transcending a life lived in time, which means a life limited by time, which in turn means a life forced to choose among projects, given that temporal limit. The value of our projects can therefore only be established in ordinal terms by the value of the opportunities that we forgo in order to live the life that we do. Without a reckoning of the value of the most cherished projects we give up, we cannot easily establish the value of the projects we do carry out. Time is the source of value in this equation, but value determined by subjective estimations of futures foregone, not labor already expended, per Marx. Our finitude is the condition of the very possibility of meaning, not its negation. Yet we feel cursed by our mortality, and we have never ceased imagining transcending it.

That we can in our minds transcend time and achieve immortality results from a cognitive error that we cannot escape. Our interest in immortality does not just come from what Lucretius described as our fear of death; our sense of immortality is not simply the result of weakness or self-delusion, for to ourselves we cannot but appear to be outside of time unlike any other animal, to alone be immortals like the gods. Whence the source of illusion? In a recent book on immortality, Steven Cave puts the point well, though it has already been suggested by Sigmund Freud: while we fear death, and the fear of death informs our lives, we actually cannot imagine our own extinction.[13] Any attempt to imagine the world without our own existence immediately revives us as a spectator, perhaps a spectral presence, but a presence or existence nonetheless—and thus inextinguishable. We fear death but cannot imagine it possible. And that we can't imagine our inexistence gives us the hook on which to hang the immortality narratives that we create in the face of our finitude. That is, the myth of immortality is both something satisfying and something believable. A sense of immortality is something we can't help ourselves from believing, just as we can't but see a straight stick in water as bent. We are to ourselves timeless creatures, necessarily so.

But the first hint as to what is troubling about immortality is already here, though Cave misses it. Note the frightening spectral existence that we can assume in our imaginations of the world beyond our own deaths. Here we exist, we have some kind of ontological status. We spectate, are spectral. We are, in Jacques Rancière's phrase, "mute speech."[14] The world does not hear our voice, and is not moved by it. We are without voice, ghostlike. We do not even have the power to change things by leaving—that is, exiting from arrangements. For our exit has no effect on the things remaining. Our voice cannot be heard. We are living dead. And this is uncanny. For too many of us, that frightening possibility of spectral existence resembles the lives that we already seem to live. We are dead-in-living, living an already social death.

There is really no more horrifying depiction of this—for what I am speaking of here is horrifying—than Alejandro Amenábar's ghost story *The Others* (2001), presumably inspired by Henry James's 1898 novella *The Turn of the Screw*. In Amenábar's film,

13. See Steve Cave, *Immortality: The Quest to Live Forever and How It Drives Civilization* (New York: Crown Books, 2012); and Sigmund Freud, "Our Attitude towards Death," in *Reflections on War and Death*, trans. A. A. Brill and Alfred B. Kuttner (New York: Moffat, Yard & Co., 1918), http://www.bartleby.com/282/2.html.

14. Jacques Rancière, *Mute Speech: Literature, Critical Theory, and Politics*, trans. James Swenson (New York: Columbia University Press, 2011).

Grace Stewart (Nicole Kidman) and her children are convinced that they are haunted by ghosts. They close doors and shut the drapes in fear. In an abandoned country house, they have awkward conversations with the staff. Fear pervades the home as Stewart and her children await the husband/father's return from war. He finally appears on the outskirts of the estate as Stewart fights through the fog to see him, only for him to disappear. Slowly we understand that he is dead, on the edge of purgatory, and that Stewart is dead and in purgatory because she committed suicide after having murdered her children. She has cast herself and her children as the spectral existences that haunt this country home. We finally see that they are the ones haunting the family that has come to live in the home; that their door-closing and drape-drawing are the mysterious acts that spook the residents. But there will be no life for them beyond this spectral existence, where they will exist for eternity. Here is a deeply troubling form of death after life; it is punishment. But even if a spectral existence were not haunted by sin in this horrifying way, it would still constitute a horrifying form of existence.

We may be horrified by the prospect of having a spectral existence after our earthly finitude. But if we then imagine that spectral existence ending, we would then be spectating on our once spectral existence. It's an infinite regress. There is no escaping our escape from time. We are born immortal. We can make sense of our immortality through notions of reincarnation or resurrection, or with the hope that our own bodies won't ever disintegrate. We can't, or at least can't easily, obliterate our sense of our immortality; we can only change the form of it. Perhaps by imagining ourselves in the pleasant state of observing our children, whom we love. Or in holding out the promise of observing a purified and indestructible race to which our children and children's children will belong. This too is a form of immortality, the religious form of racial nationalism. Or we can imagine observing some humane and inspiring legacy that outlasts our physical disintegration.

Science has also hitched its wagon to the dream of immortality more than once. In *The Immortalization Commission* (2011), John Gray tells a fascinating story of how European science merged with the occult arts at the turn of the last century to make contact psychically with our immortal souls, while the Bolsheviks dreamed of creating an immortal man through science.[15] These were not marginal projects but fundamental responses to difficulties of making sense of our delusive sense of immortality in the face of materialism.

Let me turn to another text—one that many before me have used to explore the nature of the modern quest for immortality. Here is one of the best examples of a literary work that combines the scientific quest for immortality with a republican valuation of the birth of a new Europe after the overdue death of the aristocracy. This combination of themes yields a quintessentially modernist work on immortality. I refer here to Karel Čapek's play *The Makropulos Case* (1922), which Bernard Williams discusses in his essay "The Makropulos Case: Reflections on the Tedium of Immortality" (1973).[16] Despite René Wellek's early attempt to raise Čapek's profile in the English-speaking world to the level it held in Central Europe, Čapek remains to this day under-appreciated and eclipsed by Franz Kafka, his fellow Czech.[17] Yet an entire generation of Czech artists was understood as "the Čapek generation," sandwiched between the 1890 modernists and the radical avant-garde following the catastrophe of the Great War. As Thomas Ort makes clear in his compelling intellectual history of the writer, Čapek aimed for an art that would reinforce the republican sympathies of the new Czech Republic that emerged after the termination of aristocratic titles, the breaking up of landed estates, and the nationalization of some businesses following the First World War. His literary work and political essays reflected his temperament: pluralistic, pragmatic, relativistic, empathetic, and socially engaged.[18] His republicanism, which was undergirded by pragmatism and individualism, is key to interpreting the work I shall discuss. As Ort persuasively shows in his lucidly argued study,

15. See John Gray, *Immortalization Commission: Science and the Strange Quest to Cheat Death* (New York: Farrar, Straus and Giroux, 2011).

16. See Karel Čapek, *Four Plays: R. U. R.; The Insect Play; The Makropulos Case; The White Plague*, trans. Peter Majer and Catherine Porter (Reading: Metheun Dramas, 1999); and Bernard Williams, "The Makropulos Case: Reflections on the Tedium of Immortality," in *Problems of the Self: Philosophical Papers, 1956–1972* (Cambridge: Cambridge University Press, 1973).

17. See René Wellek, "Karel Čapek," *Slavonic and Eastern European Review* 15, no. 3 (1936): 191–206.

18. See Thomas Ort, *Art and Life in Modernist Prague: Karel Čapek and His Generation, 1911–1938* (New York: Palgrave McMillan, 2013).

Čapek's greatness was in his ability to create literature that could stage debates about the contending grand philosophical ideas in a time of utter disorientation as to what humankind's guiding values should be: "Unlike Kafka, his characters sometimes lack real psychological or emotional depth, the endings of his books tend toward bathos and sentimentality. [...] But what he did well—extremely well—was to dramatize ideas. His gift (in addition to his astoundingly fertile imagination) was the ability to set ideas in motion, to enact them, to test them, to examine in art what their consequences for life might be."[19] Ort makes a good case that Čapek, twice nominated for the Nobel Prize in Literature, would have likely won if not for his unsparing and courageous criticism of the fascist forms of nationalism in his political essays.

Ort is particularly insightful about Čapek's relation to Bergson —who, Ort shows, was the dominant intellectual influence on him until his assimilation of Georg Simmel. (I shall suggest Čapek was more critical of Simmel than Ort indicates.) Ort's study of Bergson's importance to Čapek complements my own earlier study of Bergson's centrality to early twentieth-century aesthetics, and we are both indebted to Mark Antliff's study of the Bergsonism of avant-garde French visual artists.[20] As my study tries to make clear, Bergson meant many different and contradictory things to opposing groups. Ort emphasizes Čapek's development from an exponent of Bergsonian vitalism to a sympathetic critic. Once Čapek saw that in the name of élan vital people could be called to carry out aggressive and self-destructive activity, he critiqued the very idea of a transcendental force and rooted his sympathies in the lives of individuals who could not be reduced to playthings or props for forces greater than they. Čapek challenged the very idea of a life force that preceded and outlasted individual lives. In fact, as Ort makes clear, Čapek found that the rendering of life as a transcendental force made it impossible to countenance death or, put another way, transience and finitude. As Ort puts it: "Part of the appeal of Bergson's vision of life, he thought, was that it provided no space for death. Bergson had imagined life as a vital principle

19. Ort, 26.

20. See Donna V. Jones, *The Racial Discourses of Life Philosophy: Négritude, Vitalism, and Modernity* (New York: Columbia University Press, 2010); and Mark Antliff, *Inventing Bergson: Cultural Politics and the Parisian Avant-Garde* (Princeton, NJ: Princeton University Press, 1992).

inherent in all things but greater than any particular incarnation. If all life existed along a vital continuum, then death was not in fact life's negation but rather its transformation into a new and different form."[21]

Ort notes that *The Makropulos Case* put just this idea of life without death to the test. It is the story of Elina Makropulos, an opera singer and immortal who has lived 362 years under various aliases, always with the initials of E. M. (Ellian MacGregor, Eugenia Montez, Ekaterina Myshkina, Elsa Mueller, and most recently Emilia Marty). The narrative moves the reader brilliantly along to the disclosure of Elina's immortality, which solves the mystery of her uncanny knowledge of past events and her inhuman distance from her contemporaries. But re-reading with this disclosure already known does not make the story any less compelling. It is a story that takes place in time, which is to say not all at once. Time, it could be said, is that which prevents things from happening all at once. And for this reason, the narrative keeps us captivated by the struggle to transcend the limitations of the characters' understanding at a given point in time to make sense of what then puzzles them.[22]

Before I discuss Čapek's thought experiment about an immortal life, I want to note some neglected parts of the play in regard to time. The characters in the play are initially drawn to Elina for many reasons: she is beautiful, and she is an opera singer of some sublime powers. But she also first appears unexpectedly in the lawyer's office of Kolenaty and his assistant, Vitek; she has knowledge relevant to the resolution of a hundred-year-old dispute about an estate. This is how we meet her, as an informant in a case about an inheritance that remains at the center of the play. Thomas Piketty has recently read Honoré de Balzac and Jane Austen as acerbic critics of patrimonial capitalism, which is a theory of the temporal structure of the economy, that is, of the inheritance of assets already accumulated and living on immortally, as it were, and trivializing the efforts of the living.[23] Simply put, the wealth of the past, even as it is divided and passed on, can dwarf the

21. Ort, *Art and Life in Modernist Prague*, 144.

22. See William C. Dowling, *Ricoeur on Time and Narrative: An Introduction to "Temps et récit"* (Notre Dame, IN: University of Notre Dame Press, 2011).

23. See Thomas Piketty, *Capital in the Twenty-First Century*, trans. Arthur Goldhammer (Cambridge, MA: Harvard University Press, 2014).

incomes that even the most entrepreneurial can make now. This is because the rate of return on wealth is much greater than the rate at which ordinary incomes are growing. Those who can live off wealth find their status rising relative to those whose income comes from work, even if their inheritance results from the breaking up of a fortune, since that fortune has been growing robustly in their benefactors' wake. Piketty insists that this is the normal operation of a market economy and that welfare capitalism was a thirty-year anomaly due to great fortunes being destroyed by war. But they have now recovered, and Balzac and Austen describe a world of inheritance and kin that is becoming familiar again.[24]

Piketty calls this Rastignac's dilemma, which is the realization that it is better to marry well than succeed brilliantly, as depicted in Balzac's *Le Père Goriot* (1835), where the rogue Vautrin proposes to Rastignac that he'll murder the first heir of an estate so that Rastignac may marry the heiress-to-be, as long as he shares with Vautrin enough of the inheritance for the rogue to be a slave master in North America. Piketty is impressed with Balzac's realistic estimates of the extent to which the income from a great estate would exceed the greatest income Rastignac could earn as a magistrate. In his own tale of inheritance and corruption, Čapek couples a depiction of a pathetic, lingering estate battle to a story about the misery of an immortal who does immeasurable damage to all whom she touches. And in both cases, we have the power of the past over the present, the virtually dead (Emilia is spiritually dead) over the alive. This is the basic idea of the play: the nihilistic life of an immortal (as is widely discussed) is joined (as is oft ignored) to a legal battle over the inheritance of the past. The living are sacrificed to the past: Elina crowds out new talent, and human activity is perverted into legal wrangling over the inheritance of the past.

Čapek wants to let things die in the name of the new and vibrant. The estate should be broken up, and the young should make something of their lives and create a radiant future rather than fight to inherit the past. Gregor is the young man trying to reclaim the estate as the rightful heir. Čapek makes him the most pathetic character in the play, willing to commit suicide if he cannot

24. See Sylvia Yanagisako, "Kinship: Still at the Core," *Hau: Journal of Ethnographic Research* 5, no. 1 (2015): 489–94.

win an inheritance. Gregor also throws himself sexually at Elina—who, alas, is his grandmother a few generations' past. She knows that Gregor is the heir to the estate, as he is the descendant of the child she had with the Baron, whose estate it was one hundred years ago. But Elina is not the least bit concerned with Gregor's material well-being. She wants Gregor to reclaim the estate only so that he can claim secret files still there, one of which is the formula for immortality that her doctor father, Makropulos, devised three hundred years ago for a prince and that she, now finally facing death, needs again. The prince did not trust the formula and ordered that it be tested on Elina. She fell ill for a week. The prince imprisoned her father. But, as it was, she recovered nicely, living for the next three hundred years. The most sympathetic character in the play is the legal assistant Vitek, who identifies with the French Revolution and thus the theme of the death of the outdated that weighs down on the present like a nightmare. Vitek is infuriated when Elina mocks Danton for his bad teeth: "Please, I cannot permit you to speak like this ... Danton ... I beg your pardon, but you really mustn't. There'd be nothing great left in History."[25] Čapek is a republican, so it is not surprising that the demand for immortality comes from a despot.

These features of the play—the meaning of a despot's wish for immortality, the significance of the estate battle, and Čapek's republican sympathies—need to be considered as a whole. In the wake of Williams's brilliant essay, discussion has focused on whether Čapek has convincingly narrated the consequences of immortality and shown that the condition of possibility for a meaningful life is acceptance of finitude. After more than three hundred years of life, the once absorbing uncertainties of love and work have no hold on Elina. She has too many children and grandchildren to care about, none of them special to her and all of them contemptible due to their transience. She finds no joy in her technically perfect musical virtuosity (and her singing and affect reflect this); she would not rejoice in the acquiring of any new competence. She struggles to find the word that describes her state of mind: nihilism. Clearly, her life has become meaningless to her. To the extent that she can be motivated at all, only the fear of death motivates her to find the formula. The fear of

25. Čapek, *The Makropulos Case*, in *Four Plays*, 202.

death is indeed the source of her existential misery. In this way, Čapek tries to reconcile us to the wisdom of natural death. Vitek's daughter, Kristina, burns the formula. She represents the youth, and Elina's immortality has twice damaged her: the young man she would have loved commits suicide, humiliated by Elina's rejection of his sexual advances in favor of his father's, and Elina's technical but soulless artistic mastery has left Kristina, an aspiring opera singer, feeling worthless. Elina has to die for the young to live. Čapek ends the play with the characters satisfied that the immortality they long for can be achieved via progeny.

Scholarly discussion has focused on whether immortality would empty life of meaning or rather make life so potentially valuable that no risks with it would be taken. But again, I want to draw attention to usually neglected parts of the play. After the formula for immortality has been recovered, Čapek stages a Platonic dialogue about what should be done with it. Does it belong to the rightful heir, Gregor; or should it be made available to all, out of a radical democratic commitment to a truly human life for all, as the votary of the French Revolution declaims? Should the formula be sold in just the dosages the market will most handsomely reward, should it be destroyed because it will prolong the life of those who already suffer at work, or should it be reserved for the select few? Čapek gives this last position to the vile aristocrat Prus, who has illegitimately claimed and possessed the estate. He has already driven his son to suicide by exchanging the secret file for sexual favors from a sexually lifeless Elina and humiliating his son, who had become obsessed with her. He is not shaken much by the suicide of his son; nor, for that matter, is Elina, who has become maximally indifferent to human suffering.

Prus gives expression to an aristocratic view of life by saying: "Only the strongest. The most capable. For the masses even the life of a mayfly is too long. [...] I'll merely say that a normal stupid man never dies, a normal stupid man lives for ever without your help. Smallness reproduces itself without respite, like flies or mice. Only greatness dies. Only strength and talent die because they are irreplaceable. It may be in our power to preserve them, to establish an aristocracy of long life."[26] This is, I believe, Čapek's

26. Čapek, 251.

rephrasing of a key aspect of Simmel's philosophy of life, as developed in the dense, confusing chapter "On Death and Immortality." Let me quote Simmel here:

> If Goethe thus regards immorality to some extent as a prerogative of the psychic aristocracy, this means that man has need of immortality—and must justify it on the basis of special claims—to the degree that he belongs to this aristocracy, and is incomparable and qualitatively unique. Only these "unique" people die fully and completely, only their death changes the fixity of the world's image—but the death of everyday people as such does not produce this result because their essential quality, extinguished in one place, continues to exist in countless others.[27]

This is remarkable for the view that the subaltern class already enjoys immortality: subaltern life may be devalued but it may be immortal in that the denuded life it represents "continues to exist in countless others."

We could start here with what Ralph Ellison has shown us: black life, as individual life, is invisible because it is indistinguishable in the white imaginary. It has no individual importance or even features. It is not essential, singular, or irreplaceable. Here again is a paradox: black life is invisible in spite of the hyper-visibility of blacks.

Yet exactly because black life is indistinguishable, because it is reduced to a mere specimen of a type, it is immortal. Simmel refers contemptuously to the working class here, but the idea applies even more unforgivingly to the black condition. Black life is replaced by more black life over the generations. It never dies. It is only replaced in the next generation; and because it is replaced—or, to put it another way, because black life can be replaced, and it can be replaced because it is not singular—black people are thought not to die. Black life is more life, *mehr Leben.* But liberated from death, black life is denied individuality. It is because blacks, as individuals, cannot die that they are

27. Georg Simmel, *The View of Life: Four Metaphysical Essays with Journal Aphorisms*, trans. John A. Y. Andrews and Donald N. Levine (Chicago: University of Chicago Press, 2010), 83.

both immortal and oppressed. The oppressive truth of the black condition is that blacks, as individuals, are not thought to be faced with death. Immortality, more than death, haunts a black life. Blacks suffer social death paradoxically because they do not face individual mortality—in the sense that their death is not associated with the loss of anything incomparable and qualitatively unique, anything that will not be replaced through the reproduction of the species. Black life is species life. There is thought to be no tragic finitude in the black condition and thus no authentic modes of being toward death. The point is that life of a kind is never extinguished. Animal life lives on, while human life comes to an end.

In the racial imaginary, life is never something a black person has owned, something that properly has the form of her-ness or his-ness. Black life is never his or her life. It is simply life, non-individual being such that black life is thought to have no qualities that will not reappear in more black life. It follows that there is nothing of value—nothing scarce and irreplaceable—thought to be lost in the loss of a black life, which was never anyone's life, just a life. A black life has no value because black life, being immortal, does not die. *Dasein* alone has the capacity to die by facing death individually and authentically, but racist logic denies blacks the status of *Dasein*, creating a condition of being toward meaningless and nameless death.

So Prus wants immortality not for the subalterns who already enjoy it by virtue of their subalternity but for an aristocracy. Our aristocracy today is not content with faith in resurrection or reincarnation; nor does the creation of a legacy suffice. Today Western technological civilization has really only one immortality narrative on offer—the possibility of elongating life through science. It is the only response to death that can withstand the scientific undermining of traditional religion along with its corrosion by the cynicism that market competition creates. Craig Venter, who has best capitalized on sequencing the human genome, and cofounded Human Longevity Inc., thus becomes, in this reading, the leading spokesperson for our entire way of life, the Western way of the techno-human condition. The overhyped promise to elongate life (at least for some) is the only meaningful response to death that Western civilization can muster, but it too cannot withstand a moment's scrutiny.

All plans for radical longevity take us away from facing death with happiness in this life. What Theodor W. Adorno called a damaged life is built into the structures of inequality inherent to this way of life. The only promise our existing civilization has is the elongation of life in the abstract, in some promise to add aggregate years to aggregate life spans, the biological equivalent of raising GDP without any concern for distributional equality and the quality of life. The techno-hype of transhumanism is our true religion, even more than economic growth is. It is not a marginal movement; it is the deepest expression of our civilization.[28] And yet it has little hold on us. Which means that we have no meaningful narrative of our lives, no practical way of making do with our finitude. For most of us, the promise of happiness in this life is not compatible with our institutions.

But the possibility of immortality cannot be realized anyway. We cannot be resurrected, despite the promise of cryogenics. The soul cannot outlast the disintegration of the body and brain. Science can only give us so many good extra years of life. And we do not really live in our legacies, in that we can't enjoy conscious awareness of them. For Alain Badiou, the only way to raise ourselves above our animal life—the life of *zoe*, in Giorgio Agamben's terms—is through fidelity to a truth bigger than ourselves. It is only through the attempt to secure immortality in the symbolic realms of politics, art, or science that we become post-animal, if not posthuman. Badiou explicitly rejects the equivalence between radical longevity, simply more life, and immortality.[29] Epicurus questioned the longing for a longer life not because he saw it as an impoverished form of immortality but because it evinced a reluctance to live a meaningful life in our bodies, in the here and now. Epicurus would state boldly: "The correct recognition that death is nothing to us makes the mortality of life enjoyable, not by adding limitless time, but by renouncing the longing for immortality. For nothing is fearful in life to the person who is genuinely convinced that there is nothing fearful in dying."[30]

28. See Françoise Dastur, *How Are We to Confront Death? An Introduction to Philosophy*, trans. Robert Vallier (New York: Fordham University Press, 2012).

29. See Alain Badiou, "Down with Death!," trans. David Broder, *Verso Blog*, May 18, 2015, https://www.versobooks.com/blogs/2176-badiou-down-with-death.

30. Epicurus, "Letter to Menoeceus," in *The Epicurus Reader*, ed. and trans. B. Inwood, L. P. Gerson, and D. S. Hutchinson (New York: Hackett, 1994), 124.

A path forward for us, though, may be to find in our literary heritage and in our sociological literature considerations of lives already lived in death, in mute existence, in invisible and inaudible suffering. Death is not only what happens after life; it suffuses life, not simply because life is already always only the set of functions that resist death but because some lives never have the opportunity to participate in life. The way to respond to our finitude is not to obliterate finitude but to ensure life within it.

Fractal Thinking

Denise Ferreira da Silva

Hundreds of black and brown people pack onto flimsy boats; dozens charge to board trains on the border between Italy and Austria, walk along barbed-wire fences on the Croatian-Hungarian border, or are stuck in the Calais Jungle encampment. In these images, I see movement without change; the plays and the scene repeat against different backgrounds. Focus on Syrian refugees fleeing the latest war of global capital, in which Bashar al-Assad, Russia, the United States, the United Kingdom, and many smaller military groups fight to be the country's law enforcer. Arriving in Europe, having crossed the war zone that is Libya and the Mediterranean Sea, they and others fleeing wars and dispossession in Africa end up in the hands of undercover law enforcement agents from Austria and, more recently, Germany, who walk through trains stopped at the border stations asking black and brown travelers for passports and other forms of identification. Another video of an unarmed black person being killed by a police officer and another black neighborhood in revolt after the acquittal or non-indictment of another murderer occupy screens and Facebook newsfeeds.

The racial is the single most important ethico-juridical concept in the global present. National and regional wars in the Middle East and Africa and the urban and rural warfare in the economically dispossessed spaces of Africa, Latin America, the Caribbean, the United States, and Canada are neither effects nor in excess of, but rather integral to, the ethico-juridical assemblage that facilitates global capital's access to the productive resources—bodies and lands—it needs in order to thrive and reproduce.

My reading of Alain Badiou's statements on Islamophobia and Slavoj Žižek's comments on Europe's "refugee crisis" makes a case for a kind of thinking that is capable of tracing how coloniality figures in all shapes of capital, without reducing it to a linear temporality or to an accumulative or developmentally separate (parallel or subordinate) process, but instead refiguring the basic juridico-economic mechanisms of capitalist expropriation. Only complex, nonlinear thinking can trace how (a) the colonial (juridico-economic) matrix that sustained merchant capital

(b) operates through the racial (political-symbolic) arsenal that still supports industrial capital as well as (c) financial capital through racial violence. This tracing produces an ethico-juridical assemblage that includes the wars of global capital forcing millions out of their homes to cross the dangerous waters of the Mediterranean Sea and the Pacific Ocean. Anti-colonial (postcolonial or decolonial) and critical racial theory condition a reading of these images as captions of racial events.[1]

... In the Reactionary Sense

Leftist thinkers, in commenting on these events, rehearse a version of Marx's argument that the colonial plays no role in capital accumulation. When making this point in the past, I have been asked, "Who cares?" My reply is always: I care, because the historical-materialist perspective provides the best basis for the critique of capital, but only if it stops misunderstanding colonial and racial violence as an opportunistic ideological leftover of global capital. Through a reading of Badiou's and Žižek's commentaries on recent racial events, I will explain this misunderstanding as a failure to think colonial and racial violence in its full fractal complexity. In their attempts to rescue the subject (and its objects) from its Enlightenment and post-Enlightenment destiny, thinkers such as Badiou and Žižek—and their speculative-realist students—have not been able to think through/with the most significant creation of modern thought—namely, the figure of the Racial Other.[2] Both fail to comprehend the juridico-economic significance of the Racial Other in modern thought because, for them, racial/cultural difference is a given and thus need not be subjected to further scrutiny. What accounts for this failure to understand the workings of raciality in the global present? Explicitly, their failure is the result of deploying a notion of cultural difference that is too reliant upon early (twentieth-century) sociological accounts of

1. By "racial event," I mean one that is marked by racial violence. Incidentally, by "racial violence," I mean the work of the juridical and ethical apparatus of global capital, which takes the form of symbolic violence (at the level of representation, terms, and logic) and total violence (the work of the colonial modality of power, the expropriation of land, labor, and life).

2. For an account of this proposed indistinction between the racial and the cultural and racial and cultural difference, see Denise Ferreira da Silva, *Toward a Global Idea of Race* (Minneapolis: University of Minnesota Press, 2007).

racial subjugation; implicitly, the linear, or one-dimensional, thinking that subtends this deployment of cultural difference in their discourse severs the links between various incarnations of capital across the fabric of global spacetime.

In an interview published in the *International Socialist Review* in 2014, Badiou responds to questions about Islamophobia and the recent rise of the nationalist far right (the National Front) in France.[3] Linear thinking and a flawed conceptualization of cultural difference allow Badiou to negate the juridico-economic factors playing out in Islamophobia by articulating these factors while disavowing them at the same time, denying them a determining role. Badiou's linear thinking is evident in his distinction between the colonial past (Algeria) and a contemporary French context contaminated by an unbecoming ideological leftover from that past. He identifies two causes of the growth of Islamophobia in France today: the first is "of an ideological nature. It is racism that can be traced back to colonialism, this feeling of superiority of the Western world." The second cause is of a different order:

> After the war, we had a great number of workers coming into the factories in France, and these workers were in their majority Arabs and Muslims. The great majority of Arab and African workers are poor people who live in very difficult conditions in the suburbs. They are segregated because most white workers don't—and often refuse to—live in the same neighborhoods. So we have a mix between something of a racist, ideological nature and something of a social nature: a mix of ideological tradition in the reactionary sense, and something which takes the classic form of class struggle. And it is this mixture that creates a very difficult situation for Arabs and Muslims.

For Badiou, this is a situation that does not require further analysis because, he claims, it can be solved by a return to the "true Republican tradition" of equality in education. What is at

3. Alain Badiou, "A Philosophy for Militants: Alain Badiou Interviewed by Aaron Hess," *International Socialist Review*, no. 95 (Winter 2014/15), https://isreview.org/issue/95/philosophy-militants/.

work here? On the one hand, Badiou's analysis of Islamophobia rehashes the depoliticizing reasoning characteristic of early twentieth-century approaches to the sociology of race relations arising from the prejudice, discrimination, and segregation of and against Southern and Eastern European, East Asian, and black migrants in the northern and eastern cities of the United States. Badiou replays this early sociological account, which locates the causes of racial subjugation in individual prejudice and discrimination on the basis of particular physical and mental traits that were thought to be racial and mental, respectively. But what early sociologists such as Robert E. Park attributed to skin color, odor, and food,[4] Badiou blames on poverty. While Badiou's argument has all the hallmarks of a statement on juridico-economic processes, with phrases such as "something of a social nature," it loses explanatory relevance because he does not relate the poverty afflicting Arabs and Muslims to either colonial expropriation (back then and over there in Algeria) or capitalist exploitation (right here and now in France). For Badiou, once Algerians arrived in France to be exploited as workers by capital, the colonial relation with France vanished. Crossing the Mediterranean transforms the Algerian from "native," to use Fanon's term,[5] into "poor worker," allowing the French Republic to deny responsibility for the plight of Arabs and Muslims.

Žižek's "Confronting Global Capitalism"

Let me now turn to Žižek's writing on the refugee crisis as an example of an argument in which cultural difference provides the logic but is simultaneously rejected as an organizing principle of European existence. In a 2015 article, he offers four prescriptions for facing the new challenges posed by global capital. His second and fourth interest me most. Let me begin with the second:

> Europe should organize itself and impose clear rules and regulations. State control of the stream of refugees should be enforced through a vast administrative network encompassing all of the European Union (to prevent local barbarisms like

4. See Silva, *Toward a Global Idea of Race*, esp. part 2.

5. Frantz Fanon, *The Wretched of the Earth*, trans. Constance Farrington (New York: Grove Press, 1963).

> those of the authorities in Hungary or Slovakia). Refugees should be reassured of their safety, but it should also be made clear to them that they have to accept the area of living allocated to them by European authorities, plus they have to respect the laws and social norms of European states: No tolerance of religious, sexist or ethnic violence on any side, no right to impose onto others one's own way of life or religion, respect of every individual's freedom to abandon his/her communal customs, etc. If a woman chooses to cover her face, her choice should be respected, but if she chooses not to cover it, her freedom to do so has to be guaranteed. Yes, such a set of rules privileges the Western European way of life, but it is a price for European hospitality. These rules should be clearly stated and enforced, by repressive measures (against foreign fundamentalists as well as against our own anti-immigrant racists) if necessary.[6]

None of Žižek's suggestions differ from those of the European civilizers of yesteryear, who also called for and designed mechanisms of assimilation, regulation, and repression. Again, the rhetorical crutch of cultural difference and linear thinking accounts for this repetition. Žižek ignores the fact that the EU already welcomes refugees with a biopolitical apparatus of law enforcement, border protection, and other national and regional security measures, procedures, and entities. The logic of cultural difference severs the link between the violence that refugees of the wars of global capital meet in Europe right now—the building of walls, Islamophobia, deportation, and so on—and the current workings of state and capital. What I read in Žižek's text is a symptom of a common(s) case of hysterical historical blindness, an incapacity to see how raciality provides the ethical signifiers (racial and cultural difference) that collapse protection into security.[7]

Leftist thinkers of today consistently repeat an insidious pattern of modern thinking that considers the racial a referent of another time and place, an ideological vestige of the colonial past.

6. Slavoj Žižek, "We Can't Address the EU Refugee Crisis without Confronting Global Capitalism," *In These Times*, September 9, 2015, https://inthesetimes.com/article/slavoj-zizek-european-refugee-crisis-and-global-capitalism.

7. Denise Ferreira da Silva, "No-Bodies: Law, Raciality, Violence," *Griffith Law Review* 18, no. 2 (2009): 212–36.

Like Badiou, Žižek misunderstands how the colonial and the racial have always been and remain integral to the functioning of global capital, and he assumes that the architectures of total and symbolic violence that produce the figure of the Racial/Cultural Other of Europe have no juridical or economic relevance for what unfolds in the global present. In this critique of global capital, what counts is the European peasant who lost access to communal lands due to enclosures; the juridico-economic figures of the native and the slave have no significance. To summarize, Badiou's and Žižek's respective positions (a) display their rejection of the juridical and economic significance of raciality, and (b) repeat early sociological accounts of racial subjugation, which (c) explain violence as an effect of cultural difference.

The "Social Conditions That Create Refugees"

> The most difficult and important task is a radical economic change that should abolish *social conditions that create refugees*. The ultimate cause of refugees is today's global capitalism itself and its geopolitical games, and if we do not transform it radically, immigrants from Greece and other European countries will soon join African refugees. When I was young, such an organized attempt to regulate commons was called Communism. Maybe we should reinvent it. Maybe, this is, in the long term, our only solution.[8]

Reading Žižek's final recommendation, I wonder how linear thinking and the logic of cultural difference figure in the communism Žižek posits as the solution to Europe's "refugee crisis." Would the communist world establish the "rules and regulations" he demands European countries put in place in order to curb refugees' cultural "shortcomings" relative to the proper —European—values of universality and equality? And if so, how would this be different from colonialism?

Žižek's and Badiou's reframings of communism are inadequate bases for engaging global capital, owing to their incapacity to comprehend the colonial and the racial as integral to capital in all the shapes it has taken: merchant, industrial,

8. Žižek, "We Can't Address the EU Refugee Crisis"; italics in original.

and now financial. Similar to Marx's foundational texts, Žižek's thinking of communism pays no attention to the state-capital mechanisms that ensure the expropriation of the total value yielded by the productive capacity of native land and slave labor in the Americas. Deployments of racial violence, such as the conflicts in the Democratic Republic of the Congo (total violence) and the equating of Islam and brown/black bodies with terrorism (symbolic violence), are the means by which state capital reproduces itself. These forms of violence create the conditions for today's flow of refugees while at the same time justifying the enforcement of "protective" measures that result in the death and incarceration of many black and brown people.

In a discourse that masquerades as a departure from modern philosophy's foundational binaries of nature/culture, body/mind, and object/subject, the linear thinking of Žižek and Badiou nonetheless repeats the logic of cultural difference. For Badiou and his students, relinquishing a position of superiority, authority, or mastery over things or humans is a gesture sufficient to release the subject from its immanent context and to extricate the subject from that which has been made available for thinking—object and Other. In other words, announcing the possibility of knowing without the presupposition of correlation, as in the position delineated by Quentin Meillassoux, is enough to liberate "objects" from the meanings and functions attached to them in the moment of naming;[9] or announcing the appearance of a subject that is related to nothing but the event (Badiou) is enough to liberate its "Others" (those whom Badiou derides for holding on to cultural difference) from the meanings and functions attached to them in the moment of naming.[10] Part of the problem is that linear thinking addresses both state capital and its figures of authority (the party and the subject) horizontally. That is, linear thinking assumes that these political (juridical, economic, and symbolic) entities emerged and continue to thrive in a context that is historically/temporally bounded and geographically/spatially circumscribed. For this reason, it cannot help but miss the fact that, in addition to the enclosures in England, conquest (colonization/settlement)

9. Quentin Meillassoux, *After Finitude: An Essay on the Necessity of Contingency*, trans. Ray Brassier (London: Continuum, 2009).

10. Alain Badiou, *Saint Paul: The Foundation of Universalism*, trans. Ray Brassier (Stanford, CA: Stanford University Press, 2003).

and slavery are also integral moments in the founding violence of Capital.

Raw Materialism

Lately I have been considering a kind of thinking that is at least four-dimensional, and that I call "poethical" or "compositional" thinking. From a conventional historical-materialist perspective, because of the ontic presupposition of atomic-level spacetime, any instance, moment, or event has three dimensions because it happens somewhere (location) and somehow (form) in space; as such, its figuring attends to length, height, and depth all at once. From what I call a "raw materialist perspective," because of the ontic presupposition of the (particle-level) plenum, *what happens* is also a composition (or de-composition or re-composition), always a reassembling of what has happened before and of what has yet to happen.[11] Once one apprehends all that exists as a plenum, both *what happens* and *what exists* no longer have the fixed boundaries of Newton's bodies and Kant's categories (forms), and this makes it possible to think the world differently.

Three moves become possible. First, when attending to the moment of occurrence (*what happens*), instead of grasping location as a point, *where* (in space) and *when* (in time), one can attend simultaneously to all four dimensions: space (depth, width, and length) and time (Einstein's fourth dimension). Second, when attending to four dimensions without privileging time, which imposes directionality on thinking, the mind becomes capable of comprehending *what happens* as an instantaneous composition. Finally, when approaching *what happens* as a composition, it is possible to attend to its constitutive elements, which may also be part of other compositions (*what has happened* and *has yet to happen*) comprising similar elements.[12] Attention to elements exposes similarities and enables a kind of material thinking

11. My use of the term "plenum" draws from quantum physics' descriptions of the subatomic level of existence, in that quantum entities (elementary particles) enter in the composition of everything that exists in their instantiation as matter/energy. Metaphysically, it draws from Leibniz's description of the universe as a plenum, as a contingent and complex composition of entangled singularities.

12. The third move draws upon Joan Retallack's take on complexity as symmetry. See Joan Retallack, *The Poethical Wager* (Berkeley: University of California Press, 2003).

capable of reading symmetries or correspondences. Images of poethical thought are not linear (transparent, abstract, glassy, and determinate) but fractal (immanent, scalar, plenteous, and undetermined), like most of what exists in the world.

When poethical thinking contemplates the present situation in Europe, it does not image "unprecedented crisis," but rather business as usual for global capital. A poethical mapping of the present reveals the language of assimilation and the impulse to protect the White/European "way of life" to be a repetition of the terms and logic deployed a century ago, when Anglo-American workers in the East and the Midwest of the United States protested against the influx of Southern European, Eastern European, and Asian immigrants, as well as black migrants fleeing the total violence of Jim Crow, on the basis that they would not assimilate and that they would lower the existing standard of living. Poethical thinking, deployed as a creative (fractal) imaging to address colonial and racial subjugation, aims to interrupt the repetition characteristic of fractal patterns. Attention to symmetries instantaneously locates a particular event in a global context shaped by the previous and future repetitions of the founding violence of capital. Because it attends to four dimensions, fractal thinking (poethical or compositional thinking) images the global as a part of the cosmos and, as such, does not see it as constituting the ultimate ontic and ontological horizon for thinking. For since *what happens* occurs in the plenum, it is both an expression of, and expressed by, whatever exists under, above, and alongside; what has already passed, and what is yet to come. When a mode of thought graphs global capital among so many repetitive instants and instances of the deployment of colonial-racial machinery, it cannot be indifferent to racial violence in all of its iterations and expressions.

Imperial Reason, Permanent Security, and the Dawn of Everything

A. Dirk Moses

War and Realism

The Russian invasion of Ukraine that began in 2014 and intensified in 2022 has sparked a geopolitical debate about national sovereignty and the inviolability of state borders. The term "imperial reason," recently used to denote Western invasions of Muslim-majority states,[1] has found a new context as Western leaders have begun acknowledging the stark social-Darwinist logic of state competition and the necessary militarization of foreign policy. With this trend comes the masculinization of politics, the growth of the arms industry, and the degradation of the environment at a time when global politics needs to confront the impending climate catastrophe. As during the Cold War, those who advocate this seemingly realist posture decry what they call the illusion of values-led foreign policies and United Nations diplomatic leadership. Their position is reminiscent of Otto von Bismarck's dictum from 1862: "Not through speeches and majority decisions will the great questions of the day be decided—that was the great mistake of 1848 and 1849—but by iron and blood."[2] In referring to the short-lived national parliament that failed to unite German territories under liberal auspices, he was contrasting the hardheaded realism of state interests with the utopianism of politics as dialogue and consensus.

Do we face this dichotomy today? One of the most famous proponents of the international-relations theory of "realism," the political scientist John Mearsheimer, believes his position to be rational because it reflects the unwritten laws of geopolitics, namely that states pursue their own interests without much regard for universal values. He has thus warned for a decade that Ukrainian efforts to seek NATO membership would provoke an invasion from Russia because Russian leaders have consistently

1. David Slater, "The Imperial Present and the Geopolitics of Power," *Geopolitics* 1, no. 2 (2010): 191–205.

2. "Excerpt from Bismarck's 'Blood and Iron' Speech (1862)," trans. Jeremiah Riemer, German History in Documents and Images, accessed July 10, 2023, https://ghdi.ghi-dc.org/sub_document.cfm?document_id=250.

declared that such efforts threaten their statehood, which demands spheres of influence and buffer states. To ignore these threats is, by implication, irrational, even if the Russian demand is not necessarily reasonable.[3]

Recent scholarship also draws attention to realism. Matthew Specter's book *The Atlantic Realists* (2022) demonstrates that realism was not imported to the United States by German émigrés in the mid-twentieth century, as is commonly thought, but developed in a transatlantic exchange in the late nineteenth century, as both countries started to assemble overseas empires.[4] Realism, in this reading, originated in the new discipline of geopolitics, which saw established and rising empires in competition, all demanding spheres of influence for their development and permanent security. The original claim to a sphere of influence was the Monroe Doctrine, expressed by US President James Monroe in 1823. It determined that Old World intervention in the New World of the Americas threatened US security interests and would be treated as a hostile act. Such leaders—and the realists who study them—talk about "permanent security interests."[5] According to this logic, Ukrainian neutrality—or client status—is a permanent security imperative for Russia because it cannot afford to have an "anti-Russia" on its doorstep, or in its historical heartland, as Russian nationalists view Ukraine.[6]

Is this the realism we see today? Only in part. Mearsheimer does not question if Russian claims about its sphere of influence are legitimate or not; they are, for realists, an objective fact that we ignore at our peril. He invokes the Monroe Doctrine to state that

3. John J. Mearsheimer, *The Tragedy of Great Power Politics* (New York: Norton, 2001); Mearsheimer, "Why the Ukraine Crisis Is the West's Fault: The Liberal Delusions That Provoked Putin," *Foreign Affairs* 93, no. 5 (September/October 2014). See also Benjamin Schwarz and Christopher Layne, "Why Are We in Ukraine? On the Dangers of American Hubris," *Haters Magazine*, July 9, 2023, https://harpers.org/archive/2023/06/why-are-we-in-ukraine/.

4. Matthew G. Specter, *The Atlantic Realists: Empire and International Political Thought between Germany and the United States* (Stanford, CA: Stanford University Press, 2022).

5. Flemming Splidsboel-Hansen, "Past and Future Meet: Aleksandr Gorchakov and Russian Foreign Policy," *Europe-Asia Studies* 54, no. 3 (2002): 384.

6. Andrew Osborn and Alexander Marrow, "Putin Says Ukraine Is Becoming an 'Anti-Russia', Pledges Response," *Reuters*, May 14, 2022, https://www.reuters.com/world/europe/putin-says-russia-will-respond-ukraines-cleansing-political-space-2021-05-14/.

the United States would never tolerate a hostile state at its borders. So far, no one has contradicted him on this point. Like Henry Kissinger in Davos in 2022, he enjoins Ukraine to be neutral and cede territory to end the hostilities.[7] They are not advocating for escalatory warfare. Seeking to defeat and thus permanently weaken Russia, they argue, is unrealistic in view of its nuclear capacity and stated belief that a Western orientation for Ukraine poses an existential threat to Russia's survival. In Germany, the realist position, paradoxically, is the cynical combination of economic pragmatism and historical justice: buying cheap Russian energy under the cover of historical indebtedness because Nazi Germany inflicted such terrible damage on the Soviet Union. In this way, a values-led policy aligns neatly with the imperatives of German industry and the national economy. Calls to militarize German and Western politics come from liberal internationalists speaking in the name of "the West," not from classical US realists who opposed the invasion of Iraq twenty years ago and a generation earlier criticized the US campaign in Vietnam. Cold War rhetoric is being wielded anew by liberal internationalists, not by classical realists: "The future of the democratic world will be determined by whether the Ukrainian military can break a stalemate with Russia and drive the country backwards—perhaps even out of Crimea for good," write prominent US pro-war commentators.[8]

Relatedly, for the "small nations" between Germany and Russia who can invoke histories of occupation over the centuries as warranting their hard-won and jealously guarded sovereignty, the state is not the enemy but the protective shield against outside intervention. It is no accident that the concept of genocide was formed in this region by a Belorussian-born Polish-educated Jewish lawyer—Raphael Lemkin—during the Second World War. The experience of nationality as fragile and threatened by predatory occupiers is intensely recalled and felt. Freedom is not just individual but collective, indeed anti-colonial or anti-imperial: expelling invaders and establishing democratic institutions of

7. Timothy Bella, "Kissinger Says Ukraine Should Cede Territory to Russia to End War," *Washington Post*, May 24, 2022, https://www.washingtonpost.com/world/2022/05/24/henry-kissinger-ukraine-russia-territory-davos/.

8. Anne Applebaum and Jeffrey Goldberg, "The Counteroffensive," *The Atlantic*, May 1, 2023, https://www.theatlantic.com/magazine/archive/2023/06/counteroffensive-ukraine-zelensky-crimea/673781/.

self-government. Many people understand and sympathize with this impulse, identifying with Ukrainians' struggle to liberate their homeland from Russian occupation.

One of the vexing dilemmas we confront is that the impulse to support smaller states from their paranoid and aggressive neighbors can be instrumentalized by the liberal-internationalist permanent-security project that is further militarizing the West. It is often forgotten that one of the key planks of British rationale and propaganda in the First World War was ensuring the sovereignty of small states like Belgium. In doing so, the British continued nineteenth-century reasoning by imperial apologists who argued that Pax Britannica, the century of relative peace before the start of the First World War, benefited humanity by civilizing savage and barbarous peoples and ending the slave trade. Now liberal internationalists cast the current war as a rerun of the Second World War, with Putin as Hitler. In this framing, those counseling caution like Kissinger are appeasers, as Chamberlain was of Hitler. Accordingly, realists warn against sleepwalking into a new world war, as the Great Powers did in 1914. Seen this way, all parties are speaking the same language—of state interests, spheres of influence, civilizational struggle, and national survival—which ends up with what political scientists call "security dilemmas," meaning that one state's security requirements are regarded by neighboring states as a peril. Confronting this dilemma is David Graeber and David Wengrow's comprehensive book *The Dawn of Everything: A New History of Humanity* (2021). In it, they pose the question: How did we get stuck with security fears governing our lives?

How We Got Stuck

Graeber and Wengrow ask how the development of the modern state and concomitant infringements on our elementary freedom came to be seen as an inevitable and necessary trajectory of human history. It was not always so. As they demonstrate, archaeological and anthropological research indicates that humans experimented with various social arrangements for millennia that did not always violate the three human freedoms: the freedom to move and relocate, the freedom to disobey and ignore authority, and the freedom to collectively shape what they call "entirely new social realities, or shift back and forth between different ones." One of their points is to remind readers of these freedoms that "have gradually receded, to the point where a majority of people living today can barely comprehend what it might be like to live in a social order based on them."[9]

Graeber and Wengrow observe that the state is a combination of three governing principles: the control of violence, the control of information, and the control of individual charisma, which translate, respectively, to sovereignty, bureaucracy, and a competitive political field or democracy. Scholars have erred, they say, in projecting this combination back onto history, when in fact societies were usually governed by only one of them. Today we experience a unique constellation of all three: "All these accounts seem to assume that there is only one possible end point to this process: that these various types of domination were somehow bound to come together, sooner or later, in something like the particular form taken by modern states in America and France at the end of the eighteenth century, a form which was gradually imposed on the rest of the world after both world wars."[10]

They are skeptical about modern states, including putatively democratic ones, which, they observe, are dominated by elites while the population largely plays the role of spectator. If anything, they suggest, modern democracy's roots lie in aristocratic rather than Athenian traditions. How and why it came to this, they conclude, "must remain a matter for speculation."[11] Their challenge is to think non-teleologically about world history, to consider the force of contingency, so that the radical questions they pose about human freedom beyond modern states can be pondered and answered.

A point of their book is to think about these questions in different ways. For example, contrary to many accounts, they argue that warfare was not a constant of human life until relatively recently. When it does become central to certain polities, they observe the loss of freedoms and the modeling of governance on the patriarchal household.[12] Drawing on the respective work of Orlando Patterson and Franz Baermann Steiner, they trace this modular pattern to ancient Rome, in which natural freedom was

9. David Graeber and David Wengrow, *The Dawn of Everything: A New History of Humanity* (New York: Farrar, Straus and Giroux, 2021), 503.

10. Graeber and Wengrow, 367, 369.

11. Graeber and Wengrow, 504.

12. Graeber and Wengrow, 508.

defined as the male individual's ownership of property, including of enslaved peoples. The latter were often obtained in wars of conquest and became the personal property of the male head of the household, a soldier. His freedom consisted in disposing of his property as he pleased. In this way, slavery and property law intersected. The enslaved person became an object (*res*) and part of the household, joining women and children, over whom the patriarch had near absolute authority. This model of military and familial subordination linking domestic care and domination was more tightly wound in Rome than in other societies, which handled them with greater flexibility, thereby allowing more freedom, especially for women.

Did, then, the "relationship between external warfare and the internal loss of freedoms," they ask, lead to "systems of ranking and then to large systems of domination" like "dynastic kingdoms and empires"?[13] It is a difficult question to answer, they concede, but the evidence they assemble points to Roman law and its military entailments, themselves the product of an expansionary empire. The Roman historian Sallust (86–35 BCE) is apparently the first to refer to the Roman state as *imperium*. Over time, empire came to mean the domination of one society by another, usually backed by military force; imperial expansion entailed dominion whether by annexation or through less formal means, but it did not necessitate colonization.[14] Indeed, empire can exist without colonization; Ottoman rule in Egypt was not colonial because of the large measure of local self-administration and the absence of permanent settlers. Alternatively, empires often engaged in settlement and resettlement, colonizing frontier regions with loyal subjects; the Romans referred to its settlements of soldiers on conquered territory as *colonia*.

These two modalities of conquest could be combined. Alexis de Tocqueville wrote: "The Romans, in general, did both.

13. Graeber and Wengrow, 507.

14. The following exposition draws on chapter 6 of A. Dirk Moses, *The Problems of Genocide: Permanent Security and the Language of Transgression* (Cambridge: Cambridge University Press, 2021). See the lucid analysis of Ronald Grigor Suny, "The Empire Strikes Out: Imperial Russia, 'National' Identity, and Theories of Empire," in *A State of Nations: Empire and Nation-Making in the Age of Lenin and Stalin*, ed. Ronald Grigor Suny and Terry Martin (Oxford: Oxford University Press, 2001), 23–66.

They seized the country's government, and in several parts of it they founded colonies that were nothing other than far-flung little Roman societies." Tocqueville accordingly advised French authorities in subduing Algeria after 1830 to dominate the interior so the coastal regions could be settled.[15] He and other apologists denied that such wars of conquest were exterminatory in intention—they sought to use only as much force as necessary to achieve their aims. Even so, imperial conquest and warfare were governed by the logic of permanent security in various ways. In the first place, the aim of the colonizer was not just to defeat military forces but also to annex territory and rule over a foreign people. War aims were not limited, as they customarily were in intra-European wars; they were absolute. "Colonial conquerors came to stay," entailing massive disruptions to subjugated communities. Second, the colonizer often ended up waging war against the entire population because it was difficult to distinguish between combatants and noncombatants, especially when guerrilla-style resistance ensued.[16] In general, imperial troops prevailed over opponents even when outnumbered because they were regularly paid, well supplied, and trained. The ability to concentrate forces at one point was more decisive than technological superiority alone, especially if Indigenous agents could be conscripted.[17]

The most fatal logic of permanent security is the violent escalation provoked by local resistance, which leads to reprisal and revenge killing to ensure that opposition is stamped out once and for all. Rome's armies occasionally exterminated entire cities

15. Alexis de Tocqueville, *Writings on Empire and Slavery*, ed. Jennifer Pitts (Baltimore: Johns Hopkins University Press, 2001), 61, 65.

16. Horst L. Wesseling, "Colonial Wars: An Introduction," in *Imperialism and War: Essays on Colonial Wars in Asia and Africa*, ed. Jaap A. de Moor and Horst L. Wesseling (Leiden: Brill, 1988), 3; Peter Paret, "Colonial Experience and European Military Reform at the End of the Eighteenth Century," in *Warfare and Empires*, ed. Douglas M. Peters (Aldershot: Ashgate, 1997), 357–70.

17. Michael Howard, "Colonial Wars and European Wars," in De Moor and Wesseling, *Imperialism and War*, 218–23; George Raudzens, "Why Did the Amerindian Defences Fail? Parallels in the European Invasions of Hispaniola, Virginia and Beyond," *War in History* 3, no. 3 (1996): 331–52; Luke Godwin, "The Fluid Frontier: Central Queensland, 1845–63," in *Colonial Frontiers: Indigenous-European Encounters in Settler Societies*, ed. Lynette Russell (Manchester: Manchester University Press, 2001), 112.

that resisted or rebelled against its rule.[18] Punishing and avenging treachery and betrayal, experienced as an insult and expression of contempt, was another motivation for destroying a people or city. Rome's attack on Carthage, which it accused of basic breaches of trust, is a classic example. Rome withdrew the right of pity and limited warfare; vengeance and indignation drove it to impose collective capital punishment.[19] In 133 BCE, the Romans destroyed Numantia on the Iberian Peninsula for defying Roman rule, as they had Carthage thirteen years earlier. The sieges and subsequent destruction of Jerusalem between 70 BCE and 136 CE also can be seen in this light.

Terror played an important role in imperial conquest and governance. Massacring entire towns hastened the surrender of others when they heard the news. The relentless pursuit of enemy peoples is also a recurring feature of permanent security through the ages. Enemies were pursued to the extent that they no longer represented a threat or sufficient vengeance had been exacted. Sometimes the destruction was total. What these scenarios show is that real or imagined resistance to imperial or national rule can radicalize a policy of "pacification." Resistance leads to reprisals and counterinsurgency that aim at the continued destruction of a presumed enemy to achieve permanent security, so that never again would such resistance recur.[20]

Imperial thinkers devoted considerable thought to the problem of "small wars," with their pattern of conquest followed by resistance. Although they advised against exasperating the conquered population, the destruction of villages and crops was countenanced if necessary. Tocqueville's liberal scruples were not shared by many French in Algeria, as he reported in 1833:

> [In one view,] to subjugate the Arabs, we should fight them with the utmost violence and in the Turkish manner, that is to say, by killing everything we meet. I have heard

18. Benjamin Isaac, *The Invention of Racism in Classical Antiquity* (Princeton, NJ: Princeton University Press, 2004), 216.

19. David Konstan, "Anger, Hatred, and Genocide in Ancient Greece," *Common Knowledge* 13, no. 1 (2007): 170–87.

20. Benjamin A. Valentino, Paul Huth, and Dylan Balch-Lindsay, "'Draining the Sea': Mass Killing and Guerrilla Warfare," *International Organization* 58, no. 2 (2004): 375–407.

> this view supported by officers who took it to the point of bitterly regretting that we have started to take prisoners in some places, and many assured me that they encouraged their soldiers to spare no one. For my part, I returned from Africa with the distressing notion that we are now fighting far more barbarously than the Arabs themselves. For the present, it is on their side that one meets with civilization.

At the same time, he regarded burning harvests, emptying silos, and interning civilians as "unfortunate necessities […] to which any people that wants to wage war on the Arabs is obliged to submit." The reason for such extreme measures was that war was being waged on populations, not governments. Perceived "necessity" could compel liberals like Tocqueville to defend wars against entire populations.[21]

Early Modern Europe and Permanent Security

In view of Tocqueville's invocation of Roman precedent, Graeber and Wengrow rightly declare eighteenth-century France to be an inheritor of Roman traditions. As we know, early modern France normalized, even globalized, the modern state. This analysis allows us to propose an answer to the question of how security dilemmas came to define and limit our imagination of human freedom. Compressed and simplified, the story goes like this: In the sixteenth century, writers like Machiavelli advocated armed militancy and raison d'état to ensure political stability, continuity, and civic virtue. This type of thinking was enabled by the collapse of the Roman Empire long before and the splintering of Christendom into a multiplicity of realms, including small city-states, each preoccupied with its own survival. Out of this highly competitive environment, which did not characterize far richer parts of the world like China, came a military revolution and eventually the rudiments of the modern state necessary to

21. Tocqueville, *Writings on Empire and Slavery*, 70, 87. See also Jennifer Pitts, "Empire and Democracy: Tocqueville and the Algeria Question," *Journal of Political Philosophy* 8, no. 3 (2000): 295–318; Cheryl B. Welch, "Colonial Violence and the Rhetoric of Evasion: Tocqueville on Algeria," *Political Theory* 31, no. 2 (2003): 235–64; and more recently, William Gallois, *A History of Violence in the Early Algerian Colony* (Basingstoke: Palgrave Macmillan, 2013).

wage war: a tax-collecting bureaucracy and standing army so inimical to the three fundamental freedoms.

Theorists of sovereignty like Jean Bodin and Thomas Hobbes justified these developments. Self-preservation became the basic right, or even the obligation, of early modern polities. John Locke called self-preservation a "fundamental law of Nature" that trumped obligations to others. Emer de Vattel declared *un droit de sûreté* (a right to security) and the right of self-defense.[22] The link to permanent security was the doctrine of necessity: feeling forced to react when collective security was threatened. Early modern thinkers tried to limit the doctrine of necessity by linking it to immediate self-defense rather than vaguely defined self-preservation, because the latter could escalate immediate security to "permanent" security, meaning the anticipation of future threats, which would lead to endless warfare. In Article 51 of the UN Charter, ratified in 1945, the enshrinement of self-defense as the only legal justification for force stands in this tradition, as it is narrower than self-preservation, but states still reason in terms of both. The fact that it took over seventy years after the Nuremberg trials for states to agree on a definition of the crime of aggression (in 2010) indicates the subjective nature of such assessments. For example, in 1981, Israel justified its bombing of an Iraqi nuclear reactor by saying it had "performed an elementary act of self-preservation, both morally and legally," conveniently but misleadingly invoking Article 51.[23] As does Russia today.

Lest we fall into the trap of narrating the conjunctural development of the modern state as the "rise of the West," it is important to recall that in the fifteenth century even the bigger states in Europe, like Spain, Portugal, France, and England, were relatively weak in global terms. Recent research underlines how the Spanish conquistadors were effectively privateers who inserted themselves as minor players into intra-American rivalries. For all the human devastation they eventually caused, including the introduction of disease and slavery, the Spanish were comparatively few in number and dependent on local alliances. Similarly, the small number of Portuguese in the Indian Ocean were limited to coastal trading

22. Richard Tuck, *Rights of War and Peace: Political Thought and the International Order from Grotius to Kant* (Oxford: University of Oxford Press, 1999).

23. Murry Colin Alder, *The Inherent Right of Self-Defence in International Law* (Dordrecht: Springer, 2013), 141.

posts. The English and Dutch states were so poor and weak that they chartered private trading companies that had to compromise with local powers in India and the Malay Archipelago.[24] These European companies established the transatlantic slave trade that, together with the tea, sugar, and cotton extracted from India and the Americas, contributed to the beginning of the Industrial Revolution in the late eighteenth century.

This precarity led to increasingly militarized engagement with locals and the prioritization of security. The legal justification of their aggression as self-defense then laid the foundation for later imperial expansion. In the sixteenth century, for example, the Salamanca School of theologians justified Spanish depredations in the Americas by interpreting Indian resistance as aggression, thereby coding Spanish reprisals as self-defense and thus just.[25] Accordingly, the violence of imperial reason and settler accumulation was not included in the laws of nations: apart from occasional scandals, contemporaries did not see their security measures as excessive or transgressive. For this reason, the social scientist Mark Neocleous observes that the laws of war, as they developed in the early modern period, justified the crushing of Indigenous resistance as legal: "In the bourgeois mind, *the global war of primitive accumulation was the archetypal just war*." In other words, "'The class war was historically a just war. International law was a key weapon used in the global class war.'"[26]

The German jurist Carl Schmitt made this point in 1950, though from the opposite political perspective. A proponent of European empire and apologist for the Nazi state, Schmitt understood the violence of what he called *Landnahme* (land appropriation). It is the process of territorial conquest and annexation that he saw as the basis not only of European expansion but of statehood itself. The establishment of European states could be traced to what he termed *Völkerwanderung*, mass migrations of

24. Lauren Benton, *A Search for Sovereignty: Law and Geography in European Empires, 1400–1900* (Cambridge: Cambridge University Press, 2009).

25. A. Dirk Moses, "Empire Resistance and Security: International Law and the Transformative Occupation of Palestine," *Humanity: An International Journal of Human Rights, Humanitarianism, and Development* 8, no. 2 (2017): 379–409.

26. Mark Neocleous, "International Law as Primitive Accumulation; Or, the Secret of Systematic Colonization," *European Journal of International Law* 23, no. 4 (2012): 957; italics in original.

peoples tantamount to "a series of great land appropriations." The same process obtained in empire: "The history of colonialism in its entirety is as well a history of spatially determined processes of settlement in which order and orientation are combined." The legal order of European empires was predicated on control of territory that was wrested from "'wild' peoples" in colonial wars of annihilation. These wars disregarded the constraints of competition and warfare among European states, which were displaced to far-off non-European lands, thereby stabilizing Europe.[27] Combined with his influential theory of statehood as the sovereign's ability to proclaim states of emergency and violently impose order, Schmitt's notion of land appropriation made imperial conquest and settler colonialism the secret driver of Western state development.

The intensification of colonial rule over the course of the nineteenth century points to a significant transition in the history of empire and permanent security: from the land and continental empires that organized humanity for millennia with economies of tribute and taxation to the blue-water European empires that inaugurated global capitalism and centralizing bureaucratic-military states. As Tocqueville noted, both forms of foreign rule marked European expansion, beginning with the Spanish conquest of the Americas in the late fifteenth century. This was also part of what Karl Marx called *ursprüngliche Akkumulation* (often translated as "primitive accumulation," though "originary" is more accurate), the process by which English commons and church lands were privatized and agricultural producers were separated from their means of production to become wage laborers, whose surplus the landowner kept in accumulating further capital. Marx focused on the expropriation and proletarianization of the English peasantry—what he called the "classic form" of originary accumulation—because he wanted to account for the birth of industrial capitalism in England. He also observed that this English transformation was dependent on earlier imperial developments. "In actual history," declared Marx, "it is notorious that conquest, enslavement, robbery,

27. Carl Schmitt, *The Nomos of the Earth in the International Law of the Jus Publicum Europaeum*, trans. G. L. Ulmen (New York: Telos, 2003), 80–82, 132, 142. The historian Lauren Benton observes that Schmitt's distinction between European and non-European space in the application of nascent laws of war is too sharply drawn; see Benton, *Search for Sovereignty*, ch. 6.

murder, briefly force, play the great part" in originary accumulation. The violent expropriations of European empire began with the Spanish in the Americas. "The discovery of gold and silver in America, the extirpation, enslavement and entombment in mines of the aboriginal population, the beginning of the conquest and looting of the East Indies, the turning of Africa into a warren for the commercial hunting of black-skins, signalised the rosy dawn of the era of capitalist production."[28]

This list suggests that originary accumulation outside Europe mainly consisted of violent plunder: "The treasures captured outside Europe by undisguised looting, enslavement, and murder," wrote Marx, "floated back to the mother-country and were there turned into capital." He followed his contemporaries in distinguishing between colonies of exploitation and settler colonialism. The latter were "real Colonies, virgin soils, colonised by free immigrants," and "colonies properly called."[29]

But Marx was less interested in the fate of the Indigenous peoples than in the capitalist exploitation of settlers.[30] For that reason, he regarded colonies of exploitation as more brutal. "The treatment of the aborigines," he continued, "was, naturally, most frightful in plantation-colonies destined for export trade only, such as the West Indies, and in rich and well-populated countries, such as Mexico and India, that were given over to plunder."[31] Missing in his analysis was a sustained attention to the principal form of originary accumulation in settler colonies, namely the expropriation of land after the removal or destruction of its Indigenous owners.[32] In shifting the focus, we can see dispossession rather than proletarianization as the salient mode

28. Karl Marx, *Capital: A Critique of Political Economy*, ed. Friedrich Engels, trans. Samuel More and Edward Aveling (New York: Modern Library, 1906), 787, 785, 823.

29. Marx, 826, 838n1.

30. Philip McMichael, "Settlers and Primitive Accumulation: Foundations of Capitalism in Australia," *Review* 4, no. 2 (1980): 307–34. See also Gabriel Piterberg and Lorenzo Veracini, "Wakefield, Marx, and the World Turned Inside Out," *Journal of Global History* 10, no. 3 (2015): 457–78.

31. Marx, *Capital*, 825.

32. Glen Coulthard, *Red Skin, White Masks: Rejecting the Colonial Politics of Recognition* (Minneapolis: University of Minnesota Press, 2014), 19–20.

of accumulation, at least in these parts of the world, amounting to a distinctive mode of "settler accumulation."[33]

Marx noted settler-colonial violence only briefly in *Capital*, reporting how settlers in New England set premiums on "every Indian scalp and every captured red skin."[34] His remark that this practice occurred when "a certain tribe" was proclaimed "rebels" points to the logic of permanent security in colonialism and Western state building: namely, defending originary accumulation from Indigenous resistance. It is no accident that in German colonies in Africa, the authorities perpetrated mass violence in suppressing Indigenous uprisings.[35]

Resistance as Nation-State Formation

How did Indigenous people respond to this hyper-exploitation? One mode was "millenarian rebellion" directed against foreign elements perceived as threats to their survival.[36] These were not pretty affairs. Writing of the so-called Indian Mutiny, Marx thought the "infamous" conduct of the "sepoys" was "only the reflex, in a concentrated form, of England's own conduct in India, not only during the epoch of the foundation of her Eastern Empire, but even during the last ten years of a long-settled rule. [...] There is something in human history like retribution; and it is a rule of historical retribution that its instruments be forged not by the offended, but by the offender himself."[37] Writing in the same vein, Jean-Paul Sartre noted that "in Algeria and Angola, Europeans are massacred at sight; it is the moment of the boomerang; it is the

33. Nicholas A. Brown, "The Logic of Settler Accumulation in a Landscape of Perpetual Vanishing," *Settler Colonial Studies* 4, no. 1 (2014): 7.

34. Marx, *Capital*, 825–26.

35. Dominik Schaller, "From Conquest to Genocide: Colonial Rule in German Southwest Africa and German East Africa," in *Empire, Colony, Genocide: Conquest, Occupation and Subaltern Resistance in World History*, ed. A. Dirk Moses (New York: Berghahn Books, 2008), 296–324; Jürgen Zimmerer and Joachim Zeller, eds., *Genocide in German South-West Africa: The Colonial War of 1904–1908 and Its Aftermath* (Monmouth: Merlin Press, 2008).

36. Mike Davis, *Late Victorian Holocausts: El Nino Famines and the Making of the Third World* (London: Verso, 2001), 177–210; Nicholas A. Robins, *Native Insurgencies and the Genocidal Impulse in the Americas* (Bloomington: Indiana University Press, 2005); Nicholas A. Robins and Adam Jones, eds., *Genocides by the Oppressed: Subaltern Genocide in Theory and Practice* (Bloomington: Indiana University Press, 2009).

37. Karl Marx, *Karl Marx on Colonialism and Modernization*, ed. Shlomo Avineri (New York: Doubleday, 1969), 224.

third stage of violence; it comes back on us, it strikes us, and we do not realize any more than we did the other times that it's we who have launched it."[38] Frantz Fanon agreed: "The violence of the colonial regime and the counter-violence of the native balance each other and respond to each other in an extraordinary reciprocal homogeneity."[39] The Tunisian Jew Albert Memmi was also attracted to the Marxist proposition that colonialism produced its own negation by bringing forth an utterly alienated colonized population whose only prospect of dignified life was the "complete liquidation of colonization."[40]

How was the alienation of the "native" issued from colonialism generated? Does it offer a way out of "stuckness"? These Francophone anti-colonial thinkers pointed out that the foundational binary between settler and native was a colonial product. In such a "Manichean world" (Fanon) of colonialism, in which the settler cast the native as the incarnation of absolute evil, natives had to invert this value hierarchy for their own self-respect. "Colonialism creates the patriotism of the colonized," wrote Sartre.[41] Memmi explained the source of this nativism in his famous book from 1957, *The Colonizer and the Colonized.* His basic message was that "being considered and treated apart by colonialist racism, the colonized ends up accepting this Manichaean division of the colony and, by extension, of the whole world." Consequently, "in the eyes of the colonized, all Europeans in the colonies are *de facto* colonizers."[42] What's more, the practical impossibility of assimilation—because of the colonizer's refusal and because of the self-denial entailed—meant that the native inevitably resorted to traditional values as a compensatory orientation. But these values, usually familial and religious, had become petrified by colonial pressure, and did not promote social progress. Nativism was reactionary. By ontologizing collectives in the same way as

38. Jean-Paul Sartre, preface to Frantz Fanon, *Wretched of the Earth,* trans. Constance Farrington (New York: Grove Weidenfeld, 1963), 20.

39. Fanon, *Wretched of the Earth,* 88.

40. Albert Memmi, *The Colonizer and the Colonized* (Boston: Beacon Press, 1965), 151.

41. Fanon, *Wretched of the Earth,* 93; Jean-Paul Sartre, introduction to Memmi, *Colonizer and the Colonized,* xxviii; Abdul R. JanMohamed, *Manichean Aesthetics: The Politics of Literature in Colonial Africa* (Amherst: University of Massachusetts Press, 1983), 4.

42. Memmi, *Colonizer and the Colonized,* 130–31.

the settler, and "condemning each individual of that group," the colonized became "a xenophobe and racist."[43]

Sartre and Memmi did not applaud the chauvinism and racism of anti-colonialist struggles, and Fanon's aversion to nativism is well known; racism and "a legitimate desire for revenge" could not "sustain a war of liberation," he thought. Memmi eventually left Tunis for Paris because, as a Jew, he found life impossible in postcolonial Muslim Tunisia.[44] As Marxists, they were cosmopolitan internationalists who preferred a popular front of anti-colonialists that included sympathetic settlers, some closer to the liberation ideal than the Africans or Arabs. National liberation entailed transcending the terms of settler/native to create a new socialist nation of equal citizens. The colonial system needed to be transformed by expropriating the collaborating Indigenous bourgeoisie rather than simply expelling settlers.[45] They wished decolonization to be the assertion of freedom when the newly constituted people could gain political agency, enter history, and create their own authentic civilization, not just a variation of the colonizer's.

At the same time, these writers told their European reading publics that their expectation of a nonviolent, non-racist, anti-colonialist struggle was unrealistic.[46] Violent and racist anti-colonialism was a predictable phase through which colonized peoples had to pass, even if it entailed "tragic mishaps," in Fanon's words. Fanon himself was ambivalent, famously praising this violence as a "cleansing force" through which "the native frees himself from his inferiority complex and from his despair and inaction; it makes him fearless and restores his self-respect." This redemptive nationalism was necessary to assert a new postcolonial culture: "The most elementary, most savage, and the most undifferentiated

43. Memmi, 130, 139. Memmi's insight closely resembles the theory of social regression advanced by Vamik Volkan in both *Bloodlines: From Ethnic Pride to Ethnic Terrorism* (New York: Farrar, Straus and Giroux, 1997); and *Blind Trust: Large Groups and Their Leaders in Times of Crisis and Terror* (Charlottesville: University of Virginia Press, 2004).

44. Albert Memmi, *Jews and Arabs* (Chicago: J Philip O'Hara, 1975).

45. Fanon, *Wretched of the Earth*, 146, 158; Benita Parry, "Resistance Theory/Theorising Resistance or Two Cheers for Nativism," in *Colonial Discourse/Postcolonial Theory*, ed. Francis Barker, Peter Hulme, and Margaret Iversen (Manchester: University of Manchester Press, 1994), 172–91.

46. Memmi, *Colonizer and the Colonized*, 134–37; Sartre, preface to *Wretched of the Earth*, 18, 21.

nationalism is the most fervent and efficient means of defending national culture."[47] Sartre supported Fanon's rendition of the conflict with some stirring lines: the struggle's "irrepressible violence is neither sound and fury, nor the resurrection of savage instincts, nor even the effect of resentment: it is man recreating himself."[48] For all the romanticization evident here, these thinkers both expressed and explained the revolutionary violence of the colonized as the moment of salvation.

Fanon was aware that racism, far from being a transitional political emotion, was being used by the "national bourgeoisie" to secure its own position in the postcolonial order. Rather than constructing a new nation beyond race, these elites were allowing precolonial tribal rivalries to recur.[49] Moreover, the new state appeared to the liberated populations less as their own democratic creation than as a distant apparatus that was milked by a dominant rival ethnic grouping for its own benefit. Their security and identity were therefore more likely to inhere in pre-independence traditional ethnic attachments than in a chimerical supra-tribal national identity.[50] The catastrophe of postcolonial African political stability, civil war, and genocide has been blamed on this failure to transcend race during and after decolonization. Writing in the tradition of the Francophone intellectuals, the historian Mahmood Mamdani blames this failure on colonialism: "That greater crime was to politicize indigeneity, first as a settler libel against the native, and then as a native self-assertion."[51]

Anti-colonial affects like humiliation pertain to local and national uprisings against land and sea empires throughout the nineteenth century, from Haiti to Christian Ottoman provinces to the early decolonization of the Iberian territories in South America.

47. Fanon, *Wretched of the Earth*, 148, 94, 24.

48. "The native cures himself of colonial neurosis by thrusting out the settler through force of arms. When his rage boils over, he rediscovers his lost innocence and he comes to know himself in that he himself creates himself." Sartre, preface to *Wretched of the Earth*, 22.

49. Fanon, *Wretched of the Earth*, 156–59.

50. Clifford Geertz, "The Integrative Revolution: Primordial Sentiments and Civil Politics in the New States," in *Old Societies and New States: The Quest for Modernity in Asia and Africa*, ed. Clifford Geertz (New York: Free Press, 1963), 109–19.

51. Mahmood Mamdani, "Beyond Settler and Native as Political Identities: Overcoming the Political Legacy of Colonialism," *Comparative Studies in Society and History* 43, no. 4 (2001): 651–54.

Whether seeking greater autonomy from imperial rule or emphatic independence, many of these uprisings began as resistance to taxation imposed to fund the imperial war machines engaged in global struggle.[52] Thus, empires operating in this competitive and expansive environment produced their own negation, or at least made them constitutively unstable unless they accommodated local autonomy, as the Habsburg Empire managed in part until the First World War.

In western Europe, early modern traditions of resistance recalled the Dutch revolt against the Spanish Habsburg dynasty from the mid-sixteenth to mid-seventeenth century, immortalized by Johann Wolfgang von Goethe's play *Egmont* (1788) and Ludwig van Beethoven's accompanying composition. In pursuing national liberation in the nineteenth century, then, local freedom was often imagined and articulated not by moving away but by staying put. Certainly, in nomadic, sparsely settled regions, locals could try to avoid central authority, as Kazakh herders did with the Soviets into the 1930s.[53] But such regions became increasingly rare as the global population and state control grew and intensified.

Staying put and self-rule now meant buying into the Western rhetoric about civilization, which claimants, whether Egyptian or Korean nationalists, brought to Versailles in 1919, seeking national independence.[54] It also entailed adopting developmental teleologies. If the Soviet State in the 1920s and 1930s spoke about "overcoming backwardness," new African states from the 1960s onward engaged in development projects and adapted the colonial state institutions they inherited.[55] Challenging the West, for the postrevolutionary and postcolonial nations, meant a developmental state as the vehicle for national freedom and future security.

52. James C. Scott, "Resistance without Protest and without Organization: Peasant Opposition to the Islamic Zakat and the Christian Tithe," *Comparative Studies in Society and History* 29, no. 3 (1987): 412–36; Sean Redding, *Sorcery and Sovereignty: Taxation, Power, and Rebellion in Rural South Africa, 1880–1963* (Athens: Ohio University Press, 2006).

53. Sarah Cameron, *The Hungry Steppe: Famine, Violence, and the Making of Soviet Kazakhstan* (Ithaca, NY: Cornell University Press, 2018).

54. Erez Manela, *The Wilsonian Moment: Self-Determination and the International Origins of Anticolonial Nationalism* (Oxford: Oxford University Press, 2007).

55. Fred Cooper, *Citizenship between Empire and Nation: Remaking France and French Africa, 1945–1960* (Princeton, NJ: Princeton University Press, 2014).

Since the 1970s, we have been confronted with the capitalist reality of the attrition of state capacities in neoliberal revolutions. Another reality is the geopolitical dilemma with which I commenced: so-called smaller states seeking freedom by relying on "great powers" and other smaller states, making themselves clients for their own ends. Yet another is the concomitant ramping up of security apparatuses to assert state power against resistance to capitalist extraction and/or to assertions of freedom against those states, large and small.

The Fatal Temptation of National Permanent Security

It is no accident that Ukrainian President Volodomyr Zelensky idealizes the State of Israel as a model for his state's armed independence—a popular notion in Ukraine and the West, irrespective of Israel's political lurch further to the right. In an article in *Foreign Affairs* in October 2022, the former Ukrainian defense minister Andriy Zagorodnyuk quoted Zelensky as saying that the country needed to become a "big Israel" until it could join NATO.[56] Who would pay for this ultra-militarization he did not say. Nor did he mention Israel's annexation of Syrian and Palestinian territories, still less its decades-long occupation of Palestine that Israeli and international human-rights NGOs call apartheid. Zagorodnyuk focused on "Ukraine's path to victory" and "how the country can take back all its territory." His euphemistic statements about how to integrate the possibly hostile populations of the Crimea and Donbas regions are reminiscent of interwar assimilation policies by new states confronting recalcitrant national minorities. His determination to liberate occupied territory also countenances the destruction of Ukrainian cities by Russian missiles so long as the war continues. So paramount is national liberation and sovereignty, Zagorodnyuk concluded, that it was worth risking Russia's use of nuclear devices, in which case, he assured readers, "severe retaliatory measures" would be necessary.

Herewith the apotheosis of the nation-state is revealed as the embodiment of imperial security logics understood as collective freedom. Quickly forgotten in the West are the reservations many harbored about the illiberal and nationalist policies of governing

56. Andriy Zagorodnyuk, "Ukraine's Path to Victory," *Foreign Affairs*, October 12, 2022.

parties in frontline NATO states like Poland. The case of Western liberalism ("freedom") was blind to the illiberalism of some members of the Western family, whose politics regarding migration and sexual freedom resemble Russia more than proclaimed Western values. With this articulation of freedom as armed permanent security by decolonizing entities, we confront a non-dialectical end point of history: of being really, badly stuck.

There are people trying to unstick this conjuncture, indeed those who have contested the settler-colonial state project along the way—the Indigenous critiques so central to *The Dawn of Everything* indicate where to look. For example, security can be rethought: "Security takes many forms. There is the security of knowing one has a statistically smaller chance of getting shot with an arrow. And then there's the security of knowing that there are people in the world who will care deeply if one is."[57] Whether these critiques represent a negation that pries us out of the position in which we are stuck may be utopian. What is certain, however, is that the justification of stuckness by both realists and liberal internationalists cannot unstick humanity. There are good grounds, then, for thinking of other options.

57. Graeber and Wengrow, *Dawn of Everything*, 20.

War Ecologies

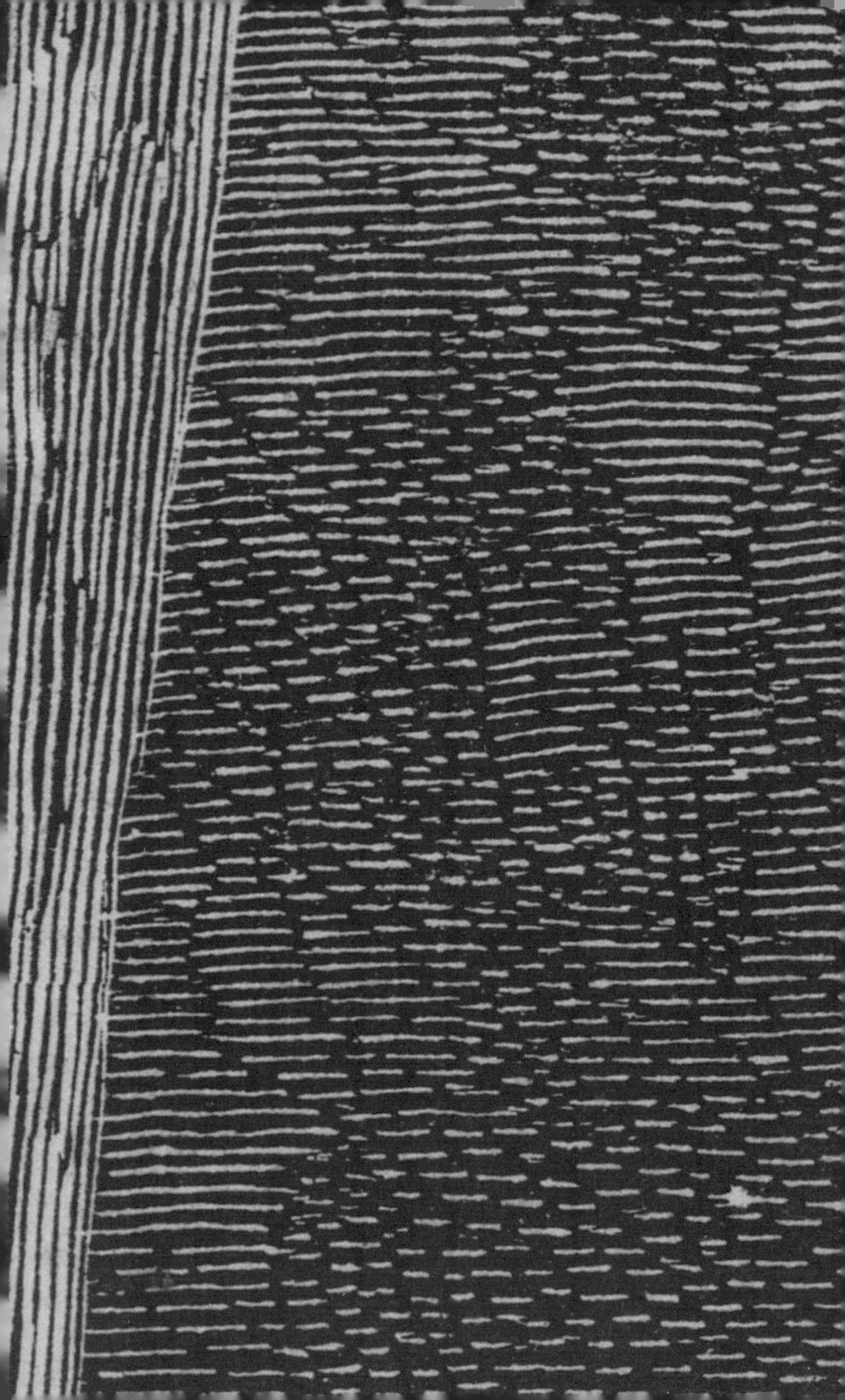

Fetishized Repression
Institutional Racism as a European Civil System
Norman Ajari

This essay presents a loose collection of thoughts prompted by a controversial expression that has given rise to much debate in France: *le racisme d'État* (state or institutional racism). Clearly this phrase is problematic, as the two notions, whose meanings are blurry even when taken separately, gain little clarity when placed side by side. It will be impossible to undertake the extensive work required to adequately define the subject in just a few pages. Instead, I shall content myself with exploring a few avenues and putting forward some hypotheses, some self-evident, some speculative. The thoughts that follow remain fragmentary and often insufficiently unified, but they are guided by a few observations set out in the form of an introduction.

Introduction

Any conversation about state or institutional racism will necessarily be controversial. Racism can almost never be objectively pinpointed within institutions and described in a way that is met with consensus. One of the most salient features of institutional racism is that it is normalized: it plays an active part in maintaining social order, it is part and parcel of ordinary, everyday reality. But any critique of the state will address the types of violence used to establish and maintain this normality. Moreover, reflecting on institutional racism involves maintaining a liberal posture as a critic who seeks to identify traces of explicit inequality in the discourse of institutions. Social conditions (forms of exposure to violence, death, exploitation, or abandonment) can guide the conversation. Essentially, institutional racism reveals itself through practices, routines, and ideas that are passed down through history and implemented by agents of the state. If, as stated in January 2018 in a report by the French Ombudsman, young Blacks and Arabs are twenty times more likely to have their ID checked by police than their white peers, it means that there is institutional racism. The existence of everyday inequality borne out by statistics and experienced by victims who testify to such treatment form the basis on which we can analyze and attempt to understand institutional racism.

Not everyone agrees on this point, however. Many journalists and politicians believe that institutional racism does not exist in France because the country's institutions allegedly have no explicitly racist ideology (a dubious statement, but let's not dwell on that for now). The problem I see in this search for hypothetical "explicit racism" is that it supplies itself with criteria that are too restrictive and often anachronistic. On this basis, the only truly satisfactory model for institutional racism, the only one that is sufficiently clear-cut, is probably the Third Reich, whose racial enemies were named, designated as enemies, and openly persecuted. Even America's racial slavery is routinely described as based on preserving the health and well-being of the enslaved as property. But in examining another historical period seen today as a prime example of institutional racism—South African apartheid—we see how stories written by the oppressors can leave us with false certainties and inaccurate hindsight.

Apartheid is now seen as a paradigm of undisputable institutional racism, but that was not always the case. Prime Minister Hendrik Verwoerd, who designed and implemented the apartheid regime in the 1950s, did not describe his project as racist. On the contrary, he talked about "separate development," hailing a policy whose aim was to promote the equality and unity of the different components of the republic. Our world has seen the triumph of the anti-apartheid party African National Congress, the political canonization of Nelson Mandela, and the elevation of Archbishop Desmond Tutu to the status of a sage. But the fifteen years that led to the regime change was a period in which Ronald Reagan recommended "constructive engagement" with the ruling party and Margaret Thatcher described Mandela's movement as a terrorist organization. The idea that South African apartheid is the quintessence of institutional racism is not the inevitable conclusion when that institution is analyzed; on the contrary, it is the product of the victory of the anti-racist movement. It is a fair bet that European and North American nations that claim to be "colorblind" and are founded on respect for equality and human dignity will, in the future, be mentioned in the same breath as Verwoerd's apartheid regime.

White Supremacy as a Founding Principle of the Modern State

The hypothesis I am seeking to corroborate is that white supremacy is a native and fundamental component of the modern state. This statement is directed at a web of institutions, cultural content, and processes of economic exchange and accumulation that help to maintain the global domination of white Europeans and their descendants—that is, the social, imaginary, and libidinal order in which the state plays an active part. The Marxist philosopher Nicos Poulantzas warned against the temptation of reducing the state to the twin ills of violent repression and misleading ideological propaganda, arguing that the state also has a creative and inventive function.[1]

Perhaps the best way to identify this function is to focus on the ideas of its proponents rather than its critics. The Nazi connections of the legal theorist Carl Schmitt are well known. A conservative Catholic, he was both an admirer of fascist regimes and an ardent defender of the European colonial project and its history. One of his major works, *The Nomos of the Earth* (1950), recounts the history of international law, demonstrating the constitutive role of the conquest of the Americas—and, more generally, the whole colonial project—in the political and legal self-definition of modern Europe. Schmitt helps us gain a better understanding of institutional racism, because in his eyes European states are neither the sole nor the primary source of the law. Ultimately, it is white supremacy, in the form of the military, political, and spiritual domination of Europe, that would constitute the very essence of modern international law. According to Schmitt, "state" law—in other words, what we usually refer to when we talk about the law that governs life in society—coexists with, and rests on, "pre-state," "extra-state," and "inter-state" law: a kind of primal legal force from which the state itself has derived its legitimacy since its foundation. This law places European self-congratulation at the heart of the role and destiny of the state. Schmitt's

1. "In short, the State also acts in a positive fashion, *creating, transforming and making* reality. It goes without saying that repression and ideological inculcation are present in the materiality of the State's current functions. But unless we are to play with words, it is hardly possible to grasp the State's economic activities by referring exclusively to this dual modality." Nicos Poulantzas, *State, Power, Socialism*, trans. Patrick Camiller (London: Verso, 2013), 30; italics in original.

description of the state's racist genesis is significant in that it does not focus on the need to eradicate racial parasites, as Nazi rhetoric does. Instead, it exudes a diffuse kind of racism in the form of the continuous, patiently elaborated affirmation of unassailable European greatness. The European state is self-congratulatory.

As one commentator notes, according to Schmitt, from the decisive year 1492 onward, "it was the great land appropriation (*Landnahme*), the conquest of the New World, that triggered the formation of an inter-state legal order in western Europe. From then on, a dozen sovereign states, all engaged in that conquest in one way or another, formed the 'Concert of Nations'; the law elaborated in the seventeenth and eighteenth centuries would formalize its legal status and structure the peaceful and warlike relationships that existed within it."[2] But this newfound solidarity was not limited to issues of shared interest. Latin American decolonial thinkers, in particular Enrique Dussel, have stressed the absurdity of using the phrase "great discoveries" to refer to contact with lands already inhabited by humans endowed with reason.[3] Schmitt, on the contrary, was fond of the phrase and defended its use, arguing that a discoverer "knows his prey better than the prey knows himself, and is able to subjugate him by means of superior education and knowledge."[4] Where Dussel highlights the incoherence of the asymmetry between the discoverer and the "discovered," Schmitt cavalierly widens the gap even further by stating that there is a radical inequality between Amerindians and Europeans, which he believes exists in the sphere of the mind, of thought, of intellect—as evidenced by the Westerners' ability to dominate.

This intellectual superiority forms the basis for two distinct relationships: first, the relationship between European states, which can oppose one another in wars governed by specific laws; and second, the relationship of these same states with non-European territories, which are seen as being ripe for appropriation, and their populations, which are seen as valueless bodies that can be

2. Jean-François Kervégan, "Carl Schmitt et 'l'unité du monde,'" *Les études philosophiques*, no. 68 (2004): 15.

3. Enrique Dussel, *The Invention of the Americas: Eclipse of "the Other" and the Myth of Modernity*, trans. Michael Barber (New York: Continuum, 1995).

4. Carl Schmitt, *The Nomos of the Earth in the International Law of Jus Publicum Europaeum*, trans. G. L. Ulmen (New York: Telos Press, 2003), 132.

massacred without remorse or reduced to servitude. This dual relationship of relative civility between European states and unfettered savagery regarding the non-European world is, in Schmitt's view, the basis and the truth of modern international law, the law of nations—what he terms the *jus publicum Europaeum.* He calls non-European lands peopled with natives "free lands."

More clearly still, eighteenth-century French jurists talked about "territories without masters." This expression underlines the fact that "non-organized territories, which were not organized politically in a way that was comparable to that which prevailed in the West, could be considered open to colonial occupation."[5] The implied overall geopolitical structure thus has two tiers: a distinction between not only European states but also those states and the rest of the world.

This contrast was exclusively based on the conviction that Europe was spiritually exceptional. Schmitt writes: "From the 16th to the 20th century, European international law considered Christian nations to be the creators and representatives of an order applicable to the whole earth. [...] *Civilization* was synonymous with *European* civilization."[6] In other words, the pre-state law that Schmitt considers to be the foundation of modern nations coincides with Europe's military and spiritual domination over the rest of the world, elevated to the status of intangible law. Elaborating on this perspective, Schmitt claims, in a lecture delivered in 1962, that each people, characterized by race, language, religion, culture, and national heritage, possesses a "spiritual substance" that it must preserve.[7] According to this philosophy, the spiritual substance of Europe lies in its global authority.

5. Dino Costantini, *Mission civilisatrice: Le rôle de l'histoire coloniale dans la construction de l'identité politique française* (Paris: La Découverte, 2008), 104.

6. Schmitt, *Nomos of the Earth*, 86.

7. Carl Schmitt, "Die Ordnung der Welt nach dem Zweiten Weltkrieg," in *Staat, Großraum, Nomos: Arbeiten aus den Jahren 1916–1969*, ed. Günter Maschke (Berlin: Duncker & Humblot, 1995), 592–618. It is not insignificant that the concept appears at the end of a paper that includes a severe critique of anti-colonialism, which Schmitt considers devoid of intelligence and imagination and berates as a sorry negation of European heritage. Though perverted by development aid and a few irksome attempts at socialization, Schmitt considers the Third World not necessarily lost, since its duty was to remain faithful to its cultural and racial substance (in other words, its ontological subservience), just as Europe has done over the four centuries the "law of nations," of which it is undeniably the center, has prevailed.

Thus, despite everything that sets modern European states apart from one another, and even despite the wars they sometimes fight, they share two features that form the basis for essential solidarity. First, they are unlike those "completely uncivilized peoples" that inhabit the Americas, Africa, and Asia, since Europe alone possesses the privilege of appropriating their lands.[8] Second, it is up to these states to defend their monopoly of legitimate violence on their own soil and to stamp out threats of civil war and revolutionary unrest. Racist colonial wars overseas are thus essentially linked to the civil war led by the state against its own population to prevent or quell uprisings.[9]

What interests me in the work of a fascist-leaning writer such as Schmitt is his attempt to base statehood on a specifically European racial rationale and intellectual power. From a materialistic or pragmatic standpoint, however, this notion of pre-state statehood is obviously pure fiction. Poulantzas rightly observes that "we cannot imagine any social phenomenon (any knowledge, power, language or writing) as posed in a state prior to the State [...]. Even if we admit that there actually was a social reality before the emergence of the State, once the latter is posited, every social reality must be conceived as maintaining constitutive relations with it."[10] In other words, the unique constitutive power that underlies the European destiny as theorized by Schmitt is, in reality, unthinkable. However, that fiction makes it possible to imagine a project for white supremacy written on the very foundations of the modern state. The spiritual superiority of Europe legitimizes, specifies, and glorifies the modern state while injecting white supremacy into Western anthropology, and even into European territoriality itself.

Fetishized Repression

The philosopher David Goldberg has shown that race was an essential part of the emergence of the modern state from 1492 onward, but he did not focus on the genealogy of the phenomenon put forward by Schmitt.[11] I think one of the values of Goldberg's work is that it demonstrates the limitations of a certain historicism

8. Schmitt, *Nomos of the Earth*, 198.

9. Éric Alliez and Maurizio Lazzarato, *Guerres et capital* (Paris: Éditions Amsterdam, 2016), 18.

10. Poulantzas, *State, Power, Socialism*, 39–40.

11. David Theo Goldberg, *The Racial State* (Malden, MA: Blackwell, 2002).

in the critique of racism. A kind of shortsightedness afflicts scholarship focusing on the racial formation of the state, its origins, the sources and history of racialization, the emergence of other discourses that are racially pejorative, and so on. But as Poulantzas suggests, it has become impossible to frame the emergence of modern racism, which is why Schmitt resorts to the fiction of pre-state law. The colonial brutality that gave birth to the modern state created a temporal rupture that Frantz Fanon analyzed in 1960: "Violence in everyday behaviour, violence against the past that is emptied of all substance, violence against the future, for the colonial regime presents itself as necessarily eternal."[12] Scholarly micro-analyses of variations in racist discourse should not have us lose sight of the fact that the emergence of the modern state is the invention of an institution that aims to ensure global European white supremacy and that intends to be eternal, not conjunctural. Racial inflections of varying intensities and instances of racial discourse only become meaningful within this horizon.

Admittedly, expressions of this white supremacy vary from period to period; the scope of what is seen as "white" (i.e., the type of humanity that has value and dignity) is modified, as is the categorization of subhumans who fall outside it. What remains constant, however, is that the modern state never stops establishing distinct types of humanity whose dignity is unequal and whose relationships with the state assume profoundly different forms. A tension runs through this operation. On the one hand, the state considers the scale of the individual relevant to its field of action because it sees individuals as having certain rights, makes them pay taxes and carry out military service, summons them to appear in court, and so on. But on the other hand, it also, sometimes simultaneously, marshals these individuals into homogenizing collective racial projects. This observation applies first and foremost to its own citizens, but not exclusively. The state deals with many individuals who are not citizens, constructing special relationships with them.

Although the modern state implements fictions such as Schmitt's pre-state law, white supremacy—its cardinal dimension—

12. Frantz Fanon, "Why We Use Violence," in *Alienation and Freedman*, ed. Jean Khalfa and Robert J. C. Young, trans. Steven Corcoran (London: Bloomsbury Academic, 2018), 654.

is too organic, too constitutive, to be thought of as a mere ideology maintained and conveyed in an ad hoc manner by the state apparatus. As the Jamaican philosopher Charles Mills writes, "Through constructions of the self, proclaimed ideals of cultural and civic identity, decisions of the state, crystallizations of juridical standing and group interests, permitted violence, and the opening and blocking of economic opportunities, race becomes 'real' and casually effective, institutionalized and materialized by white supremacy in social practices and felt phenomenologies."[13] Racism is not an ideology. In other words, race is not an imaginary relationship with real conditions of existence, to quote Louis Althusser's famous phrase, because racism generates distinct conditions of existence.[14] There is nothing imaginary about the impact of race, since modern racism deprives racialized existence, dominated by white supremacy, of any "reality" that diverges from this domination. Black people are dehumanized in many areas of their existence, and only Black thought and action can hold up their own truth to oppose that of ubiquitous white supremacy. But this is not a case of the real opposing the imaginary. On the contrary, it's a case of the political and cultural Negro imagination opposing the reality of institutional order.

Rough-hewn approaches that limit racism to a question of ideology are not alone in proposing simplistic interpretations of institutional racism. Despite the extent and interest of some critical work in the Marxist tradition, a tendency to favor a functionalist approach to race seems to me to prevent it from grasping the full extent of the problem. In this perspective, white supremacy is seen not as an end in itself but as a tool used to maintain a certain status quo. For example, according to the scholar and activist Keeanga-Yamahtta Taylor, racism in the police force is indexed to its function of defending the interests of the state and the powerful within a racial political economy. She reminds us that American police forces are rooted in a long history of controlling Black populations going back to slavery. After abolition, many

13. Charles W. Mills, "White Supremacy," in *A Companion to African-American Philosophy*, ed. Tommy L. Lott and John P. Pittman (Malden, MA: Blackwell, 2003), 273.

14. Louis Althusser, "Ideology and Ideological State Apparatuses (Notes towards an Investigation)," in *Lenin and Philosophy and Other Essays*, trans. Ben Brewster (New York: Monthly Review Press, 1971), 162.

municipalities adopted what were referred to as "Black codes": a legal arsenal that considered Black people as criminals to keep them at the mercy of planters who refused to let this newly liberated workforce escape their grasp. Taylor explains that this is how "the rampant exploitation of Black labor was contingent on the denigration of Black humanity," the preferred modality of which is criminalization.[15]

While this focus on the instrumental dimension of racism serving a capitalist state is not wrong, it is certainly partial and reductive. I find that a more accurate position was formulated by Fanon and systematized in the early 1970s by the theorist and activist Steve Biko in these terms:

> There is no doubt that the colour question in South African politics was originally introduced for economic reasons. [...] However, tradition has it that whenever a group of people has tasted the lovely fruits of wealth, security and prestige it begins to find it more comfortable to believe in the obvious lie and to accept it as normal that it alone is entitled to privilege. In order to believe this seriously, it needs to convince itself of all the arguments that support the lie. [...] White people now despise black people, not because they need to reinforce their attitude and so justify their position of privilege but simply because they actually believe that black is inferior and bad.[16]

This analysis of the South African context can be used to shed light on other situations. As evidenced in the writings of Schmitt, institutional racism is not simply a tool. It is also, and above all, what supplies the state with its coefficient of truth.

Critiques of institutional racism such as Taylor's describe the repression of the Black proletariat as motivated by the prospect of continued exploitation, but this fails to account for another dimension of this repression, which is not strictly speaking instrumental. The poet and theorist Jackie Wang convincingly

15. Keeanga-Yamahtta Taylor, *From #Blacklivesmatter to Black Liberation* (Chicago: Haymarket Books, 2016), 111.

16. Steve Biko, "Black Consciousness and the Quest for a True Humanity" (1973), in *I Write What I Like: Selected Writings*, ed. Aelred Stubbs (San Francisco: Harper & Row, 1979), 87–88.

demonstrates this: "Perhaps the desire to provide a functionalist explanation for police violence stems from an inability to face the more unsettling aspects of white supremacy: the fact that some whites—and cops in particular—get sadistic pleasure out of dominating, brutalizing, and killing black people."[17] But it is important to classify this sadism correctly and not pigeonhole it in the exotic category of BDSM or other popular tropes. Here, sadism does not immediately and solely refer to carnal pleasure resulting from the torment inflicted upon a Black body. It is, in a more abstract and radical way, a form of satisfaction caused by the negation, degradation, and humiliation of Black otherness. The theorist Frank Wilderson explains this without ambiguity: "Unlike violence against the working class, which secures an economic order, or violence against non-Black women, which secures a patriarchal order, or violence against Native Americans, which secures a colonial order, the violence of anti-Blackness secures the order of life itself; sadism in service to the prolongation of life."[18]

In other words, from the standpoint of white supremacy, the repression of non-white populations always possesses an innate positive dimension. Racist repression is reassuring for the dominant demographic and helps maintain social and national cohesion. Put another way, institutional racism relies on fetishized repression: a form of repression that is riddled with fantasy. Let us consider, for example, the *jeunes du Mantois* affair that divided French public opinion a few years ago. On December 6, 2018, during a period of nationwide protests and strikes, in the city of Mantes-la-Jolie around 150 students, most of them Black or Arab, were stopped by the police, made to kneel in submission, some for several hours, and methodically insulted and humiliated. The abuse was filmed and the videos shared by the police officers themselves, who made no attempt to hide their satisfaction and pride at their repressive tactics. Of course, their aim was to put down a strike and protect class interests, but the level of intensity and lack of restraint were only possible in the banlieues and with individuals considered to be without humanity. The extreme

17. Jackie Wang, *Carceral Capitalism* (South Pasadena, CA: Semiotext(e), 2018), 91.

18. Frank B. Wilderson III, *Afropessimism* (New York: Liveright Publishing, 2020), 92.

nature of the repression, its sordid staging, and the desire to display it on social media demonstrate that it was not just "dirty work" the police felt they had to do; instead, it played an active role in building life in the community. The subjugation did not just operate by curbing delinquency or repressing a student strike, it also made a point by tormenting and exhibiting individuals seen as creatures on the margins of humanity. The Mantois kids were targets of violence and a form of sadism that was not merely instrumental, as it directly attacked their dignity.[19] Humiliating these teens was a way of establishing or maintaining order—that of the republic—and producing a particular vision of life in the community. Institutional racism is primarily a white vision of the community, and it is a social system that prevails not only in France but in the Western world as a whole.

Translated from the French by Martyn Back

19. See Norman Ajari, *Dignity or Death: Ethics and Politics of Race*, trans. Matthew B. Smith (Cambridge: Polity, 2023).

America and the Cold War Origins of the (White) West

Nikhil Pal Singh

The conflicts and crises of the postwar period, when the cosmopolitan notion of one world shared equally by all human beings became prominent, still constellate our present. The Second World War began the dissolution of the long-standing Eurocentric world order animated by fundamental commitments to race and empire as well as the management of hierarchies across borders by a few imperial powers. At the same time, the "white West," forged through centuries of colonialism, paradoxically strengthened its power during the age of decolonization and as new nation-states formed under the pressure and direction from the world's leading power, the United States. As dispensed by the US, freedom was understood as an inheritance and capacity of those who were already secure, with some always intended to be more so than others, a division that would not only exist between nations but run through them as well.

Thus, it was not seen as a contradiction in 1947 for the US statesman Dean Acheson to promote the Truman Doctrine's "aid to free peoples" in front of a civic organization for large-scale agricultural and business interests in the Mississippi Delta, a bastion of Jim Crow segregation.[1] Any promise of future development or economic expansion in the capital-poor world (that is, the promise of "growth"), including within the US itself, implied acceptance that the past injustices that led to the impoverishment of these areas would not be actively redressed or repaired. At the same time, as the historian Odd Arne Westad notes, "American leaders consciously took on the role of leader of global capitalism and were willing to bear at least short-term burdens to ensure that the system worked."[2] These figures recognized that structural separation of economic ordering from contingent political processes—that is, the subordination of a nominally self-determining realm of politics to the ultimate sovereignty of dominant market forces—was vital. This approach

1. Dean Acheson, "The Requirements of Reconstruction," *Department of State Bulletin* 16, no. 411, May 18, 1947, 991.

2. Odd Arne Westad, introduction to *Reviewing the Cold War: Approaches, Interpretations, Theory*, ed. Odd Arne Westad (Abingdon: Frank Cass, 2000), 10.

meant that forms of direct physical coercion and discrimination, which had been the chief characteristic of colonial rule and institutionalized racism, should be avoided, even as their inherited consequences were preserved.

An additional challenge for the Western powers in the postwar years was to ensure that the reform and potential replacement of the older methods of ruling would not diminish the prerogative to exercise legitimate and durable coercive force beyond their borders. Colonial rule had always been framed as a "transitional stage to self-rule," the historian Vincente Rafael writes, with "the self that rules itself [...] only emerging by way of an intimate relationship with a colonial master who sets the standards and practices of discipline."[3] Specifically, to access nation-state sovereignty meant proving capabilities to police internal societal divisions, particularly those related to wealth and property ownership, in deference to an expanding, increasingly global arena of market rule and exchange—a kind of internal colonization. Failure to locally prioritize police over politics invited internal subversion and thus outside intervention. What could not be tolerated were efforts to achieve new societal orderings capable of resisting or fashioning local alternatives to a global architecture of capitalist rule shaped by the inequalities of the colonial past.

The tactics that the United States eventually settled on to ensure these outcomes were covert action and counterinsurgency. The Truman Doctrine, the US foreign policy to contain communism, glosses, without irony, that the liquidation of British imperial commitments across the world brought about US intervention in the Greek Civil War in the late 1940s. As Dean Rusk, at that time Truman's deputy under-secretary of state, summarized some years later, "On matters of political arrangements, the underlying thesis was that people themselves should play the decisive role as the principle of self-determination was brought to bear." In doing so, Rusk continued, the United States "turned aside from the ambitions and appetites which have historically been associated with great power."[4] Or had it? The influential US media mogul Henry

3. Vincente L. Rafael, *White Love and Other Events in Filipino History* (Durham, NC: Duke University Press, 2000), 22.

4. Dean Rusk, *The Winds of Freedom: Selections from the Speeches and Statements of Secretary Dean Rusk* (Boston: Beacon Press, 1963), 14.

Luce flatly declared that the United States "must, in Britain's place, consciously become what it has been [...] since the beginning of World War II: the champion of the remnant of Christian civilization against the forces that threatened it," a view shared by men like Rusk.[5] The right to self-determination laid out by the Atlantic Charter, signed by Roosevelt and Churchill at the beginning of the Second World War, was never a straightforward commitment by great powers to the self-rule or non-interference in the internal affairs of former colonies or subordinate states. As a principle "brought to bear" on the global situation, US foreign-policy elites understood self-determination less as a principled commitment than as a means to order the world under the auspices of the United States' own preponderance of economic and military power within the global field, and as a more effective substitute for the police power that had been exercised by imperial nations.

This insight helps cut through the implausible opposition between particularism and universalism or realism and idealism that often frames debates around the global remit of United States' foreign policy. Early Cold Warriors, much like later neoconservatives, largely disdained what the US diplomat George Kennan called a "universalistic approach" to foreign relations based on "rules and procedures which would be applicable to all countries."[6] While this view is sometimes depicted as a kind of realism in tune with the messy, uneven, riven world that emerged from the Second World War, it was also profoundly shaped by widely held skepticism toward democratic self-government at home and abroad (which was regarded as an unreliable adjunct to an elite project of global rule), as well as by commitments, both implicit and explicit, to special relationships in world politics shaped by older imperial, racial, and linguistic "amity lines."[7] Insofar as the principle of government was accepted as the consent of the governed, it was understood as

5. Henry Luce, quoted in Naoko Shibusawa, *America's Geisha Ally: Reimagining the Japanese Enemy* (Cambridge, MA: Harvard University Press, 2009), 77.

6. "Report of the Policy Planning Staff," February 24, 1948, Office of the Historian, Foreign Services Institute, United States Department of State, https://history.state.gov/historicaldocuments/frus1948v01p2/d4.

7. "Amity lines" is from Carl Schmitt, *The Nomos of the Earth in the International Law of Jus Publicum Europaeum*, trans. G. L. Ulmen (New York: Telos Press, 2003).

needing to be shaped by choice architectures designed by powerful incumbents.[8]

Just as significantly, the concept of realism fails to grasp the extent to which the members of this new "imperial brotherhood" who oversaw the development of postwar US foreign policy viewed themselves as world-makers imbued with the power of God, capital, and US military might. Such men believed unflinchingly in their capacity to fashion reality according to their own design and discretion. The global red alert on which they staked their claims to influence was built on manipulating the fears of the public against the backdrop of a devastated world. The reality that interested them—the one they sought to bring into being—was one in which the credibility of US threats of force and violence would ensure their freedom to act in service of the mobility of capital and its allied interests across an ever-widening sphere. As Acheson pronounced in 1969 in his reflections on this period, the task before men of his kind was "a bit less formidable than that described in the first chapter of Genesis. To create a world out of chaos; ours, to create half a world, a free half, out of the same material without blowing the whole to pieces in the process. The wonder of it is how much was done."[9]

Animated by increasingly doctrinaire anti-communism, assessments about how to intervene were at once global in scope and calibrated to the world's uneven development. Underpinned by speculations about return on investment, historically sedimented and racially coded assumptions further shaped the understanding of who could self-govern in a competent and trustworthy manner. In the words of a US State Department memo from 1956, nations would be judged and policed based upon whether they met "acceptable standards of civilized nations."[10] The rise of a

8. In 1980, William Appleman Williams wrote: "We were already assuming that our right to security transcended the traditional right to defend what we had and had become the right to perfect security in any imaginable future contingency. We began to define security as the natural right to empire." William Appleman Williams and Greg Grandin, "Is American Possible without Empire?," *The Nation*, March 23, 2015, http://www.thenation.com/article/200521/encounter-william-appleman-williams-and-greg-grandin.

9. Dean Acheson, preface to *Present at the Creation: My Years in the State Department* (New York: Norton, 1987), n.p.

10. Quoted in Mark Mazower, *Governing the World: A History of an Idea, 1815 to the Present* (New York: Penguin Books, 263).

moderately protectionist, pro-labor, and social-democratic government in Great Britain, in this sense, did not set off the alarms that similar orientations did when they emerged in Iran, Guatemala, or later Chile. The presence of popular large-scale communist movements in France occasioned a far more restrained US response than when this phenomenon appeared in Indonesia and was met with covert destabilization efforts by the United States in support of a vast and bloody internal repression. Some parts of the world were amenable to what the Japanese called "structured corruption," where bags of CIA cash were sufficient to buy influence within civil-society organizations and organized criminal networks that could help sow division and swing the course of elections and government transitions in favor of political parties allied with the US.[11] In others, as the situation in Vietnam demonstrated, the existence of an effective and incorruptible national-liberation movement demanded large-scale military intervention.

The presence of a democratic government that defined the "civilized" standard constituted a challenge to the operational cohesiveness of the white West. The democratic dimension of the modern state invites ongoing maintenance and renovation; crises of legitimation can alternatively lead to an unraveling of democratic process and procedure or to civil-society mobilization and political reform that broaden the ambit of justice, inclusion, distribution, and accountability. Indeed, the latter had been central to the reformist dynamic inaugurated by the New Deal in the US in response to the crises of the Great Depression. Even though the New Deal project accommodated local race and class hierarchies, colonial infrastructures, and corrupt practices—across the US South, for example, where white supremacists remained a core political constituency—it also initiated decisive political reorientations against imperialist and racist projects that defined US governance up to that time, including the first federal laws banning racial discrimination since the Reconstruction era and the granting of Philippine independence after a half-century of US occupation.

Provincial reaction, however, was not the only challenge to democratic reform from above, even when it was responsive

11. Tim Weiner, "The CIA Spent Millions to Support the Japanese Right in the 1950s and 1960s," *New York Times*, October 9, 1994.

to social movements. Processes of administrative centralization, technocratic decision-making, and rising corporate influence intensified during the period from the onset of the New Deal to the end of the Second World War, progressively insulating popular politics and eroding norms and aspirations associated with large-scale, non-elite democratic self-government. The rise of the US national security state was a crucial part of this transformation, at once friendly to domination and graft at the local level and hostile to popular politics and the consent of the governed as a defining global imperative. Thus, even as democratic struggles around racial equality and labor rights at home and anti-colonial self-determination abroad responded to crises of imperial legitimacy and inspired reformist movements in the US and across the world in the decades following the Second World War, the US state project that steadily focused on planning for war grew less accountable to the demos at home and began to accrue characteristics of what the sociologist Charles Tilly once termed "organized crime at its smoothest" in its operations overseas. "Apologists for particular governments and for government in general commonly argue, precisely, that they offer protection from local and external violence," Tilly writes. "They claim that the prices they charge barely cover the costs of protection. They call people who complain about the price of protection 'anarchists,' 'subversives,' or both at once. But consider the definition of a racketeer as someone who creates a threat and then charges for its reduction. Governments' provision of protection, by this standard, often qualifies as racketeering."[12]

The transformation of communism from the left wing of progressive politics within the US, and part of an allied global struggle against fascism, into a criminal conspiracy that would only respond to the logic of force aptly mirrors the process described by Tilly. Preserving democracy at home now required constant vigilance against subversion from within, while US capacities for fighting ostensibly defensive wars overseas morphed into an expanded machinery and propensity for anticipatory intimidation and intervention. Although US national-security discourse strove

12. Charles Tilly, "War-Making and State-Making as Organized Crime," in *Bringing the State Back In*, ed. Peter Evans, Dietrich Rueschemeyer, and Theda Skocpol (Cambridge: Cambridge University Press, 1985), 171.

to appear rational and evidence-based, strategic calculation was increasingly captive to political opportunism, paranoia, and threat inflation that hinged on other domains of thought and feeling. The Soviets, Secretary of Defense James Forrestal convinced Truman, "have the Oriental habit of misunderstanding the Western mind. [...] Their view is a long one. [...] They accept the inevitability of ultimate conflict."[13] Belying the notion that the US was guided by an ethical realism in its foreign relations after the Second World War, a historical and geographical substratum of ideas and imagery constituted by colonial rule and racist othering defined friend and enemy, trustworthiness and criminal propensity in advance of diplomatic engagement or reasoned restraint.

Race, sex, and gender, as well as their associated norms and affects, were integral to the emerging atmosphere of fear and mistrust that supported counter-subversive vigilance. Anti-communism was a variable assemblage that developed and sustained its animus through a particular alchemy of moral and emotional discourse, one sourced by familiar US hierarchies of phenotype and behavior developed from a long, intimate history of racial slavery and segregation, as well as by diverse currents of nativism, homophobia, anti-Semitism, and xenophobia, or dangers posed by an alien and unfamiliar world—especially the East, or "the Orient." For North Americans, what was denoted as the East was also what was west of the West—a moving frontier, the border of dreams and aspirations, but also a region of terror and violence. The brutal war fought in the Pacific against the Japanese provided the most immediate precedent for these fantasies and fears. However, part of the problem posed by "the Orient" was its heterogeneity—the lack of clarity about where its boundaries began and ended geographically, and related uncertainty about who was friend and who was foe. Adding to concerns of inscrutability was the potential that this once dormant or even "backward" world now harbored the potential to project a terrifying despotic power.

In his famous "long telegram" from 1946, the diplomat George Kennan offered the first influential presentation of "Soviet conduct" as an ontological threat framed in racial and sexual

13. James Forrestal, *The Forrestal Diaries*, ed. Walter Millis and E. S. Duffield (New York: Viking Press, 1951), 495.

language: the product of a "Russian-Asiatic world" that had created a "particular brand of fanaticism unmodified by any of the Anglo-Saxon traditions of compromise." The Soviet Union, according to Kennan, was "a regime of unparalleled ruthlessness and jealousy" that had sacrificed ethics and betrayed "insistent, unceasing pressure for penetration and command" over others. Those arguing for cooperation with the USSR were naive, sentimental, and soft, when only "cohesion, firmness and vigor" would suffice to counter an enemy who believed that "no permanent modus vivendi" with the West was possible. Infusing a classically Eurocentric idiom of "Oriental despotism" with the contemporary language of psychopathology, Kennan represented Soviet power as alien and neurotic, dominating and hypermasculine, with tendencies toward "unwanted intrusion" or "penetration" (a word repeated five times in his telegram) that suggested rape.[14]

Following Kennan, a style of argument linking Soviet power and communist adherence with physical violations (torture, infection, disease), deviations from white monogamous hetero-normativity (interracial sex, homosexuality, prostitution), and failures of cognitive reason (paranoia, hysteria, grandiosity) became commonplace within anti-communist discourse. The popular magazine *Life* envisioned communist operatives luring unsuspecting "Negroes" with white "party girls," and centrist liberals like the historian Arthur Schlesinger Jr. imagined the communist milieu as akin to the "sweaty and furtive" homosexuality practiced in all-male boarding schools; in response, a normative, mature, heterosexual, and realist (or in Schlesinger's words, "vital") masculinity was called for.[15] The tendency to equate communism with ill health, contagion, pathology, unreason, and perversion was fundamentally biopolitical—that is, a threat or violation of a naturalness deemed "specific to man's life in common."[16] Animated by such fears, J. Edgar Hoover's FBI employed some thirty-seven thousand informants in the 1950s and 1960s to spy on ordinary Americans.

14. Frank Costigliola, "Unceasing Pressure for Penetration: Gender, Pathology and Emotion in George Kennan's Formation of the Cold War," *Journal of American History* 83, no. 4 (1997): 1310, 1330, 1334.

15. Arthur Schlesinger Jr., *The Vital Center: The Politics of Freedom* (New York: Houghton Mifflin, 1949), 68–70.

16. Michel Foucault, *Security, Territory, Population: Lectures at the Collège de France, 1977–1978*, trans. Graham Burchell (New York: Picador, 2009), 349.

Hoover believed that the reproductive health of the American family was particularly vulnerable and increasingly prone to producing delinquent offspring.[17]

The counter-subversive inquisition launched by the Cold War led to the firing or forced resignation of at least three hundred State Department employees between 1947 and 1953 on grounds of "sexual deviance"—more than twice the rate of dismissals for suspicion of communist allegiance (the presumption being that nonnormative sexuality made one prone to blackmail by communist subversives).[18] Insofar as it challenged the public standing and private sexual prerogatives of a powerful, elite, all-male fraternity, what was later dubbed the "lavender scare" threatened to become self-consuming. "The attack of the primitives," as Dean Acheson described the McCarthyite purge years later, engendered counterattacks from public intellectuals and journalists who in turn accused the chief inquisitor, Senator Joseph McCarthy, of a kind of public indecency. Homing in on a central feature of the emerging national-security state, the journalist Anthony Lewis observed in 1954 that there was an increasingly fine line between locating criminal conspiracy and becoming one, with the "morality-security concept" morphing into a form of "blackmail by the Government itself."[19] Nevertheless, the discursive terrain of national security was by this point thoroughly saturated with anxieties about racial, sexual, and gender deviance, which was often transferred into a contest over whose "political manliness" (to use Kennan's phrase) was best suited to the defense of Western civilization.[20]

Acheson's reference to the "primitives" attests to the way racial discourse informed this contest, not least because it could unite adversaries: if the enemy within promoted mental disorientation and moral turpitude, the enemy without was still an untamed brute. At the end of the Second World War, Henry Wallace, vice president under Roosevelt, had vainly attempted to refute Forrestal and persuade Truman that efforts should be

17. Frank Donner, *The Age of Surveillance: The Aims and Methods of America's Political Intelligence System* (New York: Alfred A. Knopf, 1980), 127.

18. Robert D. Dean, *Imperial Brotherhood: Gender and the Making of Cold War Foreign Policy* (Amherst: University of Massachusetts Press, 2003), 88.

19. Quoted in Dean, 118.

20. Costigliola, "Unceasing Pressure for Penetration," 1330.

made to reassure and build trust and cooperation with the Soviets. A kind of anti-communist Orientalism, formerly the provenance of assorted isolationists and right-wing militarists and cranks like Charles Lindbergh and George Patton, however, was once again in the ascendancy. Writing to his wife from his post in Berlin in 1945, General Patton lamented that with the defeat of Germany "we have destroyed a great race and we [are] about to replace them with Mongolian savages. [...] We can no more understand a Russian than a Chinaman or a Japanese and, from what I have seen of them, I have no particular desire to understand them except to ascertain how much lead or iron it takes to kill them. In addition to his other amiable characteristics, the Russian has no regard for human life and is an all out son of a bitch, a barbarian and a chronic drunk."[21] Considered impolitic during the Second World War, expressions such as these revived as the Cold War began.

The success of the Chinese Communist Revolution in 1949 (which Acheson had previously regarded as outside the US perimeter of concern) sharply accelerated this tendency. Pundits and policymakers increasingly revived an old imperial lexicon of geopolitical and biopolitical threats emerging from the Asian rimland and extending across the "Eurasian heartland."[22] Testifying before Congress in 1950, Dean Rusk called communist China a "Slavic Manchukuo on a larger scale." That same year, General Douglas MacArthur's chief of staff warned the House Un-American Activities Committee about "the Communist 'Jehad' of pan-Slavism for the subjugation of the Western world."[23] For Senator Robert Taft, "the Russians combine with great military might and air power a fanatical devotion to communism not unlike that which inspired the Moslem invasion of Europe in the Middle Ages."[24] By the time he penned his reflections on the Cold War in 1969, even the once circumspect Acheson echoed these talking points: "The threat to Western Europe seemed to me singularly like that which Islam

21. Martin Blumenson, ed., *The Patton Papers, 1940–1945* (Boston: Da Capo Press, 1996), 731, 734.

22. Halford Mackinder, "The Geographical Pivot of History" (1904), in *Heartland: Three Essays on Geopolitics* (Katoomba: Spinebill Press, 2022).

23. Quoted in Bruce Cumings, "American Orientalism at War in Korea and the United States: A Hegemony of Racism, Repression and Amnesia," in *Orientalism and War*, ed. Tarak Barkawi (Oxford: Oxford University Press, 2013), 52.

24. Robert Taft, *A Foreign Policy for Americans* (New York: Doubleday, 1951), 19.

had posed centuries before, with its combination of ideological zeal and fighting power [...] then it had taken the same combination to meet it: Germanic power in the east and Frankish in Spain. This time it would need the added power and energy of the United States, for the drama was now being played out on a world stage."[25]

The apocalyptic tenor of much of this discourse encouraged associations with threats that linked racist elements with concerns about the collapse of Eurocentric world order and the decimation of entire populations. The US Catholic Archbishop Fulton Sheen described Chinese communists as "Chicoms," "beasts," and "scavengers of a decaying civilization" (a decade before Walt Rostow, national security advisor to President Lyndon Johnson, concealed the overtly racist element, referring to communists as "scavengers of the modernization process"). This idiom recalled World War II–era descriptions of the attack of "pan-Asian hordes" and the Japanese as "yellow-apes."[26] Even those who were already more cautious about indulging in racist flourishes were drawn into discussions of demographics that were reminiscent of the turn-of-century panic about the "yellow peril" and "race suicide." Such fears were often merged with a supremacist discourse of technological discrimination. "The only balance that we have against the overwhelming manpower of the Russians, and therefore the chief deterrent to war, is the threat of immediate retaliation with the atomic bomb," argued Forrestal in 1948. "In 1941 Stalin ruled 180 million subjects [...] in 1951 Stalin directs 800 million people. Unless our foreign policy is conducted more competently than it has been during the past ten years, our very survival is in doubt," declared Taft in his brief for Republican internationalism.[27] In early 1950, Senator Arthur Vandenberg confided that the challenge was how to "keep another billion Asiatics out of the Soviet order."[28] As an official in the Eisenhower administration

25. Acheson, *Present at the Creation,* 345.

26. See, for example, Robert A. Heinlein, *Sixth Column* (Wake Forest, NC: Baen, 2013); Walt Rostow, *Stages of Economic Growth: A Non-Communist Manifesto* (Cambridge: Cambridge University Press, 1960).

27. Taft, *Foreign Policy for Americans,* 14.

28. Arthur H. Vandenberg, *The Private Papers of Senator Vandenberg* (Boston: Houghton Mifflin, 1952), 539; see also Laurence Kaplan, *The Conversion of Arthur H. Vandenberg: From Isolation to International Engagement* (Lexington: University Press of Kentucky, 2015).

later recounted: "I always thought the Yellow Peril business was nonsense. […] Now I can visualize that Asiatics teamed up with Slavs could indeed conquer the world!"[29]

This cultural and intellectual bigotry fueled the stock-in-trade of academic modes of anti-communism, particularly on the part of aspiring public or state intellectuals. The self-described "historian of human freedom" Karl Wittfogel, a University of Washington professor and former theoretician of the German Communist Party, imported a deeply racist strand of European thinking about "Oriental despotism" as a defining attribute of Asian societies into the US scholarly and political lexicon while attacking what he termed "intellectual softness on communism."[30] Wittfogel added a veneer of historical depth by describing this mode of rule as an outgrowth of "pre-industrial," "hydraulic societies" that are characterized by an absence of private property and that ranged from the Inca Empire to China, Persia, Egypt, and even the Hopi Indians, culminating in Stalin's Soviet Union, the most "despotic variant of that system." Wittfogel's typology collapsed meaningful historical differences in a grand gesture of comparative ignorance, one that depicted all Asians as a single mass rendered supine and abject by despotic power.[31] Though a German émigré, he barely registered the recent Nazi past; instead, he claimed without irony that the main tools of the Oriental despot were state terror and "judicial torture," in contrast to "Western institutions [that] kept these inclinations from asserting themselves lastingly."[32] He issued a dire warning that "the realm of freedom is rapidly shrinking," and that only a vigorous extension of Western "cultural and intellectual heritage" to "countries of an Oriental type" could prevent the imposition of a "system of bureaucratic state slavery to two-thirds of mankind."[33]

29. Quoted in Matthew Frye Jacobson and Gaspar Gonzalez, *What Have They Built You to Do? The Manchurian Candidate and Cold War America* (Minneapolis: University of Minnesota Press, 2006), 46.

30. Karl Wittfogel, *Oriental Despotism: A Comparative Study of Total Power* (New Haven, CT: Yale University Press, 1957), 449.

31. Perry Anderson, *Lineages of the Absolutist State* (London: NLB, 1974), 494. "It is merely in the night of our ignorance that all alien shapes take on the same hue." Anderson, 549.

32. Wittfogel, *Oriental Despotism*, 145.

33. Wittfogel, 447.

A novel hermeneutic, the apocalyptic anti-communism that fixated on a menace from the East orchestrated by the Soviets (and the Chinese) combined elements of an old and a newly emerging racial order—frontier paranoia, Asian exclusion, white supremacy, and what might be thought of as a settler-colonial form of anti-imperialism—all united around the claim that the non-white enemy was, as Kennan put it, "impervious to reason" and "highly sensitive to the logic of force."[34] Here, the elements opposed by what the political theorist Judith Shklar termed "the liberalism of fear"—cruelty, torture, and arbitrary rule—were seen as the defining attributes of its main adversary.[35] Within this political ontology, racial discourse and rhetoric played an important quilting role. The illiberal enemy, now marked by behavioral rather than hereditary characteristics, was figured in historical and culturally invariant terms as contrary to an otherwise plastic and beneficent nature, and thus in need of exceptional measures, including (again without irony) arbitrary rule and cruel treatment. This is an example of how racial discourse has been periodically renewed as liberal universalism's shadow—the "ill nature" that haunts human nature—as in John Locke's original schema.[36] At the same time, to retain its liberal bona fides, this understanding was leavened with a decidedly affirmative imperative—that going forward it would be necessary to cultivate "good" and trustworthy non-white allies both at home and in the decolonizing world. Indeed, perhaps one main difference between the new emphasis on modernizing Western power and the old "yellow peril" discourse was the call to offensive action on the grounds of redeeming the people of Asia, a posture befitting a new imperial mandate framed as a defense of liberal order at a global scale. Counterinsurgency, in a remark attributed to General Edward Lansdale, who was assigned to the Philippines in the aftermath of independence to help build up a local fighting force against the Hukbalahap insurrection (before

34. Costigliola, "Unceasing Pressure for Penetration," 1331; *Eastern Europe, the Soviet Union*, Foreign Relations of the United States, vol. 6 (Washington, DC: United States Government Printing Office, 1946), 701.

35. Judith Shklar, "The Liberalism of Fear," in *Liberalism and the Moral Life*, ed. Nancy N. Rosenblum (Cambridge, MA: Harvard University Press, 1989).

36. For a discussion of Locke in this context, see Nikhil Pal Singh, *Race and America's Long War* (Berkeley: University of California Press, 2017).

moving on to do the same in Vietnam), was just another name for brotherly love.[37]

Racial anxieties and racialized fear also shaped the overriding sense during the Cold War that nothing of political consequence could be left to chance—especially contingencies of political struggles on the part of barely qualified actors either at home or in a distant land. Since all events were potentially consequential and globally interlinked, what was required was preemptive action; if that was not possible then advance intelligence needed to be secured. Wallace's jibe that Forrestal's thinking bore the hallmarks of pre–World War II isolationism was true—it betrayed the fear that the obscure world had become all too proximate, leaving US planners unsure of the borders of their country's interests, policy, and action, or even where the actual borders of the United States lay. Instead of counseling restraint or withdrawal, these politicians and thinkers were confronted with the challenge of transforming things alien and uncertain. As Acheson put it in a letter to Truman in 1945, "There can be no humanly devised method of defining precisely the geographic areas in which [… our] security interests begin or cease to exist."[38] Or as Hoyt Vandenberg, the director of the fledgling CIA and soon to become the first head of the new US Air Force, argued in testimony before Congress: "The oceans have shrunk, until today both Europe and Asia border the United States almost as do Canada and Mexico" (a line that would be repeated by George W. Bush after 9/11).[39]

The swift succession of the Chinese Communist Revolution and the Soviet detonation of an atomic bomb shattered the prospects of a durable safe zone anywhere in the world. It is easy to imagine this outcome as inevitable—who wouldn't be afraid of an enemy getting its hands on the capacity to annihilate or expanding its population base by a billion people? The politics of fear, however, was not only an explicable reaction to the catastrophic consequences of nuclear weapons (which at that time and to this day have only been used by the United States) but

37. Edward G. Lansdale, "Lessons Learned, the Philippines 1946–1953," September 26, 1962, Henry A. Kissinger Papers, part 2 (MS 1981), Manuscripts and Archives, Yale University Library, https://hdl.handle.net/10079/digcoll/561046.

38. Acheson, quoted in Mazower, *Governing the World*, 216.

39. Tim Weiner, *Legacy of Ashes: A History of the CIA* (New York: Anchor, 2018), 23.

also part and parcel of an intentionally cultivated, deeply paranoid cultural and policy outlook that was constructed over many years, fed by partisan rancor and competition, and framed with specific reference to the horrors of racial genocide and anticipated transition in the global racial order. Until the end of the Korean War, the United States' main strategy around nuclear weapons was not whether they might be used on domestic population centers by others, but whether the United States should use them again. Immediately after the Korean War's stalemate, strategic thinking in the United States turned to ways of pursuing "low intensity" wars despite the nuclear standoff. The specter of an exterminating state violence born of superior technological rationality had emanated from all parties in the Second World War—its primary symbols, the atomic bomb and the concentration camp, belonged to the two main *Western* contenders. During the Cold War, this destructive force was increasingly imagined as having an entirely different source, coming from a realm of anti-Western alterity. The concept of totalitarianism included an extended chain of reasoning about the existential dangers posed by terrorist uses of technology by those lacking proper philosophical conditioning and historical preparation for exercising state power. Thus, for mid-century Cold Warriors like the author Arthur Koestler, the "the yogi and the commissar" exemplified "the irrational credulity of all minds that have not reached the stage of science."[40] Likewise, the philosopher Karl Popper described those whose response to the shocks of modernity led to a rejection of the "anti-magical scientific empirical mode of thought," making them dangerous "enemies" of the "open society" as they gained access to modern technologies of governance and instruments of violence.[41]

As the "anchor" of Cold War discourse, the theory of totalitarianism displaced legacies of catastrophic state violence, in particular fascism, outside the main historical currents of Western moral, political, and intellectual life. The work of the most important intellectual architect of this concept, Hannah Arendt, was used to both short-circuit her otherwise forthright recognition of Nazism within the family of Western imperialisms and associate the threat

40. Nikhil Pal Singh, "Cold War," *Social Text* 27, no. 3 (Fall 2009): 97–100.

41. William Peitz, "The Postcolonialism of Cold War Discourse," *Social Text* 19/20 (Fall 1988): 55–75.

of technology-driven state terror with non-Western power. This underlines a more important claim, namely that the Cold War elaborated new associations by which heterogeneous figures of non-Western alterity could be read along a single sociological spectrum. The Cold War introduced conceptual and linguistic innovations for resolving the diverse and messy process of decolonization within a historical discourse of colonial modernity. As a belated fulfillment of what the Marxist thinker Karl Kautsky once called "ultra-imperialism," the Cold War was thus not only a coordination of military and economic affairs on a new global scale, it also marked out a correlative space of cultural and intellectual work in which the varied colonial inheritances of Western modernity were articulated into new global identities and divisions that sought to underwrite a more durable (Western) civilizational compact. By the mid-1950s, even an early skeptic of the Cold War like the political commentator Walter Lippmann worried about "the defense [...] of liberal democracy in its contracted area [...] at a time when the general civilization of the West has suffered spectacular decline and is gravely threatened."[42]

Put another way, the theory of totalitarianism was a hinge connecting the frame of US global power to the teleological door of modernization that opened and closed on new nations according to a deeply embedded set of norms and assumptions about obedience, deference, emotional "maturity," trustworthiness, rational capacity, and fitness for self-government. The ever-increasing ability to kill from a distance that constituted the economic and military infrastructure of colonial power was still unable to dispense with the vast superstructure of racist culture. Korea and Vietnam would be bombed back to the Stone Age so that Asians could finally learn to appreciate the value of human life. What Cold War historians in the United States have dubbed "the long peace" in Europe and North America was won at the price of normalizing militarized interventions—a global civil war, or as Frantz Fanon put it, a world steeped in "peaceful violence."[43] Viewed from a truly global perspective, the Cold War was framed by (the failure of) decolonization, not the reverse. Largely

42. Walter Lippman, "The Decline of Western Democracy," *The Atlantic*, February 1956, 30–31.

43. Frantz Fanon, *The Wretched of the Earth*, trans. Constance Farrington (New York: Grove Press, 1963), 81.

disregarded by US policymakers was the historian Hans Kohn's warning that "the future historian may regard as the greatest 'revolution' of the twentieth century not Lenin's overthrow of the short-lived free regime in Russia in November 1917, but the less conspicuous [...] and yet more far-reaching process which brought Europe's four hundred years old dominion of the globe to an end."[44] Whether Ho Chi Minh was "a nationalist or a commie is irrelevant," Acheson remarked in 1949. "All Stalinists in colonial areas are nationalists."[45] Nor did it matter that Stalin himself had derided Mao and Ho as "cave-dweller-like Marxists" whose nationalism made them unreliable adjuncts of the internationalist movement.[46] Here again, ironically, the criminality of the Soviet "empire of justice" mirrored that of US "empire of liberty." Both were heavily invested in bringing backward and deficient peoples into the orderings of science and state by any means necessary.[47]

Arendt argued, in *The Origins of Totalitarianism* (1951), that the authentic conflicts of our time would only become visible when totalitarianism is a thing of the past. Her ideological rival Carl Schmitt had lamented in *The Nomos of the Earth* (1950) that the two world wars had broken the compact that had once delimited war between recognized sovereigns, separating combatants and civilians and ridding war of its criminal and punitive character. As Aimé Césaire famously pointed out in "Discourse on Colonialism" (1950), what made the Nazi genocide an abomination was that it unfolded on European sovereign ground—the methods and tactics of the genocidaires had long been applied to the worlds colonized by Europeans and their settler-colonial offshoots. Schmitt similarly acknowledged that rebels, criminals, and colonial and civil conflict had remained outside the civilized world's delimitation and bracketing of war. Rather than restoring balance by universalizing national sovereignty, the post–World War II order, underwritten by nominal US support for decolonization, appeared to guarantee a future in which warfare devolved into a limitless series of asymmetrical

44. Kohn, quoted in Mazower, *Governing the World*, 244.

45. Quoted in Frederick Longevall, *Embers of War: The Fall of an Empire and the Making of America's Vietnam* (New York: Random House, 2012), 219.

46. Longevall, 227.

47. Odd Arne Westad, *The Global Cold War: Third World Interventions and the Making of Our Times* (Cambridge: Cambridge University Press, 2007).

"police actions" against subversives. Containing Soviet totalitarianism—the official US reasoning for the Cold War—might thus be viewed as a transitional phase in a longer history of colonial wars unnamed, unacknowledged, or subsumed under an expansive mandate of imperial policing.

Under the terms of the Marshall Plan, and despite proclamations of anti-colonial intent, the United States was already underwriting the continuation of British and French imperial projects, based in part on a century-long recognition "that the international economy required imperial protection."[48] In October 1945, the first French troops arrived in Indochina "aboard eight American ships. Many of the troops wore uniforms of American issue and carried American equipment."[49] That same year, Ho Chi Minh (a US intelligence asset during World War II) announced his country's independence in the language of the US Declaration of Independence and penned a series of short letters to the Truman administration asking for support. These anti-colonial pleas infamously and tragically fell on deaf ears. No less easy to ignore was the popular opinion of the US sailors transporting the French who cabled President Truman to protest the fact that "American vessels" were being used to carry "foreign combat troops to foreign soil for the purpose of engaging in hostilities to further the imperialist policies of foreign governments when there are American soldiers waiting to come home."[50]

From the standpoint of US foreign policy, however, it was already understood that the strength of the Allied powers and their place within a US-dominated world system depended on colonies, at least for the time being.[51] As the American military strategist Bernard Brodie noted, Britain's "imperial cohesion" was tied to the United States' interests: "It is important to remember that the attraction for security which the UK has so largely lost is now exerted by the United States."[52] Kennan noted that total imperial "dissolution" would not serve the interests of the US: "There were

48. William Roger Louis and Ronald Robinson, "The Imperialism of Decolonization," *Journal of Imperial and Commonwealth History* (July 2008): 495.

49. Quoted in Logevall, *Embers of War*, 119.

50. Nikhil Pal Singh, "Culture/Wars: Recoding Empire in an Age of Democracy," *American Quarterly* (Fall 1998): 488.

51. Lodge, quoted in Louis and Robinson, "Imperialism of Decolonization," 469.

52. Bernard Brodie, "How Strong Is Britain," *Foreign Affairs*, October 1948, 443.

many things that [imperial powers] could do which we could not do and which we wished them to continue doing."[53] In the face of popular anti-imperialist sentiment, the Soviet nemesis was essential to the management of decolonization, in order to assure "the American people of the innocence of their global expansion."[54] As the French observer Philippe Devillers noted just before France handed off their war in Vietnam to the Americans, it was wise for Paris to "use anti-communism to neutralize America's anti-colonialism" in order to secure continued US support for French efforts to reestablish control over their Southeast Asian colony.[55] The challenge was to shift the optics to one that framed Vietnam as an independent nation that needed saving (from Soviet imperialism) from the one that depicted it as a nation struggling against French imperialism.

Writing in 1952, the theologian and commentator Reinhold Niebuhr described the United States as the "unalloyed exemplar" of "modern liberal culture." Niebuhr was at least honest enough to admit that the United States still faced an "'imperial' problem of using power in global terms [...] that would almost certainly violate basic standards of justice."[56] Wherever one might depart from Niebuhr, who came to exemplify ethically and intellectually the liberalism he described, the moral seriousness of this thinking is commendable when set against the ossified Cold War logic of later influential thinkers who complacently argue that interventionist uses of US power have always and invariably mitigated against "something worse," in the words of the historian John Lewis Gaddis.[57]

For far too long, a simplified view of postwar Western history opposing communist totalitarianism with market freedom obscured the challenges and complexities decolonization posed to Eurocentric world order. Revisionist US historians like William Appleman Williams gradually reshaped the leftward edge of liberal scholarship by showing how the US defense of capitalism after

53. Louis and Robinson, "Imperialism of Decolonization," 499.

54. Louis and Robinson, 469.

55. Quoted in Logevall, *Embers of War*, 198.

56. Reinhold Niebuhr, *The Irony of American History* (Chicago: University of Chicago Press, 2008), xxiv, 2.

57. John Lewis Gaddis, *Surprise, Security, and the American Experience* (Cambridge, MA: Harvard University Press, 2005), 160.

the Second World War was an offensive and expansionist project underwritten by a vast "preponderance of power."[58] But this not only remains a dissenting view, it is also not well attuned to the persistence of racist and colonial legacies. The fact is that US imperial aspirations were never actually concealed, but merely hidden in plain sight. As the National Security Council paper that laid out the blueprints for the Cold War stated, the United States would have pursued the same national-security policies "even if there were no Soviet threat"—an astonishing admission.[59]

US-based Black radicals were more clear-sighted regarding the entangled roots of European and American empire. Slavery and colonialism, W. E. B. Du Bois argued in 1946, presaging Césaire, had been the greatest examples of "mass concealment" as the "sin of capitalism." They illuminated the corrupt ethical basis of the character, methods, and efforts to satisfy human wants, and constituted a

> virus […] poured into the veins of modern culture [that] fatally poisoned it. […]
>
> We have long believed without argument or reflection that the cultural status of the people of Europe and of North America represented not only the best civilization which the world had ever known, but also a goal of human effort destined to go on from triumph to triumph until the perfect accomplishment was reached. Our present nervous breakdown, nameless fear, and often despair, comes from the sudden facing of this faith with calamity. […]
>
> There was no Nazi atrocity […] which the Christian civilization of Europe had not long been practicing against colored folk in all parts of the world in the name of and for the defense of a Superior Race born to rule the world.[60]

58. Melvyn P. Leffler, *A Preponderance of Power: National Security, the Truman Administration, and the Cold War* (Stanford, CA: Stanford University Press, 1992).

59. "NSC-68, 1950," Office of the Historian, Foreign Service Institute, United States State Department, accessed September 4, 2023, https://history.state.gov/milestones/1945-1952/NSC68.

60. W. E. B. Du Bois, *The World and Africa* (Oxford: Oxford University Press, 2007), 162, 1, 15.

As the new guiding center of the West, America saw itself as the realm of freedom. Political and military violence, Niebuhr wrote (more disingenuously), "played only a secondary role" in US territorial and commercial expansion, leaving Americans "honestly deceived" about the dependencies of their allegedly post-ideological capitalism on instruments of violence and coercion against peoples (both at home and abroad) lacking capacities for self-government.[61] Williams judged more harshly, suggesting that an enduring commitment to a "frontier-expansionist conception of history" had been a way of deferring the moral, economic, and political contradictions of US capitalist development—promising to enlarge the sphere of material distribution, while also making its inequities more difficult to perceive.[62] Ultimately, both Williams and Niebuhr downplayed the imperial, racial, and colonial divisions born of invidious and targeted coercion along the color line that Du Bois emphasized, especially how they continued to define the conceptual and ethical infrastructure of the Cold War as the new strategy and container for the white West.

The diary Kennan kept during a trip to Latin America illustrates this logic. Writing in Caracas on February 28, 1950, Kennan outlined the long shadow of what might be called economic and race development in a land he described as "bilious yellow-brown": "Here was a tropical country in the subsoil of which reposed great quantities of a liquid essential to the present stage of industrialization in the U.S. Americans were extracting this liquid and hauling it away. The local population had not moved a finger to create this wealth, would have been incapable of developing it, and did not require [it] for its own needs." Miserable at the thought of this unearned wealth, which he called a tax on American "productive capacity," Kennan, like Popper, was also wary of new military, industrial, and technical capabilities that might now be extended to those whom he regarded as "unprepared," "debauched" people.

Kennan believed that disaster would ensue from this "unhappy relationship" in which the United States, as one of the "economies which are capable of developing the natural resources

61. Niebuhr, *Irony of American History*, 36.

62. William Appleman Williams, *Empire as a Way of Life* (Brooklyn, NY: IG Publishing, 2006).

of this earth," was "beholden [...] in a manner slightly disgraceful" to "other peoples who have been permitted to extend over those resources the delicate fiction of modern sovereignty." He observed that it might be better if America invested in "internal police power" to ensure "a radical and general improvement in the treatment of private U.S. capital."[63] Counterinsurgency and covert action, in short, always needed to be in the back pocket.

In 1955, a high-level US study, *The Political Economy of US Foreign Policy*, echoed Kennan while also illustrating how the white West, its imperial and colonial violence, was in the process of being transmuted into the technical jargon and bureaucratic prose of the future Group of Seven. "International economic integration," the authors wrote, "is no longer consistent with the unfettered exercise of national sovereignty," particularly when "vital Western interests" are at stake. The study indexes, much as Kennan did in his journal, a general retreat from the categorical universalism of wartime promises of self-determination: "The goal of unification of the whole free world (or, for that matter of the entire planet)," the study argues, "is not likely to be a realistic one for as long a period as a generation ahead." The creation of a unified political community and an integrated economic system by morally valid means required "an antecedent historical and moral community, which does not now exist between the West and the underdeveloped countries." As if they had already anticipated the Indonesian genocide and US invasion of Vietnam, the authors concluded, "It will not always be possible for the West to avoid interventions which are too reminiscent of colonialism to win the approval of Western and native liberals."[64]

In the final instance, the West as a unity was still a manifestation of the civilizational order of racial and economic development and its associated violence. Imperialism, to paraphrase Arendt's mid-century argument, was an effort to expand political power and rule without the foundation of a body politic. Inverting Lenin's statement that imperialism is the highest stage of capitalism,

63. "Diary Notes of Trip to South America, February to March 1950" and "Official Notes, South American Trip, Feb. 18 – Mar. 21, 1950," George F. Kennan Papers, Public Policy Papers, Department of Special Collections, Princeton University Library, Princeton, NJ.

64. William Yandell Elliott, *The Political Economy of American Foreign Policy* (New York: Henry Holt, 1955), 231.

America's post–World War II defense of global capitalism might be seen as the highest stage of imperialism. US policymakers sought to engineer a transition from a world organized through plural spheres of loosely coordinated imperial controls over non-sovereign space (and their labor, markets, and natural resources) to a single rule-bound world built on formally equal nation-states guaranteed by American military power. In doing so, as Niebuhr observed, "the liberal world [that had] opposed [...] monstrous evil [during World War II] was filled ironically with milder forms of the same pretensions," and thus permanently at risk of re-creating, another, if perhaps "less vicious version of the Nazi creed."[65]

65. Niebuhr, *Irony of American History*, 22.

Anything You Can Imagine Is Here
Rijin Sahakian

A twelve-year-old child in Sacramento, twenty miles from my home, is held down and cuffed. Although he committed no crime, he has been apprehended by a security guard who accused him of breaking into a car and called in the police. Weighing less than eighty pounds, he is kept stomach to the floor, a heavy-set female police officer bending over his small Black frame. Shouts for his parents are ignored; he spits in frustration. *You're just a little terrorist,* the officer mutters, and they bring out the white hood. The gloved hands of another officer enter the frame, pulling it down over the boy's face. *I can't breathe! Take this bag off my head! Take this bag off my head!* He is now in the back seat of a police vehicle, still hooded, still cuffed. The bystanders taking videos are shouting too. They have been shouting the whole time, witnesses to an act of torture. For those protesting the use of force, the long history of state violence was made clear in the words of the Sacramento police chief, who proudly described his officers' actions against the innocent minor as a necessary measure "to diffuse the situation."

Isaiah was arrested and hooded on April 28, 2019, exactly fifteen years to the day the torture photos from the Abu Ghraib prison were first released to the public. Among the images of men piled naked on top of one another, leashed and dragged like dogs and rushed by dogs, was that iconic hooded figure, arms outstretched. The photos sparked an outcry from the public, but far more powerfully the photos baked in, visually, tactically, that on one side were the weak and humiliated, and on the other were the strong and proud. "*Animal House* on the night shift," was how the former secretary of defense James R. Schlesinger described the findings of an investigative panel he chaired. This comparison of sexual and physical torture to a popular American comedy underlines the use of the Iraq wars, torture and all, as a fearsome display of American culture. A culture that, along with its military, is of incomparable global influence.

Animal House was the second-highest-grossing film of 1978. Though released three years after America's war with Vietnam ended, it was set prior to the conflict and satirized the military and ideas of American innocence. In 2014, three years after the official "end" of the Iraq War, the highest grossing film in the United States was *American Sniper*. Directed by the quintessential American Clint Eastwood, the critically lauded film lionized its title character, the real-life US Navy Seal Chris Kyle, who had been killed the previous year. This hero was a man who found killing "fun," who believed all Iraqis to be guilty (the film reinforces this assumption; there is not one decent portrayal of an Iraqi), and whose sole drive was to serve as his nation's most effective killing machine. Kyle had also bragged publicly about shooting "looters" from a rooftop in the devastating aftermath of Hurricane Katrina, though there is no evidence this actually took place. True or not, the act of shooting dozens of Americans, who would have been widely understood to be Black, did nothing to tarnish the view of Kyle as an American patriot.

The film is maddening but not surprising. Americans had been trained since the Gulf War in the early 1990s to dismiss Iraqi life. Iraqis were the first population to be targeted and killed by a broad international coalition on a live international broadcast—not once, not twice, but to a steady drumbeat of sanctions, bombing campaigns, and official wars over the course of two decades. During the war in 1991, America was awash in ticker-tape parades and yellow ribbons—"Support the Troops!"—despite the live footage of civilian carnage during the war and its immediate aftermath. By the time the invasion of Iraq began a decade later, global protests of the war dissipated as dramatically as the demonstrations of violence grew. The debate that followed the release of the Abu Ghraib images wasn't about justice or reparations for the Iraqis rounded up in house-to-house night raids, often without cause or due process. Like the countless uncounted atrocities committed in Iraq, there have been bitter few prosecutions of war crimes by governing officials or demands to hold accountable the private companies that embezzled billions under the cover of war. Instead, inward-looking dismissals posed as questions dominated: How do we define torture? Will this change America's standing in the world? What are we doing there? As if it were impossible to know.

By the time we see the contemporary use of hoods by police on American soil, they are no longer the heavy burlap sandbags used on foreign prisoners that reinforced the idea of Iraq as a primitive, crude site, rather than the modern nation-state it was.

For Western twenty-first-century policing, the hoods have been remade as pale plastic sheaths—compact, efficient, but no less psychologically punishing or physically strenuous.

Like the use of torture, most people think of privatized forces as shadowy players in international war games, mercenaries playing whack-a-mole with terrorists in far-flung countries. In some cases, this is true. In others, mercenaries are survivors of previous wars of mass atrocity who are now used to doing low-wage or high-risk work, or sometimes both—for instance, the former child soldiers from Sierra Leone recruited by British firms to serve as guards on American bases in Iraq. Private security is a routine sight in the US—personnel outnumber law enforcement almost two to one domestically. Their purpose is not simply to fill a demand but to allow private interests to access the power of the state, which both protects their own assets and delineates class forcibly and visibly. The security guard in the museum hall, boutique entrance, or military base signals the capital strength of each site as well as the relationship of the individual to it—viewer or collector, window-shopper or buyer, soldier or commander. The first person to apprehend Isaiah and bring him to the police was a private security guard. "Winning hearts and minds" wasn't aimed at the occupied Iraqis, but at us.

Privatized force is driven by, and made possible with, the cooperation of state and private interests, which allows for the further reach of power while staying outside or above the law within its juridical borders as easily as on foreign land. This strategy was illustrated in a deal that became public in late summer 2020.[1] A newly formed American company, Delta Crescent Energy, had signed a contract to produce and export oil in a contested area of northern Syria. The agreement was signed not with the Syrian government, which was engaged in a protracted civil war on top of a protracted dictatorship, but rather with separatist militias supported through deals enabled by American government and corporate cooperation. American soldiers stayed in Syria to assist in protecting the oil fields, now under contract with Delta Crescent, which received not only the soldiers but also a waiver from the

1. Kylie Atwood and Ryan Browne, "Former Army Delta Force Officer, US Ambassador Sign Secretive Contract to Develop Syrian Oil Fields," *CNN*, August 5, 2020, https://edition.cnn.com/2020/08/05/politics/syria-secretive-oil-contract-delta-force-ambassador/index.html.

US Treasury Department to do business in Syria despite sanctions against the country. The deal was landed by Delta Crescent's three well-connected founders—a former US ambassador to Denmark, a US oil executive, and the CEO of TigerSwan, a private security firm, who had previously been a US Delta Force commander in Iraq and Afghanistan.

Describing itself as a "global risk management" company, TigerSwan is the same firm that was hired by the developers of the Dakota Access Pipeline in 2016 after government tactics had failed to break the protest movement fighting the encroachment. TigerSwan used a different approach, that of spying, infiltration, and intimidation, using the military framework of war. The protestors were "terrorists," their nonviolent actions "attacks," and the tribal land the protests were situated on "the battlespace." The goal of their intelligence gathering, likely their contractual duty, was to "eliminate threat" (i.e., protesters).[2] Nothing about this work was illegal. In fact, when TigerSwan was taken to court, it was not for the surveillance they were conducting, which would have been illegal if done by law enforcement, but for operating without proper state licensing.

TigerSwan's CEO went from protecting the assets of an oil company in the United States to gaining ownership of an oil field overseas. Syria had become a site of domestic and multinational proxy battlefields, with the torture of civilians paving the way for multinational resource extraction. TigerSwan used the frame of war to attempt to dissolve peaceful protests in the US, but actual warfare remains the most effective means to quell, even exterminate, resistance. Chaos such as Syria's current political reality is an exceptional opportunity for arms dealers, private contractors, and oil explorers, just as the wars in Iraq have been.

Chaos is good for business. And most of the world's business today is that of social division, terrorist/militia/proxy warfare, and the accompanying record corporate gain. Before social media, divisions were often perpetuated through racist, misogynistic,

2. Allenn Brown, Will Parrish, and Alice Speri, "Leaked Documents Reveal Counterterrorism Tactics Used at Standing Rock to 'Defeat Pipeline Insurgencies,'" *The Intercept*, May 27, 2017, https://theintercept.com/2017/05/27/leaked-documents-reveal-security-firms-counterterrorism-tactics-at-standing-rock-to-defeat-pipeline-insurgencies/#:~:text=Leaked%20Documents%20Reveal%20Counterterrorism%20Tactics,opponents%20and%20infiltrated%20protest%20camps.

and nationalist film, television, and news media. Today, mainstream discourse sees social media as an unprecedented breeding ground for hate and disinformation, though these platforms rely on preexisting sociohistorical conditions and the beliefs that go along with them. Calls to "be more responsible" in preventing threats of violence or the promotion of false stories are made with the belief that this phenomenon is unparalleled, and with the idea that these corporations are not being responsible because it's "bad for business"—the more sensational and heightened the users' experience, the more clicks, data, and dollars. What is not mentioned is the big business that comes *after* creating social chaos—billions of dollars in heightened "security" needs, reconstruction bids, lucrative real estate, and trafficking (humans, drugs, energy, arms, artifacts), to name just a few.

The Trump administration's greatest feat was not in "dividing" America but in enabling greater visibility of the opportunities for wealth and exploitation when promoting division, employing an extensive array of tools—historical, corporate, and governmental—to do so. In the lead-up to the 2020 US elections, the news often reported on fears of a "civil war" that might break out over a contested outcome. This looming threat of violence was realized to some extent by the attack on the US Capitol on January 6, 2021, widely referred to as an "insurrection." Four police officers on duty that day died by suicide soon after. Couldn't this be called a form of sectarian violence, the construct that was supposed to only apply to Iraq? This construct was codified in Iraq in a hasty, American-penned constitution mandating religious quotas and ethnic divisions in what was previously a secular state—a ready-made ablution for those with little understanding of Iraq's history couched in an unwillingness to believe that the invasion was not a series of missteps but rather a how-to guide to dismantling a country for profit under the cover of determined, engineered violence.

Many were shocked by Trump's call, during the first presidential debate in 2020, for the Proud Boys, a white-supremacist group, to "stand back and stand by." But his words were not surprising considering that America's actual Civil War was centered on the determined, engineered violence of slavery. The continuation of the war is evident in far too many areas, particularly in Trump's insinuation, in order to sow further division, that white supremacy is a legitimate American force. The utilization of race and fear of socialism fueling America's newest sectarian turn is a logical strategy because it harnesses the latent divisions in the country's own history of targeting communities to divide and build profit, whether via slavery, the war on drugs, predatory financial practices, environmental degradation, or the war on terror. The Black Lives Matter movement, as a response to police violence, follows a long history of Black protest of militarized force in the United States as well as the country's history of policing, which evolved from slave patrols, militias, and vigilantism. It is devastatingly appropriate that the defense of the descendants of the enslaved who created the profits that enabled the United States' ascendancy to nation-state supremacy would serve as the catalyst for a recognition of the force that endangers life as a whole.

With the superior capacities of technology aligned with private, unregulated financial gain, we are in a space primed for universal subordination under state and non-state actors. The lines between regular and irregular force are becoming more blurred, more pervasive, more difficult to detect and fight against. In the months prior to the COVID-19 pandemic, large-scale protests for autonomy and equity around the world were met with increasingly similar tactics, uniforms, and weapons. Across America, and especially in the nation's capital, the sight of tanks, tear gas, and rubber bullets at racial-justice protests led journalists to call the scenes a "war zone" or "like Iraq."[3] But the comparison stops at the ammunition and camouflage gear; it does not extend to the engineered splintering of civil society that force accelerates.

In August 2020, on the streets of Kenosha, Wisconsin, police forces emerged from their military tanks to hand out water and words of gratitude to members of armed white vigilante groups. One of these members, the seventeen-year-old Kyle Rittenhouse, had an AK-47 strapped across his chest, which he would later use to kill two protestors. A memo with talking points sympathetic to Rittenhouse's claim of self-defense was provided to the Department of Homeland Security in a seamless display of how regular and irregular forces have been integrated in our wars overseas and at home—not simply to kill but to divide by currying favor with and protecting various groups and their respective ideologies.

3. Mark Thompson, "Why Ferguson Looks So Much Like Iraq," *Time*, August 14, 2014, https://time.com/3111455/ferguson-missouri-michael-brown-iraq/.

As the summary of the 2018 National Defense Strategy of the United States concluded, "It is now undeniable that the homeland is no longer a sanctuary."[4]

Militias, mercenaries, and armies are increasingly interchangeable in how they are defined and where they are deployed. The Proud Boys and the many militias in the US that have rapidly expanded their size and firepower in recent years are called to "stand by" not to fulfill their own agendas, as much as they may believe this to be the case, but to enable the same kind of sectarian violence, real and spectral, that enabled the comprehensive extortion of Iraq as a nation. With his professional showman's tricks honed by years as a reality star, Trump was the right president to wield this hammer. Questions about his fitness for office took precedence over the long-standing structural chaos that provides financial windfalls for those at the top of increasingly stratified economic chains. Trump made obvious the great private wealth available to those who occupy and encircle the seat of world power that is the American presidency.

In Iraq, where a new precedent of violence for profit was announced, citizens have emerged from twenty-plus years of punishing warfare from the strongest military in the world to reject the torture-for-profit scheme unfurled under the banner of "sectarianism." Some of the most prominent journalists and thinkers surmised that Iraqis simply couldn't handle "Western-style democracy" owing to their location in the Middle East, that unlucky and inherently conflict-ridden place. In fact, Iraqis must be uncannily compatible with democracy, considering that October 2019 marked the beginning of a youth-led grassroots movement that has withstood more than a thousand assassinations to protest and fight for a just representative government free from sectarian claims and lethal corruption. These are the youth who grew up under the American appetite for destruction and sadism; who came of age seeing edifices collapse under the merciless demands of extraction; who, despite everything the world has shown them, have so stubbornly and freely believed that "another world is possible" that they don't think to title conferences and books with those words, but have sacrificed their own lives and safety to demand a habitable future.

4. Jim Mattis, *National Defense Strategy of the United States Unclassified Summary* (Washington, DC: Department of Defense, 2018).

The ramifications of these recent wars cannot be fully considered without contemplating their related violence and environmental impact, and the inevitable outcome of both: the constriction of inhabitable land. Brown University's Costs of War research group estimates that at least thirty-seven million people have been displaced by the war on terror.[5] As armed conflicts and climate change intensify, so too has the fight over ever-scarcer resources, creating more and more frequent waves of climate and battle-scarred refugees. The expected rise in these numbers is taking place as immigration controls become more restrictive in Europe, the United States, and Australia. Images circulate the globe of migrants from Latin America, Africa, and Southwest Asia held in cages, drowned at sea, washed up on shores, spending their lives in sprawling, desolate refugee camps, or fleeing those that have been burned to the ground. The public is growing as accustomed to these images as to those of Aleppo and Mosul in absolute ruin. The term "doom-scrolling" has been coined in America to describe the experience of consuming a stream of interminable apocalyptic events on social media. What these users do not acknowledge is that their own government has created actual apocalyptic worlds meant to be as captivating as they are quotidian, starting with the bombardment of Baghdad in 2003, the first assault one could watch while having a beer at a sports bar. It is grotesque but not impossible to imagine how acclimated we may become to the sight of the devastation of bodies both on-screen and off-, in the mass population losses to come.

The cessation of wars and the demilitarization of the police are notably absent from climate-change remedies, which too often focus on consumer activities such as recycling and buying electric cars. Another finding in the Costs of War report is that "the DOD [Department of Defense] is the single largest consumer of energy in the US, and in fact, the world's single largest institutional consumer of petroleum," with over four hundred million metric tons of greenhouse gasses emitted since 2001 through war-related

5. David Vine et al., "Creating Refugees: Displacement Caused by the United States' Post-9/11 Wars," Watson Institute for International and Public Affairs, Brown University, Providence, RI, September 2020.

efforts.[6] This plain measurement sits alongside datasets on the impact of toxic fumes, depleted uranium, trauma to human and nonhuman life, deforestation, water mismanagement, and munitions residue and buildup, which can result in fetal deformities and habitat destruction. The fight to slow climate change in the US has gained traction, but mainstream groups and nonprofits still neglect to include demilitarization and a global fight against unregulated capitalism as a necessary strategy, despite the limitless profit motive that serves as the bedrock of anti-green pro-war efforts.

In 2020, the largest wildfires in California's recent history raged over one hundred million acres. I, along with many others, mourned the loss of life and land, stunned by the enormity and physical transformation wrought by the fires' fury. It had been years since I was last in Baghdad, and I was living again in the northern California town I'd immigrated to as a child. Its trails and walkways were choked with smoke, and ash fell for weeks, blanketing the grass and windows in a kind of alien snow. A renowned writer and climate-change activist based in San Francisco shared a story on social media about the fires and Baghdad. I thought for a moment that the connection between the extreme environmental costs of waging war on bodies and the earth, and its implications for sites beyond Iraq's borders, had been made. But the story was not about Iraq's burning oil fields, the soaring emissions of heavy military machinery, the razing of trees and foliage, or the less understood future implications of the loss of life and destroyed geography. Instead, the story was about a man in the US who felt the need to go outside and breathe in the hazardous air, just like in the thirteenth century, when Iraq was invaded by the Mongols who burned the Grand Library of Baghdad and threw countless numbers of books in the river. Ink from the books turned the river black, and residents drank its waters in order to retain some of the knowledge from their pages.

I wonder when we will drink from the waters, or breathe in the air, of all that has burned in our recent wars in Iraq; when will we retain any of the volumes of knowledge that fall heavier than the ash from our wildfires. There is a saying that became popular

6. Neta C. Crawford, "Pentagon Fuel Use, Climate Change, and the Costs of War," Watson Institute of International and Public Affairs, Brown University, Providence, RI, November 2019.

in Iraq in the years since the invasion: "Anything you can imagine is here." These words are typically used to describe vacation spots, utopias. In Iraq, this adage speaks to the details of the future we keep dreading and discussing, as if it would only relate to unbearable heat and species extinction. Iraqis have always dealt with unbearable heat, expanded the species despite it. The future we can't imagine isn't in the extra days of glaring sunlight, dead and decaying fish, or dwindling honeybee population. We don't have to speculate about the Anthropocene or dystopias, or question what the edge of climate change, capitalism, policing, and warfare looks like. We don't have to look for evidence in paper trails or forensic reconstructions. We don't have to keep pretending that this is something we can't imagine. It has all been laid bare for us, in torture videos, mass graves, civic fissures, and private glee, images of sulfur-dioxide levels equivalent to volcanic eruptions taken from space. In the moment a child's voice shifts from defiant to desperate, the shroud is laid. We know, already, what the answer to mercy will be.

Blue Land
Olivier Marboeuf

Places

An ultramarine blue space, blue smoke, white tear gas,
the red of fruits thrown onto a stage, a seminar, an art centre,
a dwelling, it depends.
The environs are not described. Just a night, filled with fire.

The characters

The Voices of Solitude, the woman rock, a liquid storyteller,
Phantom Matter.
Alternately or at the same time.
A chorus is in charge of the soundtrack: imitation of explosions,
beatbox, cries of fear and pleasure, counterfeit poetry.

Oh!

Where begins
Where to begin?
That's the question
That's the vain
question
It's the blue
vein
that vibrates
under the surface of black skin

Who's talking?
From what underwater
and lost country
Ocean

will you return me
The bone
and the eye,
The mouth
And the sound

[Performance.

He repeats the same thing
modulating the tone
and pitch of his voice,
over a scrim of overseas blue
with precious gems
in his mouth.
A ceramic pineapple
balanced on his head.
Smile my treasure!
It's an artistic performance.

It's fun.
It's cool.
A mauve light
and slide projections of seashells.
Shitty Caribbean, cobbled together
for the loving eyes of the West.
To pay the rent on a lousy room
in a European capital;
he consents
and watches himself on Instagram,
and watches his life,
a brief, empty, ephemeral story;
he consents.
A life in the prison of an eye
which isn't his.
He consents.
And to think: "What I want is to come"
and finding it beautiful
and finding it clever.
And one day he'll find that everything is old.
Already.]

It's not the vein
No
the vain question
It's not
coquetry
either.
Where to begin
Where in space do you plant your eyes
Where in time
do you breathe?
fresh air
What air?
Where to carve out a space?
On the frozen surface
of the ocean
a woman
thrown overboard

a long time ago   a very long time
rises up
shows her chest
covered with worms and mollusks.
Mouth open
to the sky

beard of foam,
a living island
fossil
and vegetal
she pierced
the dark
blue
abyss
of death.

There she is more alive
amid the remains
of a boat
that floats
in the eye of sharks

She sees again
She speaks
and de-speaks

[Fossil archive. Raise up your statues, affix your plaques, pour out men on horseback with African metal, distribute busts of the resistant Delgrès in towns, in Guadeloupe, plant gardens in the name of Solitude and plant statues of rebel slaves, here and there, plant in Paris, and don't forget to topple a slave seller in Bristol on his head, it doesn't cost anything and it's always a pleasure, to drown him in the port with all his secrets. Irony and diversion. And then when calm returns, plant instead a Black woman with a fist raised, even for a moment, as if she's pretending.

A Black woman will do the trick, with her fist raised, it's better, it's cool.]

The chorus repeats a stanza from Derek Walcott's poem "The Sea Is History"

Where are your monuments, your battles, martyrs?
Where is your tribal memory? Sirs,
in this grey vault. The sea. The sea
has locked them up. The sea is History.

[Let them do it. They have to do something.
But don't forget to break Schœlcher's arm in Cayenne,
the one that points at the Middle Passage to show the
future, breaks irony and breaks diversion, make the proud
abolitionist of Martinique topple over onto his teeth
and don't put anything back up, wait, don't plant anything.
Wait and welcome the explosion and the smoke that
ceaselessly changes form and direction.
Those are our monuments,
the voice that recedes or rises up from the floor
grey blue
fossil blue
of the ocean, in the cave, in the landscape
concrete blue
of tower blocks,
accordioned sheet-metal roofs of shabby allotments,
the silhouette that cuts through the night on a mini-moto,
and the scar inside a mouth that glows red
blue red
of the bad gaze that defies the police
and the gaze that writhes in the chaabi of factories,
the cut hand
and the hand
Cobalt blue
Mine blue
Charcoal blue
Green blue
and blue red

Talbot Blue
Algerian Blue
Blue 83
which is another Blue 61
Blue Seine
Blue 82
Caribbean Blue
the beloved neck and the neck broken in a haze of sweat,
infinite football where time no longer exists
Marius Trésor
arms crossed
Jesus!
In Sevilla.
Go Blues!
There they are, our monuments
living-dead.
Living.
Living blue.]

Oh!

In what period
and at what distance

You think that it begins

you think someone sees
something
that doesn't need to be
the start.
I leave you the start
the origin,
man
I'll let you recount your *life*
woman
I leave you
your little property to you, you, you
I leave you History
and its diversions

You have all the means
of production
to tell it
and to have it told
your History
again

and again

to fill our eyes
and our hands
with your grandeur
and your whining.

Now

I see
other worlds
with the new
and putrid eye
of the dead woman

in decomposition
who is my liquid
continent.

And that
you can't imitate it
because you can't imitate life
under death
in the worlds of death
the life of death
which is life
which is breath
from which
you hear me
speak to you.

Boom!

Oh!
I don't lower my eyes
however
I don't lower arms
cut off
and breath
the same
Beneath the capitalist sky
inlaid with precious
gems
mineral knowledge
speech treasure
words
extracted from the depths of the mine
of the throat
immediately circulate in veins
circulate
supple and
fluid
repeat repeat repeat
and acquire value
in armpits
and thighs
and brown torsos

Take!
We have nothing to hide
We have no words
I swear
We have nothing
that isn't our own

and that we could hide
We have nothing but dirty hands
where nothing lingers

Take!

All the white guys

can be Black women

queer

now

And the white women

too

It's easy

and it's cool

You can serve yourself

You just

tap

on available matter

Take!

in the gold

of sweat

lick tears on the surface of eyes

Audre Lorde

My dear!

Octavia Butler

My heart!

Hortense Spillers

Oh!

bell

hooks!

my little kitten

Meow!

Meow!

Voilà!

You want it, you have it!

Everyone wants it

Everyone wants

to be a Black woman

and if possible

queer

and brilliant

and shiny
and fluid.
Endless matter
amicable
and

available

Oh!
Saidiya!
in the mauve
mauve light
But without
this hell
and this eye
without the immense
wasteland that haunts
the head
painted in monochrome orange-Blue
of night
on the National highway
head lost
at the ends of the world
a map-less
periphery

in the shadow of a door

Rodney,
did you fall asleep
there?
on the edge of the expressway,
Weird guy!

Adama,
did you put your handsome profile
on backwards,
big guy?
on the tarmac, why?

In order to say what,
to do what?

Catch your breath.

Catch it!

Do it!

What accident did you get yourself into, Théo?
What did you get into?

Who squeezes, who knocks
at the door
of your nerves?
No one wants to be
this pile of criminal bones,
I'm telling you
everyone wants,
but not that

stop bothering us
Everyone wants to be bothered
but not that

wake up from your delirium
wake up!
No one wants to see
your life
spread out
in this stroboscopic
and liquid
light
no one wants to see
your life.

Who painted your eye
that scintillating blue?
What would you call it?
Overseas blue?

Cobalt?
Royal?
Limoges
porcelain blue
or Toulouse?

Who moved your mouth
in
the French landscape?
Who squeezed your dangerous
muscles
who smashed
the dangerous door
of your dangerous breath?

Catch
Catch
If you want it,
you have it.

The chorus sings
an anonymous, ageless
song of the people
"We have a duty of melancholy"

Oh!
Pile of breathless
bones
tossed in the morning
a lighter blue air presently
almost sky
watercolour
of the West
Plastic bag blue

Blue that shoots
White

shoots at
Red

Bang!

And dies.

Everyone wants

but
No one wants you.

There
I'll tell you
in this ocean
Marine blue
Petroleum blue
Atlantic blue
At the bottom of abysses
There where there is no sky
Where there are never eyes,
our monuments
are lying.
There!

Sculptures
or fossils
it depends
mouth against the floor
of the world.
Conquest dub
Beatbox
Poorly spoken infra-basses
de-speaking waves
trembling.

Here we are

Boom!

A collection of explosions
invades the mouths of the chorus,
a night blue story
landscape of sounds
Delgrès kills himself
with his three hundred companions
the Danglemont plantation house
explodes and rains down
noisily

at the base of La Soufrière
mouths clattering
whistling between teeth
which is also
the History of the banlieues
which is the History of the Seine
and thus the History of Algeria
and thus the History of iron
of railroad switch points
and thus the History of wastelands
and thus the History of dirty faces
of Mali and the Ivory Coast
of Tunisia
But we won't know it until the end,
all this noise,
this smoke and roar
it's a story
about what must explode
to open up a space
and breathe.

The chorus throws rotten
pomegranates on the stage.
All of this noise serves as intermission
Then things continue
with renewed vigour.

Boom!

I am not
your little sugar archive
I'm not your beautiful quotation
Your *pretty native informant*
darling
Go ahead!
I'm not
your wallpaper

rifleman blue

I'm not
your matter
indestructible
and beloved

I'm not
your crazy dancer
Neon blue
Liquid blue

I'm out of that.
I remove myself from that.

On my tongue
there are landscapes   of night
oranges and blues

and there's the din

of an angry ocean,
of a celebration.

My story is
hidden
behind the noise
and behind
the images,
in the decor,
my story is
hidden
and my breath
is
hidden.

[Film outline: It's not the story of a Black cowboy, so free that he kills anyone who gets in his way, anyone who wants to prevent him from having and coming – what I want is to come – it's not the dazzling life of a Black armed cowboy who lives out the fantasy that was implanted inside him, the fantasy of becoming a man, in this way, of becoming a man through violence and possession, thereby leaving that crawling matter with dark eyes that burns its hands gathering cotton, unable, unlike him, to come, unable to revolt as he can, not to be free, but to enjoy this right to violence and this right to death, which is in the Constitution, the right to destroy all obstacles and to possess, the right to break down all resistance, the right to reduce all enemies into this primary matter of death. History of the unchained hero, not of the mass in chains, that swarming and frightened pile on which the always too hot head of the master lies down. Remains, decor, waste. There is what serves no purpose to the story and there is the hero, who is spectacle, who is murder and who is thus, History. The hero and the sea. For the sea is History and we are locked up in this grey blue vault. What survives this History we will call hallucination. Have you seen it? Have you heard it? We call it monument, we call it delirious archive.

Have you seen it?
Have you heard it?

Whose road is this?
It's our road!
Whose road is this?
It's our road!
Whose street is this?
It's our street!
This street?
Our street!
Whose wound is this?
It's our wound!
Whose breath is this?
It's our breath!
This breath?
Our breath!
Survive and breathe,
this is the rebellion
and collective History
of the black matter
and of its life in the decor
of films
and the landscape
of films
where the hero kills
to come
as the master tells him
to come
better perhaps
even more implacable
to become this man
entirely free
to give
death
to shoot bullets
that pierce
resistance
to what he wants
to what he believes he wants
because he's free to kill
And he's free
to come.

There's no other History
Except maybe there
in what remains
and the decor
in the trash
and smoking
rubble
of the crime scene
which is the scene
of endless
orgasm
there is
a surviving
eye
there is
the beginning of a place.]

The air has a pale blue tint
The trails of tear-gas bombs
trace arcs
that rebound on the ground.

Forget then
the origin

the beginning
and the idea of the beginning

and seek rather
the critical moment

the primitive scene

that then repeats.
In echoes
that are less and less powerful

less and less visible

but still hover

the ghost

of the primitive scene

which is perfect
which is terrible and perfect

terribly perfect.

The plantation.

Oh!

That's where we'll begin

like Malcom Ferdinand

but for other reasons.

[Personal diary. One day I participated in a fascist seminar – it was the first time. I didn't know it at first, I wasn't sure when I read the invitation if I understood exactly what the people who invited me were trying to say, but in the end, it was a seminar about the possibility of racism and the possibility of fascism, in Belgium, in art, despite the embarrassed air, that's what it was about: fascism, white Europe, contemporary art, future and melancholy. I exhibited a diagram that represented the visual economy of the plantation: a history of the eye, of the men and women who lived within it, under the empire of a gaze, a history of the visible, a history of the invisible, of what is thrown into the shadows and of what survives in shadow, of those who are the light, of those who imitate them. At another seminar, somewhere else, I showed the diagram. And at the end of the panel I was participating in, a white woman stood up. She didn't come toward me.

She gathered into her arms one of the female participants, a Black academic, onstage, in front of everyone, in the empire of her gaze. In her arms. She hugged her very tight against her chest, the way you hug a friend, a parent – Mum! She clung to her with all her strength, so as not to sink. Maybe she was afraid of sinking. And what she found was a Black woman, the hull of a ship in freezing water, a bit of hull or a rock. And barely had this same black rock finished speaking – on the same panel where I showed the plantation diagram, the emotional and invisible violence of the master's house – than this smiling white woman came onstage with all her distress to hug her close, as if to tell her, it's okay, as if to tell her, it's okay kitten, come give me some of your warmth, just after the slide projection of the diagram which shows the plan for an emotional extraction zone, the plantation, where violence in the fields and at the pillory dazzles the person who does not see what this violence is a diversion for, what it prevents us from seeing of the heat and shade of the master's house. (Here's something Saidiya Hartman wants to see and that maybe Malcolm X misses: the cost paid by those who rub shoulders with the masters and owe them attention, sexual services and spectacle; the economy of this attention, of this care, this availability, a debt.) And so just after the diagram, there's the scene with woman who wraps herself around black flesh, as if she were hugging her beloved nanny, somewhere in the history of shadow, in a place with no witness, but that becomes a performance now. And just after the diagram again, but somewhere else this time around, back at the fascist seminar, the white director of a museum shakes my hand and says, we're all Maroons, we are the Maroons, all of this is right, all of this is terribly right, the plantation and all that, thank you, thank you, it's incredibly right, the luminous scene that chases the ecology of shadow, the delicate hand that emerges from the matter of the ship's hold to divert and escape, that's the art world we hold so dear, except for one thing, it's us, we the Maroons. But this time in the fascist seminar, he doesn't take me into his arms, it's not the place for it, it's not the right moment, but mostly, mostly he knows I'm not going to save him, that I'm not a Black woman who saves the white directors of Belgian museums who are Maroons, that I can't do, I'm not that rock, I'm not a piece of the hull of a huge cruise ship, a floating city, a European city that smashes into an iceberg, that's beyond my strength, and so I watch him let go of my hand and sink deep into the dark waters of this fascist seminar. He disappears.]

The chorus
(in an ocean sound à la Turner):
Splash!

The plantation
in the Caribbean

that's where we'll start

for we have to start somewhere
far from staring eyes
at the peripheries of the Empire
there where everything is more intense and naked
a primitive scene

intense and naked

terribly perfect

And it's there that we see
clearly
all the collections
all the delicate
motifs
of violence
exposed without fear
and without
shame
But it isn't
the only story

in the performance

Unsustainable
and its dazzling
diversions
It isn't
the only story
of the shooting
that delights the eye of the Black cowboy
which is the eye
of another
with his body attached to it

And it isn't the only
ghost scene
of this moment of orgasm

a lynching
burned wood
coal hung from a tree
strange fruit

*ripe to burst**

It isn't
the only story

of a police officer who gets lost
and falls asleep

on a pile,
a dark mineral
a shining mountain of petroleum
hard
and resistant

* *Mûr à crever* is a 2004 novel by the Haitian poet Frankétienne. It was translated by Kaiama L. Glover and published by Archipelago Books in 2014 as *Ripe to Burst.*

until it falls in
on itself
and becomes a lifeless

thing
by accident
in the exercise of his functions
of death
and performance.

It is not just
and it is not only.

It's also the story
of what happens in the familiar and warm
shadow
of the home

the kitchen,

the bedroom
the cold cellar
the sanctuary

my dear
my sweet

Everyone wants to be

a Black woman,
but

Oh!

in the half-light of the plantation house

where hands
are available

and comb
blond hair endlessly

where lips
are available

and without a word

where buttocks,

breasts genitals

legs

are available

and also the pierced eye

into which dramas

are poured
the immense vulnerability
of masters
and the impossible comfort

which never has enough
hands

my dear

that's our house

our home
that's how

our world is

and there is no other world

We must care for it
and understand it and
accept it
in all its light

and in all its darkness

Very dark blue
What would you say?
Black with bluish reflections
Like the feathers
around the eye
of a bird.

Come!
You'll make me a promise
Don't ever go away again
Never
Stay here so I can feel you
Give me
your cool hands

to wipe my fever
You'll be my twin sister

And we'll found a sky
of sorority
in the fading afternoon

behind the hills

Why don't you love me

with a true love?
Like me, I love you
Why that idiotic smile?

These lifeless arms
and that nod of the head
And that stupid slowness

with which you drag
your stupid feet
when I call you?

Why am I so tired and weary
of you refusing me?

Don't you want to do
what I ask?

Don't you want to be
my collective work
my speaking installation
my collaboration?

[And repeat the same thing
modulating the tone
and pitch of your voice,
against a scrim of overseas blue
with precious gems
in your mouth.
A ceramic pineapple
balanced on your head.
Smile, my sugar,
my treasure!
It's very beautiful.
Don't move.

A mauve light
and slide projections of seashells.
Stifling landscape of these damned islands
where we've come aground
you
and me
my sister.

Go sleep on your shabby pallet
in a dream of Europe,
but first, consent to this life,
brief, empty, ephemeral,
consent.
To live in my friendly gaze
and to watch me come.
Everything is old now.
The palm trees are covered
with the ashes
of an explosion.
Up there at the base of La Soufrière,
the rebels have exploded
the Danglemont plantation house.
It's the end.
Boom!]

But we are
a family.
Aren't we a family?

A big family
loving and just?

There's nothing to see outside but ashes
floating over this paradise
ugly and grey.

There's no reason
we're leaving
the master's house
There's no reason

No
that we leave the scene

I can tell you
we won't leave it
because we are

the arch.
What would you do outside
where burned-alive apes now scream?
in a forest of uprooted trees

There is nothing

There has never
been anything
but hallucinations
There is no other world
For we are the arch
and we are the Maroons.

[A reading note. Please make donations, obligations, co-optation, small privileges, preferences, concurring desire. (These interactions) are the means to make racial supremacy bearable and to generate it. In my view they indicate the dimension of symbolic violence when it substitutes itself for physical brutality, as the place where subjection is fabricated in a hidden manner, in the routinization of domination. Christine Chivallon, *L'esclavage, du souvenir à la mémoire: Contribution à une anthropologie de la Caraïbe* (Éditions Karthala, 2012)]

And that is what we must learn
to see with a new eye
green and brown
beyond diversions
the whirlwind of ashes

and invent gestures
so we won't become

the last captures

of what disappears
and must
disappear.

Splash!

You won't go
far
it's not worth it
Over here
Over there
Not far
There's no other world
There's only this world
Leave the plantation
a moment
outside
is not
another world
but learn to breathe
to taste the air
and listen
to those who speak softly
a monument of whispers
and low masses.

It's here where our voices intermingle
with other sounds,
Creaks
and cries

We must learn
to breathe
inside of all this

and outside of this familiar
eye that calls

Who calls you?

That is a language
for a place
that is not yet there
for there is no other world

and yet we must breathe
right next to this world
as it is

Our skin comes off
Stay calm
smile at your enemies
show your teeth
and slide softly towards the outside,
fill your blood
with fear
fill your lungs
with fire

It's the place that comes

and we speak loudly
now

we de-speak it

It is the unsure
fragile

place
that comes

Amid the decomposition

something

rises and stands up
something escapes too

let escape
what needs to escape

it will return
when it finds its moment
and its music
when it finds
its dance

Nothing consents
in this place.

Forget the origin
and desire for a home
a palace
for false heat
and what tires you and bends you
What I want is to come.

Uproot your desire
for these old stories
Stay calm
and smile at your enemies
undo the anger
which is desire for power

desire of kings of queens
desire for children
kings and queens
save the other anger
which is bloody
monument
and don't set yourself either

immediately
to braiding

as you've always had to braid
endlessly
before
because you were afraid
of not being part

everyone wants to be, but

Don't offer your hands anymore
forget that you're being called

Who is calling you?

Take back your desire
and your eyes

and let come

what rises

a form
that no one decides on
rises up presently
with no master
by the mere
swarming presence
of worms
in the blue black matter
of the living
and the dead
it is our language

the beginning of our language
which begins everywhere
and which always begins
somewhere

in particular
in the shadow
of that which was not
seen
of that which was not
said

our monuments
which never cease to grow
now
now collapsing
have neither face
nor horse
under the orange grey
sky
where float the ashes
of those
who wanted to live
and breathe

Boom!

there is a place
the beginnings of a celebration
without spectacle
in the clacking of our bones
in the gurgling of our empty stomachs

there is a place.

Translated from the French by Liz Young
Editorial review by Shela Sheikh

Aesthetic Currencies

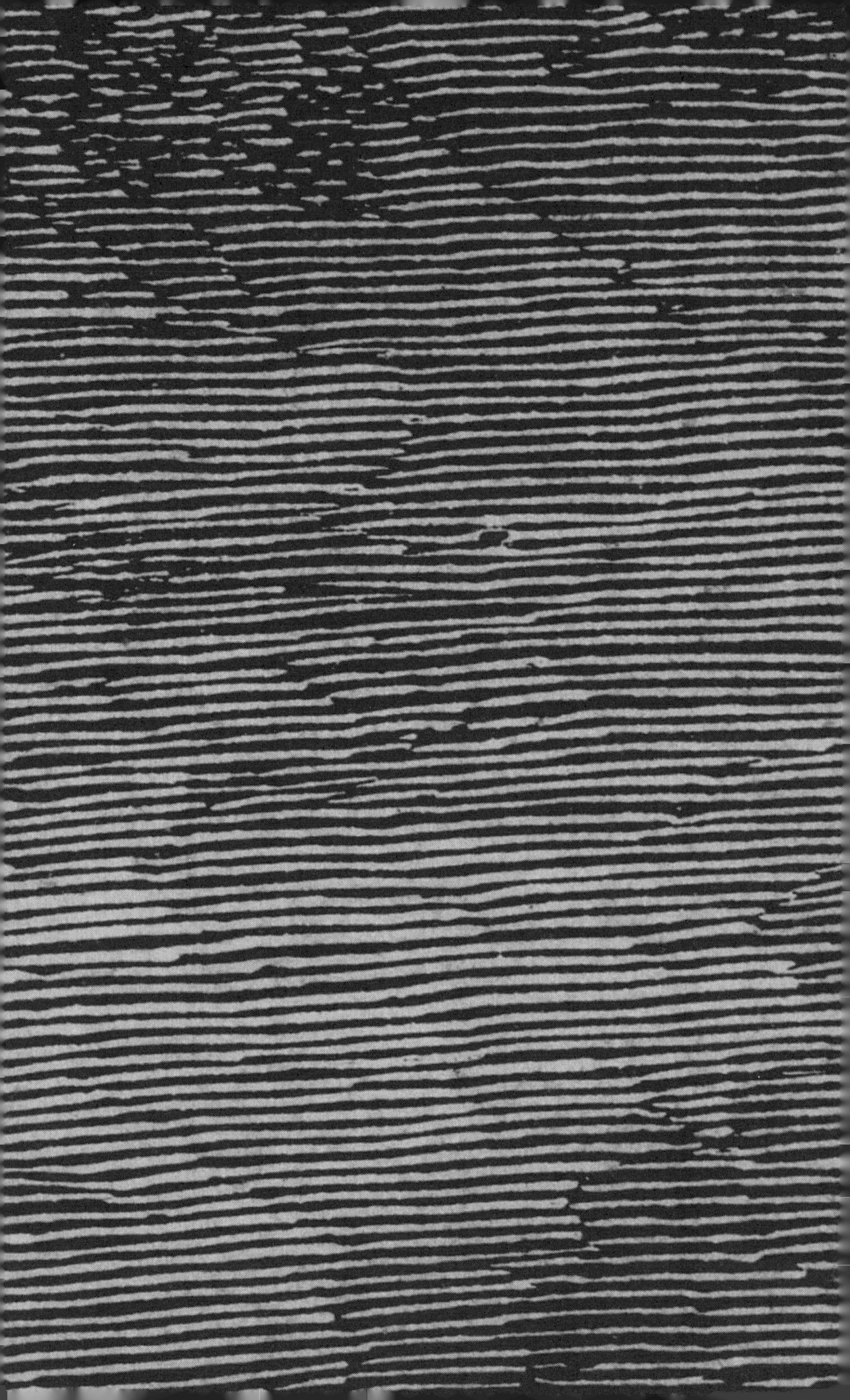

The Promise of the Nonhuman
An Existentialist Trope in the Anthropocene

Sladja Blazan

Current academic publications concerned with looming environmental collapse seem to be pulled in opposite directions. On the one hand, the increase in the intensity and frequency of natural catastrophes is producing a large influx of papers calling for humanity to unify in immediate response. On the other, decolonial scholars are joining feminist and postcolonial voices in greater numbers to warn that the current crisis can only be curtailed by a "delinking" from the "totality of Western epistemology."[1] Fusion or separation? Or is there a way to respond to both?

The concept of the nonhuman is often brought forward as a way of reconciling the two opposing views. By drawing attention to the elementary ways in which the concept of the human is shaped by the nonhuman, the thinking goes, Western ontologies of human stewardship can be overturned. If the fatal separation between the human and the nonhuman—and the related dominance of eco-phobia in the Western imaginary—is the base for the exploitation of human and nonhuman resources, overcoming the binary of culture and environment should be the first step toward a more just ontology. Pressed by the horsemen of the Anthropocene, Western scholarship is awakening to the lethal consequences of the imposed dichotomy between humans and their environment, which gives hope that social change begins in the act of embracing the nonhuman.

In this essay, I will take a closer look at two representations of the nonhuman—Jean-Paul Sartre's *Nausea* (1938) and Jeff VanderMeer's *Annihilation* (2015)—both of which have been celebrated for their emancipatory potential. Highlighting the connections between the two will demonstrate how anthropocentric and Eurocentric figurations of the universal human smoothly transition into the recently established discourse of the Anthropocene with the help of the nonhuman. While the nonhuman certainly

1. Walter D. Mignolo, "DELINKING: The Rhetoric of Modernity, the Logic of Coloniality and the Grammar of De-coloniality," *Cultural Studies* 21, no. 2 (2007): 449–514.

holds the potential for dismantling colonial conceptualizations of Man that pose as universal, the Anthropocene umbrella, as the geographer Kathryn Yusoff succinctly argues, "neatly erases histories of racism that were incubated through the regulatory structure of geologic relations."[2] The environmental discourse's urgency threatens to create self-reproducing figurations of the human through ethnocentric narrative frameworks.

The gender studies scholar Michelle Rowley has warned that we need to attend to a theory's "politics and conditions of emergence," as inherited structures that used to be liberating but now might be damaging will necessarily be part of future visions.[3] In response to such cautioning, I want to underline how imperial taxonomies are structurally inscribed into a discourse that claims to be novel and emancipatory. As the Anthropocene quickly transforms into the meta-narrative of our times, the need for reflection and criticism grows.

The Nonhuman Turn?

Theories abound that account for culture as an ecological niche within which humans live. Invested in finding spaces "beyond humanity" (Tim Ingold) or among "more-than-human geographies" (Beth Greenhough) and "other-than-human critters" (Donna Haraway), environmental scholars expand the sphere of agency to encompass more and more representatives.[4] Hybridization and entanglement are the modi operandi that promise to enable a critical positioning of the human within the environment. As a category that appears to respond to the demands of the Anthropocene, the nonhuman has proven helpful in filling the void left by the human. It is therefore not surprising that more and more examples in literature, film, and the visual arts attest to this sentiment. To artists, directors, and writers who seek to find a

2. Kathryn Yusoff, *A Billion Black Anthropocenes or None* (Minneapolis: University of Minnesota Press, 2019), ch. 1.

3. Michelle Rowley, "Feminist Visions for Women in a New Era: An Interview with Peggy Antrobus," *Feminist Studies* 33, no. 1 (2007): 83.

4. Tim Ingold, "Anthropology beyond Humanity," *Suomen Antropologi: Journal of the Finnish Anthropological Society* 38, no. 3 (2013): 5–23; Beth Greenhough, "More-than-Human Geographies," in *The SAGE Handbook of Human Geography*, ed. Roger Lee et al. (London: SAGE Publications, 2014), 94–119; Donna J. Haraway, *Staying with the Trouble: Making Kin in the Chthulucene* (Durham, NC: Duke University Press, 2016).

space outside the realm of problematic humanity, the nonhuman is an inviting alternative.[5]

Owing to the concept's interdisciplinary framework—an asset for analyzing contemporary socioenvironmental issues—the humanities scholar Richard Grusin has proposed that we are currently in a "nonhuman turn." In his introduction to the eponymous 2015 anthology, Grusin compiles an inventory of "intellectual and theoretical developments" that have led to nonhuman theory, including actor-network theory, affect theory, animal studies, assemblage theory, new media theory, new materialism, speculative and object-oriented realism, and systems theory.[6] What connects these diverse fields is a sense of novelty. The fusion of fresh perspectives provides contemporary scholars with the new interdisciplinary approach necessary to account for modern conceptualizations of the human. Thus, if nonhuman theories are, as introduced by Grusin, "a way forward for the arts, humanities, and social sciences in light of the difficult challenges of the twenty-first century," who would want to look back to the wasteland of the once dominant human?[7]

I consider this celebratory rapid development alarming, and understand it as a call for critical reflection. Grusin's list tellingly excludes fields such as Black feminist theory, despite its long history of questioning the Western concept of the human. In an era of accelerating environmental catastrophe that produces an overwhelming sense of urgency, it is understandable that there is little time for rummaging through the past and looking for gaps that grew out of epistemic erasures and ontological intrusions. Yet the ways in which the nonhuman, turn or no turn, is employed to decenter the human, at least in a transatlantic cultural context, often confirm the centrality of the universal figure of the human. In other words, the nonhuman accommodates a return to the human of the Enlightenment, namely the white European male. Cloaked in the mantle of the Anthropocene, the nonhuman

5. Even a medium that is grounded in human perception such as cinema seeks to abolish the human condition and circumvent subjectivity. See Gilles Deleuze, *Cinema 1: The Movement-Image*, trans. Hugh Tomlinson and Barbara Habberjam (Minneapolis: University of Minnesota Press, 1986).

6. Richard Grusin, introduction to *The Nonhuman Turn*, ed. Richard Grusin (Minneapolis: University of Minnesota Press, 2015), viii–ix.

7. Grusin, vii.

threatens to become a runaway concept that, in the worst case, perpetuates social structures that have brought us to this bleak moment.

The Root

Before we had the Anthropocene, there was existentialism. One of the most famous passages in Sartre's novel *Nausea* depicts its protagonist, Antoine Roquentin, sitting on a park bench and staring at the tree roots "plunged into the ground just underneath" his feet. As fear begins to creep up his body, he reflects: "I was sitting, slightly bent, my head bowed, alone in front of that black, knotty mass, which was utterly crude and frightened me. And then I had this revelation." As the root of the chestnut tree "pressed itself against [his] eyes," "existence had suddenly unveiled itself."[8] The root exists in an independent and non-relational way; it is unintelligible to the human observer. This realization, which comes at the end of a long introspective meandering on the narrator's otherwise affectless being-in-the-world, stirs everything up. If the root exists without context, then so does Antoine himself.

It is here, at the intersection of the thinking subject and the unintelligible root, that phenomenology was formed; this central passage has come to symbolize the moment that existentialism came into being.[9] Roquentin continues to speculate about the "revelation" the root provoked in him, whereas the descriptions take a curiously material turn: "The soft sound of the water in the Masqueret Fountain flowed into my ears and made a nest there, filling them with sighs; my nostrils overflowed with a green, putrid smell." This material situatedness in a non-relational world framing the experiencing subject is much more than a central literary example of phenomenology that only leads us to acknowledge the nonhuman's existence in its own right. Looked at more closely, the nonhuman permeates the human, even if cognitively. Roquentin,

8. Jean-Paul Sartre, *Nausea*, trans. Robert Baldick (New York: Penguin, 2000), 182–83.

9. Alistair Rolls and Elizabeth Rechniewski, "Uprooting the Chestnut Tree: *Nausea* Today," in *Sartre's Nausea: Text, Context, Intertext*, ed. Alistair Rolls and Elizabeth Rechniewski (Amsterdam: Rodopi, 2005), 1–28; Robert C. Solomon, "Meditations on *Nausea*: Sartre's Phenomenological Ontology," in *Dark Feelings, Grim Thoughts: Experience and Reflection in Camus and Sartre* (Oxford: Oxford University Press, 2021).

after all, realizes that he is also part of the "monstrous masses, in disorder—naked, in a frightening, obscene nakedness."[10] Centering on self-realization, the text relies on a radical and active separation from the nonhuman. It is at this intersection that Sartre's universal human emerges.

Existentialism is often discredited in contemporary thought. In the early 1980s, Erazim Kohak warned that in Sartre's oeuvre "the nonhuman appears as also inhuman, absurd and nauseating."[11] In his 2004 study *Seeing Through God: A Geophenomenology*, John Llewelyn invokes Sartre in passing, suggesting that the ecological philosophy that takes existentialism as its starting point cannot ultimately escape the "at least figurative dominion of the ego." He continues: "Shallow ecologism thus described would be an environmentalism that sees the nonhuman as the environment of the human." Scholars like Llewelyn are disturbed by a form of environmentalism that instrumentalizes the care for the nonhuman Other to justify the authority of the Self. The problem they highlight is that the nonhuman is acknowledged as the material condition for human experience and needs to be preserved for that reason only. As Llewelyn puts it, "The Sartrian Ego in the end always points to itself."[12]

I want to propose that it is this element of existentialism—environmentalism that decenters the human by promoting the well-being of the nonhuman, a "shallow ecologism" that circles back to the ego—that continues to dominate transatlantic attempts at narrativizing the nonhuman. Returning to Sartrian universal humanism, these imaginaries ultimately reinforce the binary between the self and the "monstrous masses—in disorder." However, the updated version of Sartre's concept does not affirm the self in the *negation* of the nonhuman but promotes a confirmation of the self *in* the nonhuman. With this move into the non-human, the non-relational assimilation produced, as Isabelle Stengers has put it, a "future perfect continuous" tense that "swallows" the whole messy history that has led us to this moment in time

10. Sartre, *Nausea*, 183.

11. Erazim Kohak, *The Embers and the Stars: A Philosophical Inquiry into the Moral Sense of Nature* (Chicago: University of Chicago Press, 1984), 4.

12. John Llewelyn, *Seeing Through God: A Geophenomenology* (Bloomington: Indiana University Press, 2004), 5.

and can now be simply forgotten.[13] In a sweeping erasure of long histories of violence that have produced the Western concept of the nonhuman, Anthropocene figurations revert back to a Sartrian confirmation of the contextless Self *in* the nonhuman.

Seen from an ecocritical perspective, Sartre had already paved the way for environmentally engaged scholarship in his catchy eco-phobic transcorporeality that grounds his aesthetics-turned-ethics. Leveling his own materiality with everything around him, Roquentin begins to grasp flat ontology. He leads his reader to the Anthropocene, providing an addressee for his existential angst: "I am afraid of towns. But you mustn't leave them. If you go too far, you come up to the Vegetation Belt. The Vegetation has crawled for mile after mile towards the towns. It is waiting. When the town dies, the Vegetation will invade it, it will clamber over the stones, it will grip them, search them, burst them open with its long black pincers; it will blind the holes and hang its green paws everywhere."[14]

This fusion of nonhuman living matter into a "Vegetation Belt" instills a sense of liminality as well as the potential for transgression. It is the whole of vegetation that appears "absurd: irreducible; nothing—not even a profound, secret aberration of nature—could explain that."[15] The Vegetation Belt, in all its grandiosity, bursts with the nothingness exemplified by the root. In the face of what is fused under the term "Vegetation," the Human is erected in the body of a white European able-bodied cisgender affluent rational man caught in a moment of reflection on the senselessness of the world. He extracts his negation, and thus dialectical confirmation, from the threatening image of the Vegetation. It is this performative act of engendering a universal (anxious) self in the face of the nonhuman that leads to the Anthropocene. Even more to the point, the nonhuman, today more than ever, stands as the material condition for the possibility of *human* experience, as nature/technology threatens to replace/erase

13. Isabelle Stengers in conversation with Heather Davis and Etienne Turpin, "Matters of Cosmopolitics: On the Provocations of Gaïa," in *Architecture in the Anthropocene: Encounters among Design, Deep Time, Science and Philosophy*, ed. Etienne Turpin (Open Humanities Press, 2013), 178, http://dx.doi.org/10.3998/ohp.12527215.0001.001.

14. Sartre, *Nausea*, 221–22.

15. Sartre, 185.

its existence. As I will demonstrate in the next example, current trends in narrativizing the nonhuman with the aim of addressing "unthinkable" climate change manage to clearly imagine, and thus not much depart from, Sartre's universe.[16]

The Shimmer

In the world of the Anthropocene, the Vegetation Belt has spread to the realm of the city. A telling example can be found in Jeff VanderMeer's novel *Annihilation* (2014), the first part of his Southern Reach Trilogy, and the film adaptation directed by Alex Garland in 2018; both are widely celebrated as narratives of the Anthropocene.[17] VanderMeer describes the book as "fiction about climate change and the environmental crisis," written in "the hope to push us out of our complacency."[18] The popularity of the novels and the film has moved the Southern Reach Trilogy to the forefront of ecocritical science fiction. The ideas of the radical environmentalist Derrick Jensen, whom VanderMeer has identified as a major influence, shifts the books into the realm of political literature, as Jensen is known to push for writers to "help to create a literature of morality and resistance."[19]

Given the prominence of this piece of literature, we should analyze the kind of morality and resistance promoted in the novel. Finola Prendergast reads the book in Jensen's terms as "an ethical work: it assumes biodiversity's inherent value and, from that assumption, imagines a model for sustainable human-nonhuman communities that respect both the autonomy and the relational subjectivity of their members."[20] To disentangle this point, I want to take a closer look at these types of communities and

16. Amitav Ghosh, *The Great Derangement: Climate Change and the Unthinkable* (Chicago: University of Chicago Press, 2016).

17. Miranda Jeanne Marie Iossifidis and Lisa Garforth, "Reimagining Climate Futures: Reading *Annihilation*," *Geoforum*, no. 137 (December 2022): 248–57.

18. "Jeff VanderMeer on *Annihilation*, Utopia and Climate Change," *The Atlantic*, May 7, 2018, https://www.theatlantic.com/video/index/559790/jeff-vandermeer/#.

19. Jeff VanderMeer, "The Nature of Reading: 10 Influences on the Southern Reach Trilogy," *HuffPost*, May 27, 2014, https://www.huffpost.com/entry/southern-reach-trilogy_b_5381331; Derrick Jensen, preface to *The Derrick Jensen Reader: Writings on Environmental Revolution*, ed. Lierre Keith (New York: Seven Stories Press, 2012), 10.

20. Finola Anne Prendergast, "Revising Nonhuman Ethics in Jeff VanderMeer's *Annihilation*," *Contemporary Literature* 58, no. 3 (Fall 2017): 344.

intersubjectivities. It is my intention to demonstrate that, despite better intentions, this self-proclaimed fiction about climate change does not depart from the Sartrian anthropocentric framework, thus promoting a questionable ethics and setting a problematic example. My aim is not to indict VanderMeer's novel but rather to caution against the Anthropocene framework of future imaginaries that do not extrapolate from history, promoting instead a conceptual leap into apocalyptic survival fantasies.

Annihilation docks onto a long history of horror stories set in uncanny sentient natural environments—one of the first, John W. Campbell's 1938 novella *Who Goes There?*, initiated a series of eco-horror plotlines set in Antarctica. Keeping in sync with the demands of science fiction, particularly its Lovecraftian branch, the undefinable power of the earth is taking over ever-larger landscapes. VanderMeer's eco-horror, however, sets itself apart from similar narratives that rely on monstrous creatures hidden in permafrost or growing in swamps by transforming the whole of nature into the monstrous, immersing the protagonist and the entire planet in this peculiar environment. Early in the novel it becomes obvious that a rainbow-colored substance refracts the DNA of all bodies that enter Area X, which in the film is called "the Shimmer." This realm reconfigures all living matter into new combinations, resulting in spectacular images of human–nonhuman hybrids. This move away from external monstrosity to internalization by navigating the narrative directly through the belly of the beast received critical praise, and rightly so. Rejecting individuality, Area X promotes the dividual.

As predicted by Sartre in *Nausea*, the Vegetation is predatory. The narrative of *Annihilation* begins after the natural environment has already taken over part of the earth. We learn about it from the diary of the narrator, a biologist who was sent by the government for research purposes into Area X along with a psychologist, an anthropologist, and a surveyor. Together they enter the flourishing "transitional environment," now an abandoned area that encompasses a black-pine forest, a swamp, marsh flats, and an ocean.[21] Sartre had predicted that Vegetation's dangerous "pincers" will be lethal; all expedition members apart from the biologist die.

21. Jeff VanderMeer, *Annihilation* (New York: Farrar, Straus and Giroux, 2014), 8.

Science, in *Annihilation*, poses a false promise. The novel follows the development of a narrator who progressively merges with the environment, yet different from her team members, she appears to do so willingly, and not only physically but also cognitively. She finds herself "contaminated" after inhaling "golden spores" that "spewed out" of a nodule on the wall, which leads to her mental and physical transformation, including heightened senses and a brightness she feels emanating from her chest. The reader learns that this inner illumination is the Shimmer inside of her—the narrator is in sync with the eerie environment. More importantly, the narrator is established as a character who has always felt alienated by society and closer to "nature." After her contamination, she experiences a new clarity that leads to a sense of completion rather than dissolution, as suggested by the chapter title with the same name.

The biologist is an identification figure for the reader, who longs for something more-than-human along with her; together they continue "descending into an organism" that is the earth itself.[22] The meaning of the word is to be taken literally, as the environment consists of diffracted animals, plants, and human bodies that all together compose what is referred to as "the Zone" (with a nod to Andrei Tarkovsky's 1979 film *Stalker*). Departing from animistic readings, *Annihilation* employs a scientist who detects human tissue in the environment under the magnification glass of her microscope. However, just like pre-Enlightenment animists, she finds confirmation of something that she intuitively knew but couldn't accommodate in scientific lingo: the environment is alive. Her description comes close to Roquentin's experience: "The wind was like something alive, it entered every pore of me and it, too, had a smell, carrying with it the earthiness of the marsh reeds."[23] Finding a way back to her true self without leaving the confines of science, she finally can embrace the nature that she is.

Sartre's Roquentin, in fact, had insisted that human relationships are kept up "to delay the collapse of the human world of measures, of quantities, of bearing."[24] This world of measuring and

22. VanderMeer, 28.
23. VanderMeer, 4.
24. Sartre, *Nausea*, 184.

taxonomizing becomes increasingly redundant in the narrative of *Annihilation*, to the point where it finally collapses. The story traces the final steps of a scientist accepting the implications of a radical human-material entanglement with natural environments. And this is where VanderMeer's book takes an environmental turn. The separation from nature and culture that was expressed in the inability of science to account for the natural environment in Area X is reversed in the very materiality of the human that extends itself into the nonhuman. The horror of personal dissolution is gradually transformed into the instability of form. Like the biologist, the reader is left to wonder if becoming "part" of nature is a horrific or progressive scenario.

While highlighting the porosity of human bodies and their environments is a necessary step toward understanding people's implications in their environments, I want to question what has been discussed as the "relational subjectivity" promoted in this text. What do we learn in terms of kinship or affiliation, or even in terms of climate change? Crossing into what is called the Zone or the Shimmer—which I would like to call the Vegetation Belt—is a military endeavor presented as an act of penetration. The scientists seem to be aware of Sartre's warning: they arrive equipped with measuring instruments, heavy weaponry, mobile devices, and field notebooks to help them define and hopefully tame the unruly vegetation. Their intention is to taxonomize, name, report, and explain what cannot be understood. All but the one who knew not to try to comprehend fail and disappear into the void that is Nature. The biologist survives because of her inability to subscribe to the language of science, despite her professional success. Appealing to a readership wary of Enlightenment anthropocentrism, this protagonist, since childhood, intuited how to accept the illegibility of ecosystems. The diffusion into the environment of the Shimmer initiates the alternative epistemology she longed for. This openness allows for her transformation from the position of a scientist who seeks to control to a living creature that seeks to cohabit.

The narrator's predisposition gives her an exclusive insight. She describes the Zone as "a kind of brightness of its own, a sort of refracted phosphorescence, that did not bear thinking about. That I could see it, that I had an affinity to it, agitated me. I was certain no one else left here, not the surveyor, not the psychologist, could see that stirring of the inexplicable."[25] Her acceptance of the inexplicable is reminiscent of Roquentin's embrace of nothingness. Her existence is confirmed in the intelligibility of everything that is. The biologist reflects on a starfish she studied long before entering the Zone: "There was something about my mood and its dark glow that eclipsed sense, that made me see this creature, which had indeed been assigned a place in the taxonomy—catalogued, studied, and described—irreducible down to any of that. And if I kept looking, I knew that ultimately I would have to admit I knew less than nothing about myself as well, whether that was a lie or the truth."[26]

The biologist's contentment with the opacity of life secures her survival. Roquentin similarly acknowledged: "I am in the midst of Things, which cannot be given names."[27] His embrace of meaningless existence prevents his suicide and therefore, as with the biologist, enables his survival. The Anthropocene imaginary that fuses Nature with Man can be interpreted as the next stage in a linear development—after the "great mass of hair" in *Nausea* that stretches its "green paws" and threatens to "devour" everything.[28] While the existential nonhuman was kept at the gate, the Anthropocene nonhuman burst through. In keeping with the Western tradition, this version of the nonhuman has only one function—the affirmation of the (universal) human in Nature.

In the aesthetics of the Shimmer, *Annihilation* erases history. The Shimmer refracts all living matter, reforming it into a shared form and setting it up for a new beginning. All life continues in a different form, ignorant of its prior life. This usage recalls, but departs from, the more common application of the shimmer to mark the presence of death. The anthropologist Jennifer Deger writes about the artistic device of the shimmer for the Yolngu, an Aboriginal culture mainly located in northeastern Australia: in Yolngu paintings, the shimmer commonly signifies the presence of death in life, thus reanimating the memory of former lives.[29]

25. VanderMeer, *Annihilation*, 69.

26. VanderMeer, 114.

27. Sartre, *Nausea*, 180.

28. Sartre, 221.

29. Jennifer Deger, "Shimmer," in *The International Encyclopedia of Anthropology*, ed. Hilary Callan and Simon Coleman, September 5, 2018, https://doi.org/10.1002/9781118924396.wbiea2043.

Annihilation too references the presence of death, but life is not seen as a memory. Literal writing on the wall, a vine of fungi, reads: "That which dies shall still know life in death for all that decay is not forgotten and reanimated shall walk the world in a bliss of not-knowing."[30] Upon closer examination, the fungi letters turn out to partially consist of human tissue, suggesting a metempsychosis, an indication that nothing dies in the Zone. All life continues, but with the "bliss" of erasing history. Therefore, the Shimmer will not save humanity from climate change, but a changed climate will save the human(s). The end is a clean slate, a new beginning.

Instead of a violent apocalypse, *Annihilation* uses the Zone, a "sudden impression of a fizzing block of light, fast fading," to reconfigure what is present rather than to erase or replace the human.[31] The aesthetics of the Shimmer is grounded in the presence of the invisible; not solely the absence of visibility, the invisible receives a dimension of its own. Scholars have offered emancipatory interpretations. Cameron Butler, for instance, reads the Shimmer as the staging for "posthumanist entanglements" able to break "Western ontological and material violence," while Chase Alexander Menaker, in his queer reading, interprets it as a fluid border of bodies, and Bill McClanahan sees it as "an ecology without purpose."[32] Butler is the only one of the three who accounts for the colonial history of the wetlands where *Annihilation* is set; he also sees in the Shimmer a means of collapsing Western binaries and exploring the porosity of seemingly firm bodies. Yet the area does not mark the presence of death in life; it rather erases the past and determines who will live and who will die. In this description by the biologist, the alarming similarity with Sartre's Vegetation Belt comes to the fore: "As that shimmering white rectangle became larger but no more distinct, I was filled with such a feeling of *wrongness* that I suffered nausea. The idea of a *trap* grew in my mind, that this floating light in the darkness was not a

30. VanderMeer, *Annihilation*, 114.

31. VanderMeer, 8.

32. Cameron Butler, "Shimmering in the Swamp: Wetlands, Danger, and Ecological Refractions in *Annihilation*," *ISLE: Interdisciplinary Studies in Literature and Environment* 29, no. 4 (Winter 2022): 1143; Chase Alexander Menaker, "Queer New Media" (MA thesis, San Francisco State University, 2019); Bill McClanahan, "Alex Garland (dir.) (2018) *Annihilation*: A Film Review," *Crime, Media, Culture: An International Journal* 15, no. 2 (2019): 363–66.

door at all but the maw of some beast, and if I entered through it to the other side, it would devour me."[33]

Just like Sartre's "great mass of hair," the Shimmer is the mode of vegetation that absorbs everything. The "inexplicable," which in Sartre's novel is "nothingness," needs to be acknowledged for one's own existence to be affirmed. Butler writes: "In being simultaneously miasma, pathogen, and pollutant, the Shimmer exceeds Western scientific legibility and containment protocols."[34] However, avoiding Western protocols does not automatically burst Western frameworks. Rather than departing from Western models, the Shimmer allows for a structural reconfiguration of the human in Nature at a moment when this very concept is threatened by extinction. Being able to go beyond Western humanism, therefore, will have to begin with the acknowledgment that the category of the human has relied on the exclusion of the nonhuman.

Capitalism and the conditions of the Anthropocene, as Anna Lowenhaupt Tsing has put it, no longer create the conditions for life.[35] Under unlivable conditions, it is the nonhuman or Other that is exploited yet again for hegemonic survival fantasies. *Annihilation* does not depart from most popular apocalyptic scenarios. The novel's investment in a protagonist who is the sole survivor confirms the trend in popular eco-collapse narratives that center on humanity prevailing in the individual, even under "unlivable" conditions. Such narratives appeal to the affective demands of an audience for a reconciliation with vegetation without giving up humanity. Sympathizing with an inquisitive biologist who has been wary of the nature–culture divide that science exemplifies, the reader is invited to explore life beyond the human without extending their imaginary toward the nonhuman. Rather than diversifying ecology, *Annihilation* adds the human to the "great mass of hair" that is Nature, securing a place for threatened humanity among the stranger taking over the world. How is the excessive libidinal fantasy of hybridization in current eco-horror different from narratives of human adaptation? The sentient environment that the biologist learns to accept functions as a backdrop for her reconfiguration.

33. VanderMeer, 121.

34. Butler, "Shimmering in the Swamp," 1127.

35. Anna Lowenhaupt Tsing, *The Mushroom at the End of the World: On the Possibility of Life in Capitalist Ruins* (Durham, NC: Duke University Press, 2015).

It is in the Vegetation that Man finds what is necessary to define who "we" are.

Thrown back to the universal ego, all scenes that engage in descriptions of the Zone focus on the human component. While learning little about the environment, the reader becomes certain that the biologist, in fact, will somehow, even if transformed, master existential dread by embracing the environment-in-herself. Like Roquentin before, who found confirmation of his existence in the undeniable presence of the "superfluous" root, the biologist receives her humanist affirmation in her confirmation of Nature's excess.

The Strange/r

VanderMeer's novel and Garland's film adaptation are indicative of narratives that seek to locate horror in relational geographies by finding ways to depict an invisible or unintelligible agent (the films *The Fog*, 1980, *The Thing*, 1982, *Interstellar*, 2014, and *Arrival*, 2016, to name a few) to shock readers and viewers out of a sense of complacency. Sartre pitted the human against vegetation, which resulted in his protagonist recognizing his individuality and his being-in-the-world, his implication in environments both social and historical. VanderMeer expanded this vision by materially inscribing the human into the environment, but the result does not depart significantly from the existentialist struggle for self-creation, and the nonhuman serves the individual human as a foil for self-affirmation. Harking back to the existential claim that existence is always a being-in-the-world, the biologist can finally authenticate her existence.

Comparing these two significant steps in the Western cultural imaginary (*human vs. Nature* and *human as Nature*), and the ways in which they stage themselves temporally and spatially within an exclusive or inclusive framework, exposes how the colonial fantasy of the universal human that defines itself against the image of the nonhuman can readily move from existentialism to theories of the Anthropocene. While the multispecies creations of human–plant and human–animal formations may seem to reexamine human exceptionalism, they in fact secure a continuation of exclusive personhood in a reconfigured subjectivity. Certain human lives continue, and these will need the body of another.

The shift from a narrator sitting on a park bench, staring at the roots of a tree, "paralyzed" by the realization this sight triggers, and dreading the potential takeover by Vegetation (an image central to modernity's discourse), to a narrator who initiates that fusion, effectively merging with the same root without losing her humanity (an image central to Anthropocene discourse), poses numerous epistemological problems. In both cases, the unintelligibility of the nonhuman, often described as strange, is promoted for the sake of highlighting the strangeness within oneself. Ever since Julia Kristeva's theory of the relationship with the internal other as the origin of xenophobia, the acknowledgment of internal estrangement has been considered a necessary step toward a meaningful relation with others in society.[36] *Annihilation* follows the same trajectory by promoting the perspective of an alienated scientist who acknowledged the "strangers to ourselves" and proceeded to merge with the Other/Nature.

In *Strange Encounters* (2000), a study of the problematic Western ontology of the strange, Sara Ahmed points out that recognizing the intra-subjective stranger minimizes historical and political sources of alienation. Ahmed explains how it can be necessary to become the stranger—or even eat the stranger—to assert one's own humanity, which extends into the nonhuman. Thinking about figurations of "the alien" in relation to "the stranger," she writes:

> The alien is a source of fascination and desire: making friends with aliens, eating with aliens, or even eating one (up), might enable us to transcend the very limits and frailties of an all-too-human form. Or, by allowing some aliens to co-exist "with us," we might expand our community: we might prove our advancement into or beyond the human; we might demonstrate our willingness to accept difference and to make it our own. Being hospitable to aliens might, in this way, allow us to become human. It could even allow us to become alien, to gain access to alien worlds, previously uncharted by other humans.[37]

36. Julia Kristeva, *Strangers to Ourselves*, trans. Leon S. Roudiez (New York: Columbia University Press, 1991).

37. Sara Ahmed, *Strange Encounters: Embodied Others in Post-coloniality* (London: Routledge, 2000), 2.

For Ahmed, such encounters are troublesome because the stranger is produced as a means for self-discovery. VanderMeer's biologist speaks on behalf of his Western readership, standing at the threshold of uncharted climate territory. Like them, she has been wary of her "all-too-human form" since childhood. Her stranger—the nonhuman as irreducible singularities and material agencies—allows her to embrace the stranger within herself. It is an act of self-discovery that affirms human mastery. Before she disappears into the vegetation, the narrator abandons the readers:

> This part I will do alone, leaving you behind. Don't follow. I'm well beyond you now, and traveling very fast.
>
> Has there always been someone like me to bury the bodies, to have regrets, to carry on after everyone else was dead?
>
> [...]
>
> I am not returning home.[38]

In the Zone, a universal nonhumanity is constructed against which the reconfigured human can erect itself in full negation; this chosen human can "bury the bodies," "have regrets," and "carry on after everyone else was dead." The reader remains behind, painfully and plainly human, but with the security of a redeemed humanity in the face of the nonhuman.

I want to pose this question again: What do we learn about climate change from stories such as *Annihilation*? The chapter titled "Dissolution" suggests a state beyond entanglement, a reconfigured subjectivity. Rather than dissolving, the biologist is surviving, becoming part of the strange vegetation and therefore becoming her true self, the self that has always known a "death that would not mean being dead."[39] After escaping the violence of urban artifice, she can finally affirm her authenticity by becoming one with Nature. But if subjectivity is a matter of inhabiting a certain body, [40] what does it mean for this scientist to reconfigure her self in the body of another that now extends to Nature?

38. VanderMeer, *Annihilation*, 128.

39. VanderMeer, 24.

40. For John Locke, subjectivity depends on matter "vitally untied to the same organised body." John Locke, *An Essay Concerning Human Understanding*, ed. A. D. Woozley (New York: Meridian, 1943), 210.

The literary scholar Monique Allewaert's study on personhood and colonialism can advance the understanding of this repeated scenario. In *Ariel's Ecology*, she describes colonial fantasies of "disaggregation" that, despite the disassembling of the body, "holds open the apparently paradoxical possibility that personhood is not vanished by this disaggregation but instead changed." Allewaert considers the "transformation of human and other bodies" to be a "key anxiety of Anglo-European writing in and about the American colonies."[41] Reading *Annihilation* in this tradition points to the alternate materialism of the body that the biologist has been aching for all along. As Allewaert demonstrates, becoming subject to a "different kind of organisation of matter and thus a different kind of being" has been part of the philosophical discourse from the earliest times of American colonialism. It features prominently in Benjamin Franklin's *Dissertation on Liberty and Necessity, Pleasure and Pain* (1725), whereas "interstitial life between humans, animals, objects, and sometimes even plants" in colonial texts was considered to be the domain of "African descended human beings."[42] A reconfiguration of human subjectivity in interspecies hybrids could thus be a continuation of this colonial imaginary. Envisioning a broader ecosystem that includes the human in transformed variants would then be nothing but a colonial reversal. The problem with such posthuman reconfiguration is that, rather than exposing a massive suppression of the diversity of all living species for the sake of just one of them, the narrative promotes a violent merging of diverse forms of life with the human. Multiplying its figures and twisting linear life spans serves the purpose of extending the life of those humans who know how to instrumentalize the nonhuman. What appears to be a transformation of human history in radically unforeseeable ways turns out to be yet another reappropriation of the colonial nonhuman in the face of the erasure of the human in the Anthropocene.

The Universal Nonhuman

Drowned in the need for alternative ontologies, the nonhuman threatens to create the space for the very category it seeks to

41. Monique Allewaert, *Ariel's Ecology: Plantations, Personhood, and Colonialism in the American Tropics* (Minneapolis: University of Minnesota Press, 2013), 2.

42. Quoted in Allewaert, 6.

avoid—namely, the Western concept of the universal human that suppresses all other forms of life. The universal human that erects itself against the Other has been scrutinized by the philosopher Sylvia Wynter as a convenient "cover-up for Man," which she exposes as an "ethnoclass (i.e. Western bourgeois) conception of the human, Man, which overrepresents itself as if it were the human itself."[43] A large part of Wynter's writing functions as a warning that the well-being of the human species depends on the "unsettling of this overrepresentation."

The Anthropocene comes with its own set of aesthetic recodifications. The human has progressed into the strange and curious universal nonhuman. As a trope in science fiction and eco-horror, this enforced plurality through assimilation at first appears as a more democratic way of representing collective consciousness across species and time. Yet it remains in keeping with linear progress, which reverts the initial separation, by replacing it with a fusion without losing its hierarchical qualification. Wynter traces a long history of establishing the centrality of the so-called human that goes back to the beginning of colonialism in the fifteenth century. Allewaert similarly traces human disintegration images to early colonialist fears. Under the conditions of the Anthropocene, the universal human is extending into the uncharted territory of the nonhuman without leaving the confines of colonialism, ultimately expanding its conceptual and bodily reach, and in so doing eliminating the rest of the world.

The philosopher John Dewey wrote, "Failure to examine the conceptual structures and frames of reference which are unconsciously implicated in even the seemingly most innocent factual inquiries is the single greatest defect that can be found in any inquiry."[44] The Anthropocene is barely a problem of the imagination, as suggested by Amitav Ghosh; it is rather a problem of representation bound to "capitalist realism" (Mark Fisher), which in its suffocating death throes stubbornly holds on to structures of domination. An imaginary of the Anthropocene

43. Sylvia Wynter, "Unsettling the Coloniality of Being/Power/Truth/Freedom: Towards the Human, After Man, Its Overrepresentation—An Argument," *CR: The New Centennial Review* 3, no. 3 (2003): 260.

44. John Dewey, *The Later Works of John Dewey, 1925–1953*, ed. Jo Ann Boydston, vol. 12, *1938* (Carbondale: Southern Illinois University Press, 2008), 501.

reproduces a society of self-reflexivity and individuation. Narratives that fail to pay attention to the historicity of the events that have led to the Anthropocene, or promote imaginaries that enable historical erasure, consolidate existing power structures, transforming the nonhuman into an active collaborator in the necropolitics of power.

Neither Sartre nor VanderMeer uses the nonhuman as a simple Other against which the ideals of modern liberal humanism unfold. Both writers propose a flat ontology that acknowledges the irreducibility of the nonhuman. However, by failing to diversify human and nonhuman lives, they fail to provide a relational ethics that will lead to alternative consciousness. They remain caught in the Western humanist ideal that fails to pay immanent attention to the politics of varied matters. Until this work is done, the lingering specters of colonialism in environmental destruction will remain neatly coated with glimmering—or rather shimmering—lights, blinding us to the rubble piling up underneath. As long as the nonhuman is a means for self-discovery, there will be no meaningful reconfiguration of the human.

The Art Right

Larne Abse Gogarty

Author's Note: This article was written and published in *Art Monthly* in 2017, in the immediate aftermath of the events surrounding the LD50 gallery. For this publication, it has been lightly edited for clarity and style, with footnotes added. The ideas in this article, and the political consequences of the LD50 story within the broader developments of post-internet art, are further examined in the first chapter of my book *What We Do Is Secret: Contemporary Art and the Antinomies of Conspiracy* (2023).

In February 2017, a flurry of discussion and activity emerged in the London art scene concerning the activities of a small, previously unremarkable East End gallery called LD50. The gallery opened in 2013 in Bethnal Green before moving a couple of miles north to Dalston in Hackney. It has held exhibitions by artists including Deanna Havas, Jake and Dinos Chapman, Juliette Bonneviot and Christopher Kulendran Thomas, and Jesse Darling and Brace Brace. By hosting collaborative shows, billing itself as a "project space," and organizing public programs on fashionable art-theory subjects such as genetics and technology, LD50 cohered with London's contemporary art landscape and its location in Dalston, a neighborhood that has been tagged by estate agents as the "coolest place in Britain" since at least the early 2010s.

However, despite visible signs of growing wealth, Hackney remains the eleventh most-deprived local authority in the UK. Though an improvement from its second-place ranking in 2010, it is easy to surmise that after more than five years of austerity measures, such so-called progress is partially enabled by the shifting of poorer individuals and families out of the borough. Hackney has a long history of repression and resistance. Stoke Newington Police Station, for instance, has long been notorious for racist police brutality. More recently, following the police shooting of Mark Duggan in the neighboring borough of Haringey in 2011, the riots that erupted represented a flash point within the grinding forms of dispossession that persist, despite the borough's bourgeois makeover.

So, when it emerged that LD50 had been organizing talks by right-wing extremists, it was unsurprising that the demonstration called against the gallery was well attended, with many locals taking part who had long-standing involvement in anti-racist work. Hackney residents also took to LD50's Facebook page to stress that "you don't really get Hackney. It's not a playground for fascists and sympathisers." I begin this article here because it is important to situate LD50 as materially located in the real world. While anti-fascist groups and local residents viewed the events organized by LD50 as something to be challenged, the art world mostly prevaricated over the "complexity" of the situation, often viewing the campaign against the gallery as a worrying impingement on free speech.

The story of LD50 broke after the artist Sophie Jung published online a private conversation with Lucia Diego, the gallery's director. In the conversation, Diego explained that she wasn't sure if she opposed President Trump's travel ban and bemoaned the recent rehang at the Museum of Modern Art in New York that highlighted works by artists from countries included in the ban, suggesting that this amounted to diminishing "Western culture and tradition." In the comment thread that followed, people quickly related Diego's message to the gallery's recent hosting of an "alt-right" exhibition and far-right speakers. Things swiftly escalated, as Diego responded by posting the entire thread on the gallery's website, which was then uploaded to the nationalist website Amerika.org, which is run by Brett Stevens, one of the speakers hosted at LD50 in August 2016.

Diego's posting of the thread on LD50's website—and her feeding of this information to Stevens—closely corresponds with the tactics of websites such as Redwatch, which was inspired by the earlier print magazine of the same title published by the neo-Nazi terrorist group Combat 18. Redwatch uploads photographs of and identifies leftist activists, anti-racist campaigners, and trade unionists with the purpose of intimidation and inciting violence. The uploading of the Facebook thread by Diego is comparable, particularly due to its continued presence on Amerika.org, a website run by a man who has said that he is "fond" of Anders Breivik (the far-right terrorist who killed seventy-seven people in Norway) because he shot "members of Us"—by which he means whites—that had "turned to leftism."

At this point, the campaign against LD50 grew as further details emerged about the talks organized by the gallery. In contrast with the public nature of LD50's program on genetics, the conference that hosted far-right speakers was secretive. While LD50 noted on its Facebook page on July 18, 2016, that it was excited to announce that "Nick Land will be with us at LD50," no specific details were given. On July 24, LD50 sent a mail-out inviting recipients to "a conference on Reactionary and Neoreactionary thought," noting that the events were "by invitation only." Those who wished to attend had to follow a link and enter a password provided in the email.

This level of security contradicts Diego's statements on Vanessa Feltz's BBC Radio London show on February 24, 2017, where she claimed that the talks "didn't really cause any struggle in the neighborhood or amongst anyone. Everyone was quite happy to learn about this at the time." However, since the talks were not made public on the gallery's website or Facebook page until after they finished, this assertion is patently false. The only public announcement of the conference was posted to Amerika.org, where an open invitation kept the name of the venue secret, but described it as being "hosted at a gallery in east London" and organized by a "brave group of arts community members." If readers wished to attend, the notice explained, they should email an address hosted by Amerika.org that would be redirected to the organizers "who will remain anonymous until they are able to verify your good faith participation." This announcement—coupled with the password-protected invitation—evidences the secrecy LD50 built up around the conference. It also demonstrates an organizational partnership between Stevens and Diego, contradicting Diego's statement that the role of the talks was to simply "explore contemporary discourse." Instead, the only public promotion of the event appeared on a far-right website run by a man who admires a notorious far-right terrorist and mass killer.

There were five speakers hosted at LD50 between July 24 and August 7, 2016. In chronological order, they were Iben Thranholm, Peter Brimelow, Brett Stevens, Mark Citadel, and Nick Land. While Thranholm's talk was organized before the conference, the last four speakers were programmed together. Citadel's bizarre, meandering talk decried the left, comparing public accusations of racism to medieval heresy, while complaining about nation-states that were not based on ethnicity. Like Thranholm, his ideology is based on a crusader-like Christian traditionalism that emphasizes Western supremacy and traditional gender roles. Stevens's talk was entitled "The Black Pill" in reference to debates within the "manosphere." Within this online community of men's-rights activists, anti-feminists, and "pick-up artists," an analogy has been developed from the movie *The Matrix*: taking the "red pill" refers to accepting the truth of the manosphere's ideology, and those who take the "blue pill" disagree with their misogyny and are often equated with "beta males." Stevens draws on a further elaboration of this dichotomy with the "black pill," referring to a total nihilism that rejects "illusion" and "positive action."

Brimelow runs the far-right nationalist website VDare.com, named for the first white child born in America. His talk is the only audio recording that includes audience questions, which makes it helpful in gauging the composition and response of those attending.[1] One audience member asks Brimelow whether the "root cause of the present situation in the US and Europe is the result of Jewish, Talmudist, supremacist ideology and of course the financial power the Jewish community clearly has." Brimelow responds by stressing that "in the US, Jews are about 2 to 3 percent of the population yet are immensely powerful. [...] It has displaced the WASPs and the Ivy League—the Ivy League is now basically a Jewish institution, looking at the numbers. But on the other hand, Trump's key speechwriter, Steve Miller, is Jewish, you find them on all sides of every question." At another point, he describes the "problematic Jewish portion of the Democratic vote." That the majority of the audience was sympathetic to Brimelow is also audible in their agreement with his argument that nation-states should be ethnically specific.

This event cannot be described as a neutral exploration of ideas, not least because the audience is audibly invested in far-right politics, with only one dissenting voice that quickly retreats. The invitation was secretive and private. Stevens promoted the events and assisted with the email administration. Diego closes the event with Brimelow by saying "Thank you so much for your time" and "We'll be in touch," indicating a continuing correspondence with LD50.

The final talk in the series was delivered by Land, a long-term darling of the art world and academia because of his work with the Cybernetic Culture Research Unit (CCRU) in the 1990s. Land is

1. A recording of this talk was hosted on the now-defunct website of LD50.

a key proponent of accelerationism's central tenet that capitalism must exceed its own limits through a devouring, all-encompassing growth. His later theoretical work—before he moved to China to work as a journalist after CCRU disbanded—engaged with esoteric Kabbalist number systems and the QWERTY keyboard. This work remains attractive to many in the art world and academia, offering the frisson of esoteric obscurantism and cold nihilism. Land's current interests have seen him become a philosophical guru for elements of white supremacy and nationalism. His exceptionally turgid text "The Dark Enlightenment" (2012) describes the murder of Trayvon Martin as "too good to be true" for progressives, decries the "politically awakened masses as a howling irrational mob," and coldly emphasizes measurable intelligence as a mark of supremacy among humans. He takes a conspiratorial view, describing Western society as being maintained by "the Cathedral," a term used to describe values of democracy, tolerance, and equal rights. Land's presence at the conference epitomizes one of the ways the art world regularly flirts with elements of fascist thinking. The combination of Land with Brimelow, Stevens, Thranholm, and Citadel is a coherent attempt to link already-present art-world discourses with their ideological cousins—in other words, it presents a milieu.

After the conference was over, LD50 held an exhibition titled "71822666," after the name of a thread on 4chan predicting Trump's election victory. The invitation included a photograph of the pop star Taylor Swift with a quote from Adolf Hitler and the logo of the Afrikaner Resistance Movement and the Blood and Honour group, both neo-Nazi organizations. While Swift has no professed allegiance to such groups, she has become a symbol for white supremacists and white nationalists who describe her as a "perfect Aryan goddess." The exhibition was composed of tweets and memes by contributors including @realDonaldTrump alongside alt-right Twitter personalities such as @BronzeAgePerv, @kantbot2000, and @Kekpriest. Also included was the mass shooter Elliot Rodger's video manifesto, which detailed his anger at having been rejected by women, produced before he killed six people in Santa Barbara in 2014. On Instagram, LD50 described these contributors as "our new artists." The exhibition combined these aspects with candles, altars, flowers, a robot-like sculpture, and Top Trumps–style playing cards that listed the "attributes" of various neoreactionary and alt-right figureheads, including Land and Richard Spencer. The show's combination of far-right material with new technologies and esoteric new-age imagery signals how LD50's rightward turn coheres with the broader field of contemporary art the gallery had engaged with since it opened in 2013.

In Morgan Quaintance's article "Cultic Cultures," he examines the appeal of the occult within London's young art scene, stressing feminist and queer engagements, while arguing that we need to consider the appeal of magic and mysticism for the far right.[2] The same concern applies to the accelerationist obsession with new technologies—particularly "the singularity," the idea that artificial intelligence will grow exponentially and become so powerful that it will result in the wholesale transformation of human life. Notable artists who engage with these tropes include Daniel Keller, Ed Fornieles, Yngve Holen, and Simon Denny, as well as publications and curatorial collectives such as Dis. Indeed, we could view the 9th Berlin Biennale as the apex of this aesthetic —in its blending of online health and lifestyle cultures, marketing tools, new technologies (particularly those that adapt the human body), conspiracy theories, and new-age subcultures.

Importantly, this aesthetic also characterizes musical subcultures that grew online in the early 2010s, principally vaporwave, a nostalgia-heavy and techno-orientalist genre inspired by anemic corporate mood music. As with LD50's neoreactionary turn, a similar phenomenon has emerged through the development of the micro music genres "fashwave" and "Trumpwave." While currently a small subculture, it is becoming a key soundtrack for the far right, with Andrew Anglin, founder of the Daily Stormer, one of the principal neo-Nazi sites, praising it as "the Whitest music ever" for its ostensible lack of "African rhythmic influence," as reported in an article by Penn Bullock and Eli Kerry on Vice Media's Thump.com. Alt-right figurehead Spencer has spoken approvingly of the genre, stating that he listens to the artist Cyber Nazi while working and is pleased that "we have our own culture, even if it's small."

The significance of building a cultural wing is described by posters on the 4chan /pol/ forum, a central arena for the alt-right. One poster links to a Google Doc entitled "Westhetica," which acts

2. Morgan Quaintance, "Cultic Cultures," *Art Monthly*, no. 404, March 2017.

as a kind of instruction manual for the production of alt-right (with the title emphasizing "Western") aesthetics. The anonymous author suggests "synthesising [...] futuristic themes with a classical greco-roman base [...] 80s retro neon vibrancy [...] postmodernism and distinct irony" alongside new-age imagery. These tropes are associated with vaporwave and post-internet art, and the document further stresses the idea that "emphasis on aesthetics helps separate the notion of white identity from fat spergs/skin heads and dorky cuckservative stiffs in order to gain wider appeal." The aim is to "appeal to the more Bohemian type of people [...]. They could be drawn in by the aesthetics and then get redpilled with incremental exposure to the ideas of the alt-right." This stands as an attempt to rebrand the culture typically associated with white supremacy in order to assist in the goal of entryism among the young white bourgeoisie.

If we think more carefully about the aesthetic tropes of mysticism and technological accelerationism, we can see that they are steeped in entanglements between avant-gardism and politics dating back to the interwar years in Europe. Rudolf Laban, a Dada Zurich associate and pioneer of modern dance, established and lived in the esoteric, back-to-nature Monte Verità commune near Ascona in Switzerland, where he worked with others such as Mary Wigman, whose work engaged with ritual, witchcraft, and East Asian dance. After 1933, both Laban and Wigman collaborated with the Nazi regime, Laban becoming head of the Deutsche Tanzbühne and Wigman choreographing a mass dance for the notorious 1936 Summer Olympics in Berlin. While both Wigman and Laban fell out of favor with the Nazis by the end of the 1930s, what is important here is the convergence of their mysticism with Nazism, a connection resting on the invocation of an idealized archaic, "pre-modern" era. In terms of the accelerationist impulse that undergirds the commonality between contemporary art and far-right aesthetics, a well-known precedent lies in Futurism's valorization of speed, war, and death, which was famously described by Walter Benjamin as the aestheticization of politics.

The third element emphasized in the "Westhetica" document is irony, the primary tonal register for many artists associated with post-internet practice.[3] Irony has typified much popular culture

3. See Morgan Quaintance, "Right Shift," *Art Monthly*, no. 387, June 2015.

since the 1990s, and is often associated with the influence of *Vice* magazine, which has since grown into a much larger media platform and dissociated itself from the rampant misogyny and "jokey" racism that defined its millennial so-called edginess. If Land cannot be called an "eccentric" intellectual after reports that Steve Bannon (chief strategist in the Trump administration) admires his work, racism and misogyny should never have been imagined as "ironic" while states and capital consistently maintain and reproduce these structures. This is what is missed by commentators such as the former *Art Monthly* contributor Daniel Miller when he defended LD50 in a one-man counterprotest, declaring on Facebook: "A non-conformist in the art world – they aren't extinct – incredible! – who would have thought?" Racism and misogyny are not "non-conforming" ideologies, and I don't need to waste space here describing the reality of how they are reproduced in and through the art world, which, unfortunately for certain fantasists within its orbit, happens to be part of the wider world.

This is also the problem with the "free speech" argument mobilized by J. J. Charlesworth and Jonathan Jones in their defenses of LD50 published in *ArtReview* and the *Guardian*, respectively.[4] Like Miller, Charlesworth seems to believe that culture in the West is governed by a strangling political correctness. He dismisses the campaign Shut Down LD50 as being based on "wild assumptions," which he believes he has broken down by speaking to Diego. This peculiar argument is made even more so by Charlesworth's claim that no "conference" was held, after Diego told him so. His acceptance of her claims rests on the argument that three of the talks (Branholm, Brimelow, and Land) were Skype calls, and the other two were presented as recorded texts read by "digital avatars." The idea that a conference is not a conference because some people called in through Skype is laughable, let alone the fact that had Charlesworth bothered reading the material gathered by Shut Down LD50, he would have seen the invitation to a "conference on Reactionary and Neoreactionary thought" sent out by LD50.

4. J. J. Charlesworth, "The Strange Case of the 'Alt-Right' Art Gallery," *ArtReview*, March 3, 2017; Jonathan Jones, "No One Should Demand the Closure of Galleries—Even for Far-Right Artworks," *Guardian*, February 22, 2017.

Jones's defense positioned the Shut Down LD50 campaign as "absolutist" and dogmatic, a threat to the values of art. Charlesworth, Jones, and Miller all defend the gallery from the perspective of free speech, yet if nothing else I hope this article clears up the fact that there was nothing "free" about how these ideas were presented. The audio of Brimelow's talk confirms that the audience was already on board with anti-Semitism and ethno-nationalism, which is what makes it a conference. It was a gathering of like-minded individuals with the desire of furthering their interests and connections.

Defenses of far-right white-supremacist ideas made in the name of free speech imagine that such debates can be held neutrally. What they fail to understand is that while the art world likes to imagine itself as a free space for the liberal exploration of ideas, this is a delusion only permissible to those who never have to feel vulnerable on the street. Even more galling is the idea that vulnerability exists in the figure of the "endangered" white man who is imagined as particularly "at risk"—and thus heroic—when he defends free speech. This notion is particularly dangerous in that it has become a central tenet of the contemporary far right and the Trump administration, and it is being persistently mobilized to increase the risk of violence against those who do not conform to such an identitarian position. That the art world is an arena for the furthering of such positions should come as no surprise, and unfortunately those of us who want to halt their growth probably need to be prepared to repeatedly intervene with strength and clarity in the coming years.

Formless Labor

Kerstin Stakemeier

In Labor

In the *Economic and Philosophic Manuscripts of 1844*, Karl Marx anchors social labor at the center of his ontology of modern life. It is on this basis that the capitalist horizon of modern human self-alienation unfolds. For Marx, this special status of labor does not mark it as a vitalistically charged capacity; on the contrary, it makes labor manifest in its role as "abstract social domination," as the violent relation of an undead form.[1] Whereas vitalistic politicizations of human labor understand it as fettered potential whose liberation would be equivalent to that of humanity, Moishe Postone and others emphasize—as Marx himself writes—that labor as *property* itself implies "vitality as a sacrifice of life." The world "of estranged labor, of estranged life" is thus "a result of the *movement of private property*."[2] It is this *ownership* of labor that even today, in the state of "mass underemployment,"[3] maintains what Postone calls the spell of "abstract social domination," the violence of which is reproduced in a fully real sense as the "sacrifice of life" on the part of its (re)producers.

In contrast to the critique of capital from the perspective of its all-encompassing exchange relations that Alfred Sohn-Rethel formulated from the 1950s onward,[4] Postone and others object that it is ultimately not the historically variable abstractions of exchange that govern modernity—its animisms and its deathliness—but rather the isolation of abstract labor itself as an equivalent form.[5] Labor is modern *as* a form of exchange. This modern labor is even today the historical core of a more-than-dubious humanism;

1. Moishe Postone, *Time, Labor and Social Domination: A Reinterpretation of Marx's Critical Theory* (Cambridge: Cambridge University Press, 1992), 152–55.

2. Karl Marx, *Economic and Philosophic Manuscripts of 1844* (Moscow: Progress Publishers, 1977), 80, 89; italics in original.

3. Aaron Benanav, "Automation and the Future of Work—2," *New Left Review*, no. 120 (November/December 2019): 121–24.

4. See Alfred Sohn-Rethel, *Intellectual and Manual Labour: A Critique of Epistemology*, trans. Martin Sohn-Rethel (Atlantic Highlands, NJ: Humanities Press, 1978).

5. See Marina Vishmidt, *Speculation as a Mode of Production: Forms of Value Subjectivity in Art and Capital* (Leiden: Brill, 2019), 64n75.

it exists as the *social equivalent form* of its domination.[6] Labor *as* exchange. From abstract labor, Marx projects a society of negatively interrelated self-realization inhabited by a modern subject bound and trapped within the equivalent forms of its own questionable reproducibility.[7] Within the horizon of capital, labor is self-realization as self-alienation:[8] it forms a self-alienating humanity with very clearly outlined barriers.

Self-possession presupposes its own alienation; its stabilization is identical with that of its own capitalistic externalization. In this horizon, the lack of self-possession corresponds not to unexhausted potential labor power but rather to its absence, a lack of social vitality.

Yet in Marx there is also an attempt to grasp modern labor from the perspective of its beyond. At the end of the 1970s, for instance, Diane Elson cited one of Marx's formulations in the 1858 *Grundrisse*: "Labour is the living, form-giving fire; it is the transitoriness of things, their temporality, as their formation by living time."[9] Far from protecting a humanistic core, Marx by contrast presents labor in the horizon of its own vitality as well-nigh cosmological. He does *not* oppose the modern ontology of abstract social labour to a utopian concretion of its metabolisms within the same horizon; rather, he formulates a kind of extra-ontological contemporaneity of labor, a kind of cosmological

6. "The commodities' social form is their relationship to one another as *equal labour*, hence—since the *equality* of *toto coelo* [utterly] *different* labours can only consist in an *abstraction from their inequality* their relationship to one another as *human labour* in general." Karl Marx, *Capital: A Critique of Political Economy*, 1st ed., trans. Albert Dragstedt, in Marx, *Value: Studies by Marx* (London: New Park Publications, 1976), 32.

7. Negatively, because the value relation as the social binding of capitalist societies in practice destroys the solidarity of their private-property owners, putting them into competition in an antisocial value relation that is oriented to systemic rather than individual reproducibility. See Frank Kuhne, *Begriff und Zitat bei Marx: Die idealistische Struktur des Kapitals und ihre nicht-idealistische Darstellung* (Lüneburg: zu Klampen Verlag, 1995).

8. See Marx, "Estranged Labour," in *Economic and Philosophic Manuscripts of 1844*.

9. Karl Marx, *Grundrisse: Foundations of the Critique of Political Economy (Rough Draft)* (London: Penguin Books, 1973), 361; quoted in Diane Elson, "The Value Theory of Labour," in *Value: The Representation of Labour in Capitalism*, ed. Diane Elson (London: CSE Books, 1979), 128.

labor, as the intersection of living temporality and positioning (*Verortung*). In her book *In the Place of Origins* (2000), Rosalind Morris introduces us to the cosmological world: "It is not simply that the cosmological world submits space to time, or even that it assumes the primacy of locality when compared to a modernity wherein time is subsumed by global space that has expunged the local. [...] A cosmological orientation permits practices in which presencing [...] is assumed to be possible. Thus, the world dominated by time is also one in which time can be absolutely transcended."[10]

Even if there is no question that Marx himself did not conceptualize labor in terms of its debordering as a cosmic lever, from the standpoint of our contemporary moment we can nonetheless suggest such a cosmological reading of labor. The sources of such monistic ideas of labor are widely dispersed in history. In Alexander Bogdanov's early writings—for example, *Empiriomonism* (1904–6)—there is an attempt to translate Marx's materialism into a "monistic methodology of perception."[11] Building on Ernst Mach's 1866 work *The Analysis of Sensations*, Bogdanov pushed beyond Mach's theories of radical psycho-physical receptivity toward a monistic materialism. He was convinced that "criticism cannot be the final goal, the end product at which life can come to a stop. [...] The task of criticism is to provide space for these forms [...] but it cannot create those forms."[12] A materialism of the form of labor about which Marx wrote in the *Grundrisse*, a materialism in which the world is derived not from the critique of capital but from the "socio-morphisms" of a debordered understanding of labor, in the context of which the continuous reproduction of "abstract social domination" no longer gives critique its form but rather "the interconnectedness of the elements of experience in cognition has as its basis the correlation of the elements of social activity

10. Rosalind Morris, *In the Place of Origins: Modernity and Its Mediums in Northern Thailand* (Durham, NC: Duke University Press, 2000), 161.

11. Alexander Bogdanov, *Empiriomonism: Essays in Philosophy*, vol. 1–3 (Leiden: Brill, 2010), xxv.

12. Bogdanov, 4.

in the labour process."[13] In his early writings, Bogdanov is thinking toward a cosmological materialism, in contrast to Marx, whose critique applied to the ontology of capital.[14]

Marx observed the materialization of an "abstract social domination" of undead measure. He saw himself amid the onset of an ontology of capital, against which he formulated his critique. Now, however, it is evident that the historical primordial forms of this ontology, when seen from the perspective of its own extinct liberalism (which nonetheless has not ceased to reproduce itself), drive much deeper into the past—toward the point where Denise Ferreira da Silva, Saidiya Hartman, David Lloyd, Rosalind Morris, Cedric Robinson, and Sylvia Wynter locate the colonial production of its subject, in the externalizing violence of enslavement and the internalized fear that is the modern legal regulation of life and labor.[15] In a cosmological break whose ontological critique unwillingly confirms the extent to which modern life here lies immobilized in its framework. Deviating from this immanent function of critique necessitates a breaking through of our modern

13. Alexander Bogdanov, *The Philosophy of Living Experience: Popular Outlines* (Leiden: Brill, 2016), 219–21.

14. Bogdanov's early reflections on psychophysical materialism are methodologically crucial to us because he attempts to leave these open to a radical receptivity, a production of reception. Bogdanov was later the cofounder of the Proletkult, a mass organization that, from 1917 onward, attempted to realize decentralized artistic production on the part of all workers, a practical cultural revolution of labor, in opposition to the Bolshevik Party. In any case, Bogdanov's "empiriomonism" congealed a few years later into a "tektology" (1912–17), a proto-cybernetics, in which the open monism of laboring experience closed into a system of absolute labor.

15. Denise Ferreira da Silva, "Toward a Black Feminist Poethics: The Quest(ion) of Blackness toward the End of the World," *The Black Scholar* 44, no. 2 (2014): 81–97; Denise Ferreira da Silva, *Toward a Global Idea of Race* (Minneapolis: University of Minnesota Press, 2007); Saidiya V. Hartman, *Scenes of Subjection: Terror, Slavery, and Self-Making in Nineteenth-Century America* (Oxford: Oxford University Press, 1997); David Lloyd, *Under Representation: The Racial Regime of Aesthetics* (New York: Fordham University Press, 2019); Rosalind C. Morris and Daniel H. Leonard, *The Returns of Fetishism: Charles de Brosses and the Afterlives of an Idea* (Chicago: University of Chicago Press, 2017); Cedric J. Robinson, *The Terms of Order: Political Science and the Myth of Leadership* (Chapel Hill: University of North Carolina Press, 2016); Cedric Robinson, *Black Marxism: The Making of the Black Radical Tradition* (Chapel Hill: University of North Carolina Press, 2003); Sylvia Wynter, "The Ceremony Must Be Found: After Humanism," *boundary 2* 12, no. 3 / 13, no. 1 (Spring/Fall 1984): 19–70.

temporal horizon together—instead of criticizing it, letting it run back to its primordial forms, in order to materialize its contemporary ends out of its cosmological ruptures.[16] This entails not the abandonment of labor as a materialist nucleus but turning against the modern ontology of its social character, against the undead violence of its humanism; leaving the door open to the formless entry of monistic "life-works."[17]

Out of Labor

Labor requires "determination," as Elson writes, yet "only with industrialisation does the fluidity of labour become immediately *apparent*":[18] its possible formlessness is first produced in the Global North in the horizon of its determination as a value form. Elson's argument that in these modern times "social labour" is always ultimately abstract, in Postone's sense, that it only exists as its equivalent form, renders it prior to its often politically idealized counterpart "concrete labor" and its privatization in capital.[19] There never was such a thing as concrete labor that was abstracted through capitalization; its individuation only followed as a result of (value) abstraction.[20] The realization of "the entire life-work of a person" as opposed to professionalization that Lu Märten called for in 1905 as well as the political potential of "shared labor" that Aaron Benanav discussed in 2019 in view of rampant automation in the end necessarily imply a convergent loss of form in *both* social *and* concrete labor, an opening toward Marx's undreamed-of cosmological "formation by living

16. This is not entirely unlike Donna Haraway's call for a "technoscience," except that Haraway aims to produce an illegibility of the "Greatest Story Ever Told" opposed to one's own narrative, whereas today we presume that this illegibility must include ourselves too. Donna Haraway, *Modest_Witness@Second_Millennium.FemaleMan_Meets_OncoMouse: Feminism and Technoscience* (London: Routledge, 1997), 4, 12.

17. See Jenny Nachtigall and Kerstin Stakemeier, "Lu Märten: An Introduction to Four Texts" and "Art Work as Life Work: Lu Märten's Feminist 'Objectivity,'" *October*, no. 178 (2021): 3–14, 35–54.

18. Elson, "Value Theory of Labour," 128.

19. On this relation, see Elson, 145. See also I. L. Rubin, *Essays on Marx' Theory of Value* (Montreal: Black Rose Books, 1973), 64.

20. In feudalism it was only an "assignment," not "labor."

time."[21] The more that we, with Märten and Benanav, emphasize the determinacy of our own contemporaneity, the more this gives way to moments of being-contemporary, presences, graspable as the possibility of cosmological worlds that Morris describes. As a political horizon, such a re-temporalization stages a passing loss of the form of labor in the contemporary moment: a loss of the form of our labor, for indeed what is art need not remain art. As a modern site of desire for concrete (private) labor, art does not intersect its abstract (social) contrary but only complements it. And as Marina Vishmidt argues, in contemporary art, where social labor and private labor run in parallel as equivalently capitalized, "the 'generic' has supplanted 'genius' as the operative category of art's self-understanding and its relationship to its outside. [...] Just as 'abstract labour' is labour performed under conditions of private property [...] the movement of the content of artistic labour into the category of the 'generic' secures its access to symbolic and economic valuation through the private property relations of authorship, provenance and the consistency of the 'oeuvre' as a unit of subjective and objective validation."[22]

In other words, contemporary art only convincingly appears as private labor when it makes itself exchangeable, to the extent it takes on the content of abstract labor. Thus, so long as a loss of form that breaks up this labor relation *in* art remains absent, its concrete labor remains a purely private effect of abstract labor, the privatism of which is not merely a limitation but above all a privilege. The privacy of concrete labor ornaments precisely that nervous interiority whose European origin is to be found in institutional nationalization, colonization, sexuation, ableization, and racialization—an order of violence. Vishmidt emphasizes that even today "genius remains the foundation of artistic subjectivity, its principle of identity (and non-identity)," although the "generic" has become the measure of its production.[23] Labor as the "living, form-giving fire," in Marx's words, can today no longer be experienced within the exclusive linearity of this bourgeois

21. Lu Märten, "Die künstlerischen Momente der Arbeit in alter und neuer Zeit" (1903), in *Formen für den Alltag: Schriften, Aufsätze, Vorträge* (Dresden: Verlag der Kunst, 1982), 14; Benanav, "Automation and the Future of Work," 138. Quotations have been translated by the author unless otherwise noted.

22. Vishmidt, *Speculation as a Mode of Production*, 225.

23. Vishmidt, 225.

privacy. Art demonstrates precisely this, as a site that is persistently idealized toward these ends. The various arts today, as a social exceptionalism, and as the most open site for private labor and its generic connection to the social, thus effectively constitute the space of a shared problematic not a suggested solution: a mutual work on losses of form within our artistic privacy, on scenarios for concretizing the social beyond the generic, on linkages between its contemporaneities and presences.

Primordial Form (*Urform*)

The artistic "life-work" of the early twentieth century, the "shared labor" of the present, must ultimately be projected beyond the horizon of capitalized life into other times and spaces; their determination must take up arms against the ontology of modern life after Marx. In Märten, this role is taken on by a series of "primordial forms" (*Urformen*) that she places at the head of her chapters as historical anchors.[24] They replace the borders of artistic genres with their material "causes" (or *Ursachen*, "primordial things") in the literal sense, "because the effect of form causally corresponds to the excitation of reality, and because every revolutionary instinct today grasps forms of reality beyond any kind of art—as causally revolutionary."[25] Art is traced back to reality as its cause (*Ursache*); bourgeois art is for Märten only a kind of receptive transitional stage. Primordial forms, in this context, do not legitimate any origin (*Ursprung*), but rather demonstrate that what today is art need not necessarily remain art. They are references to function—for Märten, to "life-works" in which various times and places open in their linkage; in our contemporary moment, perhaps rather to figures of a sort of "death-work" within which the capitalizations strewn throughout these times and spaces are brought to a head. No defeatism, then, but rather the hope for a horizon of the formlessness of solidarity toward the end of modern work(s).

Where the contemporary relation between private (concrete) and social (abstract) labor today breaks into the formless, perspectives open for us toward primordial forms that, as Märten

24. Chryssoula Kambas, *Die Werkstatt als Utopie: Lu Märtens literarische Arbeit und Formästhetik seit 1900* (Tübingen: Max Niemeyer Verlag, 1988), 164.

25. Lu Märten, *Wesen und Veränderung der Formen/Künste: Resultate historisch materialistischer Untersuchungen* (Frankfurt am Main: Taifun Verlag, 1924), 280.

puts it (in a quotation from Engels at the beginning of her book), continuously change their function "in universal interrelations, where causes and clouds continuously change places."[26] In this sense, we need primordial forms too: they serve not only as figures of legitimation but also as navigation points for an "impetus" that is "causally revolutionary." Even if Märten's gestural language (and her modernity) are untimely today, the radical receptivity of artistic forms of production in the beyond of genre boundaries—the "life-work" of a "classless art," as Märten calls it[27]—breaks into our contemporary moment, with which it corresponds. In place of romantic projections of concrete labor appear those unmodern anchors, those primordial forms of our now only nominally liberal life, whose horizon leaves our contemporary labor formless: the unintended cosmology in Marx, which breaks through in the present downfall of the ontology of labor, foregrounding perceptibilities of unmodern life amid the atrocious violence of liberalism in its death throes. And hence the central question for us, as Vishmidt argues, is ultimately not whether capital can be explained by labor (following Elson) or by exchange (following Sohn-Rethel) but whether "an exact description of the *quality* of the mutual determinations" can be produced,[28] a description that makes it possible to understand a heightened concrete temporality, an "excitation of reality."

Un-form

Out of what, in the modern narrative, is described as the tragedy of modern subjectivity and its alienation, its constant fear for its title to (self-)property, there spools out a series of working ruptures, a series of impossible exchanges. Ruptures that mark this bourgeois self-alienation as a privilege, as an ontological hurdle, beyond which primitivizations, animisms, sexualizations, and biologisms were determined. Life in the beyond of labor in the

26. Märten, 8.

27. Lu Märten, "Kunst und Proletariat," *Die Aktion* 12 (1925): 663–68; repr. in *Alternative* 16, no. 89 (April 1973): 54–59. See also Kambas, *Werkstatt als Utopie*, 162–64, 170–73; Rainhard May, "Theorie der 'Formen' wider Theorie der 'Künste'? Lu Märtens Versuch, eine marxistische ästhetische Theorie in Deutschland, Anfang der zwangziger Jahre zu konzipieren," in *Kunst im Klassenkampf: Arbeitstagung zur proletarisch-revolutionären Kunst*, ed. Autorenkollektiv (January 1979), 84–92.

28. Vishmidt, *Speculation as a Mode of Production*, 64.

private bound to the powers of socially fragmentary self-property. What Avery Gordon once termed "complex personhood" qualifies precisely this state of permanent becoming-transgressed as the possible life of a "critique of privately purchased rights" that "might guide an attempt to drive a wedge into lives and visions of freedom ruled by the nexus of market exchange." Gordon's perspective is also cosmologically oriented; it "means that even those called 'Other' are never never that."[29] The afflictions Gordon writes about, like Morris's "presencing," represent a horizon of the power of imagination in which Marx's "labour [as] the living, form-giving fire [...] the transitoriness of things, their temporality, as their formation by living time" can return in wholly unmodern form. Here it is a matter of ontological gaps that cannot be framed as self-criticism of the modern horizon, but which rather expand by breaking the frame itself. The social, abstract labor in the capitalist value relation, as Postone and Elson describe it, becomes marginal from the perspective of this "complex personhood," because personhood is only social in this sense as an uncomplicated vested right. The concern of this text is not least to escalate openings of the sort Gordon calls for. Not to envision a panorama of utopian propertylessness extrapolated from the present on the basis of the same social abstraction, but rather amid the *membra disjecta* of liberalism to gather the social site of art as a point of concentration for an actualized "life-work," a "shared labor," as a series of ends. An (art)work whose point of departure is a radicalized receptivity, a "perception" that, as Bogdanov writes, "is no different from other realms of human labour; it is creativity and struggle and not mere record keeping."[30] No "critique of experience" is required here, for there is "no need to throw anything out of the content of experience, but it must simply be presented in its actual and precise interconnectedness." What Elson discusses as the determinacy of labor is confronted with an altered starting position: Bogdanov calls for the work of an indiscriminate, sociomorphically determining "creativity."[31]

Through this "actual and precise interconnectedness" also run those historical powers toward whose decentering our primordial

29. Avery F. Gordon, *Ghostly Matters: Haunting and the Sociological Imagination* (Minneapolis: University of Minnesota Press, 1997), 4–5.

30. Bogdanov, *Philosophy of Living Experience*, 147.

31. Bogdanov, 137.

forms are oriented, or more precisely the "capitalism(s) which emerged through the specific institutions of transatlantic slavery and globalized colonial ventures."[32] Modernity is their effect. In *The Poverty of Philosophy* (1847), Marx notes that slavery is "an economic category of the greatest importance," taking a clear position against it.[33] But with his identification of slavery as an *economic* category he inadvertently stabilizes enslavement as an ontological category.[34] Ultimately, in Marx's horizon it is only liberation *into* social abstraction that promises a transition from the economic to the anthropological sphere.[35] Within a modern ontology of labor, enslaved workers remain unrepresentable, beyond both abstract social labor and concrete private labor.[36] According to Elson, the fluidity of labor that first emerged from this historical split, however, consequently has as its primordial form realization as ontological dedifferentiation, the unavoidable downfall of labor. Otherwise, in Marx's tragedy of self-alienation the violence of alienation from without ultimately becomes what Orlando Patterson has described as "the slave's natal alienation" in a state of "social death."[37] In the modern ontology of labor, the enslaved person plays the role of the living dead, a "thingliness" that for Ferreira da Silva, Fred Moten, and David Lloyd becomes the necessary point of departure for

32. "The Colonial Lives of Property, Abolitionist Struggles, and Alternative Imaginaries: Brenna Bhandar in Conversation with Daniel Loick," *Texte zur Kunst*, no. 117 (March 2020), https://www.textezurkunst.de/en/117/colonial-lives-property-abolitionist-struggles-and-alternative-imaginaries/.

33. Karl Marx, *The Poverty of Philosophy* (Moscow: Progress Publishers, 1955), 97.

34. See Frank B. Wilderson III, "The Prison Slave as Hegemony's (Silent) Scandal," *Social Justice* 30, no. 2 (2003): 18–27; and Frank B. Wilderson III, *Red, White & Black: Cinema and the Structure of U.S. Antagonism* (Durham, NC: Duke University Press, 2014).

35. What's more, Marx discusses slavery as a historical predecessor of wage labor; that is, he neutralizes four hundred years of the slave trade as a form of primitive accumulation in advance of capital. See David Neilson and Michael A. Peters, "Capitalism's Slavery," *Educational Philosophy and Theory* (April 2019): 475–89.

36. For an attempt to open up this discussion, see David Lloyd, "The Racial Thing: On Appropriation, Black Studies and Thingliness," *Texte zur Kunst*, no. 117 (March 2020): 75–96.

37. Orlando Patterson, *Slavery and Social Death: A Comparative Study* (Cambridge, MA: Harvard University Press, 1982), 5–10.

a delinearization of contemporary experience.[38] Toward a *certain* rupture. Marx's tragic ontology of self-property "transgresses," each time in a specific way, all *racialized* as well as all feminized bodies, but also sexualized bodies, pathologized bodies, disenfranchised life.[39] Its ontological weight is determined by the specific questionability of its vitality; it becomes measurable as the limit of its externalizing, social labor. The limit of its modern vitality is that of its participation in the most modern of all forms of exchange, that of labor. Life with damaged self-property in the modern horizon lacks social abstraction precisely as much as it lacks the protection that nervous labor offers to privacy, whose alienation reproduces the tragedy of the "possessive individualism" (Raymond Williams) of bourgeois, liberal life: an order not of the fear of violence, but rather of the certainty of its reach.

Primordially Funny (*Urkomisch*)

In his 1950s critique of work, Georges Bataille also called for solidarity in the self-transgression of that alienated privacy he might well have called his own, though from a fundamentally different perspective—that of an unwillingly modern subject. Bataille stages its systematic self-brutalization, its making-public, *as* a form of violence of social abstraction. For him, it is the tragedy and comedy, tears and laughter, that temporarily take possession of the human body that become the points of departure for its underemployment, its formlessness effected in the face of social abstraction.[40] Bataille invokes a tragedy that does not continually reproduce itself as fear and mourning for one's own privacy, but rather one that expends itself, that becomes a killing joke.

38. In "The Racial Thing," Lloyd mentions, among others, Hortense J. Spillers, *Black, White, and in Color: Essays on American Literature and Culture* (Chicago: University of Chicago Press, 2003); and Fred Moten, *The Universal Machine*, vol. 3 of *Consent Not to Be a Single Being* (Durham, NC: Duke University Press, 2018).

39. Self-property is not the same as private property, as *objectified, externalized* ownership.

40. Bataille argues this since he opposes debordered labor, which he degrades to the status of a mere means, a hardly less debordered eroticism. Within its horizon laughter and tears occur, outbreaks close to the "little death" of desire, which Bataille takes as the goal of human life. Here we must postpone gauging the consequences of substituting eroticism for labor, or asking whether the former today would occupy the same place that Bataille accords it. Georges Bataille, *The Tears of Eros*, trans. Peter Conor (San Francisco: City Lights Books, 1990).

A melodramatic externalization of one's own inwardness as farce, such as Ulrike Ottinger, Rainer Werner Fassbinder, and later Christoph Schlingensief were to repeatedly perform as the deathliness of nationalized and sexuated life in the Federal Republic of Germany. What binds all of them is a life-work on *deproduction*, a question of a determinacy that is not only unproductive but deals with expenditure, in the horizon that Elson opened for determinacy between social abstraction and the private concretion of modern labor. Today this horizon is occupied by the "mass underemployment" (Benanav) of undead liberalism, and thus expenditure and participation in "abstract social domination" (Postone) are less and less differentiated: they are indeed becoming indistinguishable. Their figures of production become figures of deproduction, a dismantling of the modern human. It is precisely in this sense that Vishmidt, for example, offers the old Hegelian figure of "speculation" as an "open negativity," as a "mode of social, cultural and conceptual production that can operate on and in reality; that displaces the specular relation between representation and the real."[41] Vishmidt deploys the figure of speculation as a primordial form, in Märten's sense, of our present moment, as a cliché of the modern thinking that has (barely) survived its own abstraction. If, for Märten in the early 1920s, the primordial forms were openings to the possibility of a contemporary life-work that revises the past from a distance, these return in our time as figures of deproduction, as a hope for the production of temporary formlessness.

Vishmidt is reaching for the "open negativity" of speculation in a changed temporal horizon, that of the (un)dead liberalism in which Gordon's "complex personhood" is a general horizon of experience: not a chosen perspective, but rather one of the material demodernization of the present moment. Joshua Clover has recently demonstrated that the predetermined breaking points of the subject of alienated labor noted by Bataille—tragedy and comedy—are today becoming indistinct not only in the figures of (self-)expropriation, that they are indistinguishable not only on the level of the subject but also on the level of their abstraction in capital, on the level of their economic forms of reproduction. What's more, the capacity for their individuation was ultimately

41. Vishmidt, *Speculation as a Mode of Production*, 230.

always one of (well-)managed self-property. Clover starts his text with Marx's famous pronouncement that "Hegel remarks somewhere that all great world-historic facts and personages appear, so to speak, twice. He forgot to add: the first time as tragedy, the second time as farce."[42] Clover traces how the two in the meantime have become wholly indistinguishable. In our present moment of financialized capitalism in its variable state of exception, "crisis is the mediation that allows tragedy at one level to return as comedy at a higher level." But "comedy in this regard is not tragedy plus time, exactly. Comedy is tragedy plus scale."[43] Elson's social labor on value abstraction develops into a permanent tragedy of private expenditures whose comedy is now only staged as its value. In contrast to Bataille's pushing of tragedy into transgressive self-ruin in which laughter accompanies the exploded fragments of self-expropriation, for Clover comedy takes that stage as social abstraction: the rictus of a self-alienation that recognizes its self-property on every level—as well as that which has been divorced from it, toward which tragedy becomes absolute. A way of life that for Robert Hullot-Kentor, writing in 2018, was exemplified in the figure of Donald Trump's life in a "hall of mirrors," as a purely virtual self, and which Jarett Kobek (referring to the same person) in 2019 identified as the stage of fully realized virtuality, as the life of Jean Baudrillard's "hyperreality."[44] To identify with the side of this comedy as a self-forgotten form of expropriation is the privilege of remaining representable, repeatable within the ontology of capital's world. It is the laughter of social sadism.[45]

Breakthrough

In the breakdown of liberalism in which we exist today, the modern determinacy of labor as the motor of reproductive externalization increasingly loses its form. With the systematic questioning of its reproducibility, abstract social labor becomes

42. Karl Marx, *The Eighteenth Brumaire of Louis Bonaparte* (New York: Mondial, 1994), 15.

43. Joshua Clover, "Genres of the Dialectic," *Critical Inquiry* 43 (Winter 2017): 447.

44. Robert Hullot-Kentor, "Metric of Rebarbarization: Real Time in the Authoritarian Personality," *South Atlantic Quarterly* 117, no. 4 (2018): 722; Jarrett Kobek, *Only Americans Burn in Hell* (London: Serpent's Tail, 2020), 6–12.

45. See Ana Teixeira Pinto and Kerstin Stakemeier, "A Brief Glossary of Social Sadism," *Texte zur Kunst*, no. 116 (December 2019).

ever more a liminal experience of (unwilled) private expenditure. In the stage of "mass underemployment" (Benanav), social labor becomes psychosocial trauma. An ontological order of coherent and incoherent, dead and dying parts whose own primordial form, liberalism, is losing its ontological legibility and that from our perspective becomes increasingly cosmological. According to Fritz Kramer, "The cross-over point between cosmology and psychology is to be found in the microcosmic refractions of the powers within the individual. These would normally be called not *passiones*, but rather possession, being moved or being filled with emotion."[46] The epistemic ontology of psychology transitions from possessions to being-possessed, a cosmological order.[47] The property of social workers, their private determination, loses itself in dependency on abstract labor itself, the social bindingness of which becomes a concrete, privatized, exceptional phenomenon. In "mass underemployment" it increasingly loses its reproductive and social core. In the *Grundrisse*, Marx writes that "indifference towards specific labours corresponds to a form of society in which individuals can with ease transfer from one labour to another, and where the specific kind is a matter of chance for them, hence of indifference." This "ease" derives from the determination of modern labor *as* abstraction. It is only by becoming general that it becomes social and hence that "the abstraction of the category [...] becomes true in practice." Marx continues, "Even the most abstract categories, despite their validity—precisely because of their abstractness—for all epochs, are nevertheless, in the specific character of this abstraction, themselves likewise a product of historic relations, and possess their full validity only for and within these relations."[48] One question is whether the death of liberalism which we have been inhabiting renders the cosmological end of these relations thinkable at last. Its extinction in the ever-more private dysfunctions of our social labor, our collection of primordial forms as ends of our contemporary moment, the expansion of cosmological ruptures into formlessness—all of these are points of departure for questions of form put to the contemporary life-work that binds us: the remains of liberalism that flow through our present moment

46. Fritz Kramer, *The Red Fez: On Art and Possession in Africa*, trans. Malcolm E. Green (London: Verso, 1993), 59–60.

47. See Alenka Zupančič, *Warum Psychoanalyse?* (Berlin: Diaphanes, 2009).

48. Marx, *Grundrisse*, 104–5.

let us sense a determination in which our common labor promises (but also threatens) a temporary formlessness, whose primordial forms are to be our materialism.

Märten used the modern "self-essence of the individual varieties of art that differentiates itself from the historical law of change" only as a template. The isolated forms of the varieties of art made it possible for her to discover the primordial forms as animations of working complexes in the beyond of art. As we perceive it, the function of the primordial forms today is less the importing of a premodern vitality into our undead present moment, but rather the calling forth of expanded forms of appearance of their possible ends. Not as defeatism, but rather as the production of a shared formlessness. For it is only here that what art is must not remain art. As Märten writes: "Revolutionary art is not when, retaining the existing means of art, one demands from them only unambiguous slogans for specific feelings or lines of thought while silently passing over all forms incapable of providing this, but rather consists in liberating oneself entirely from the obsessive idea of 'art,' here keeping in mind as well […] that with consciousness one 'brings to an end' a 'labor of humanity' that is different from one directed by capitalistic interests."[49]

49. Märten, *Wesen und Veränderung*, 56.

Automating Apartheid

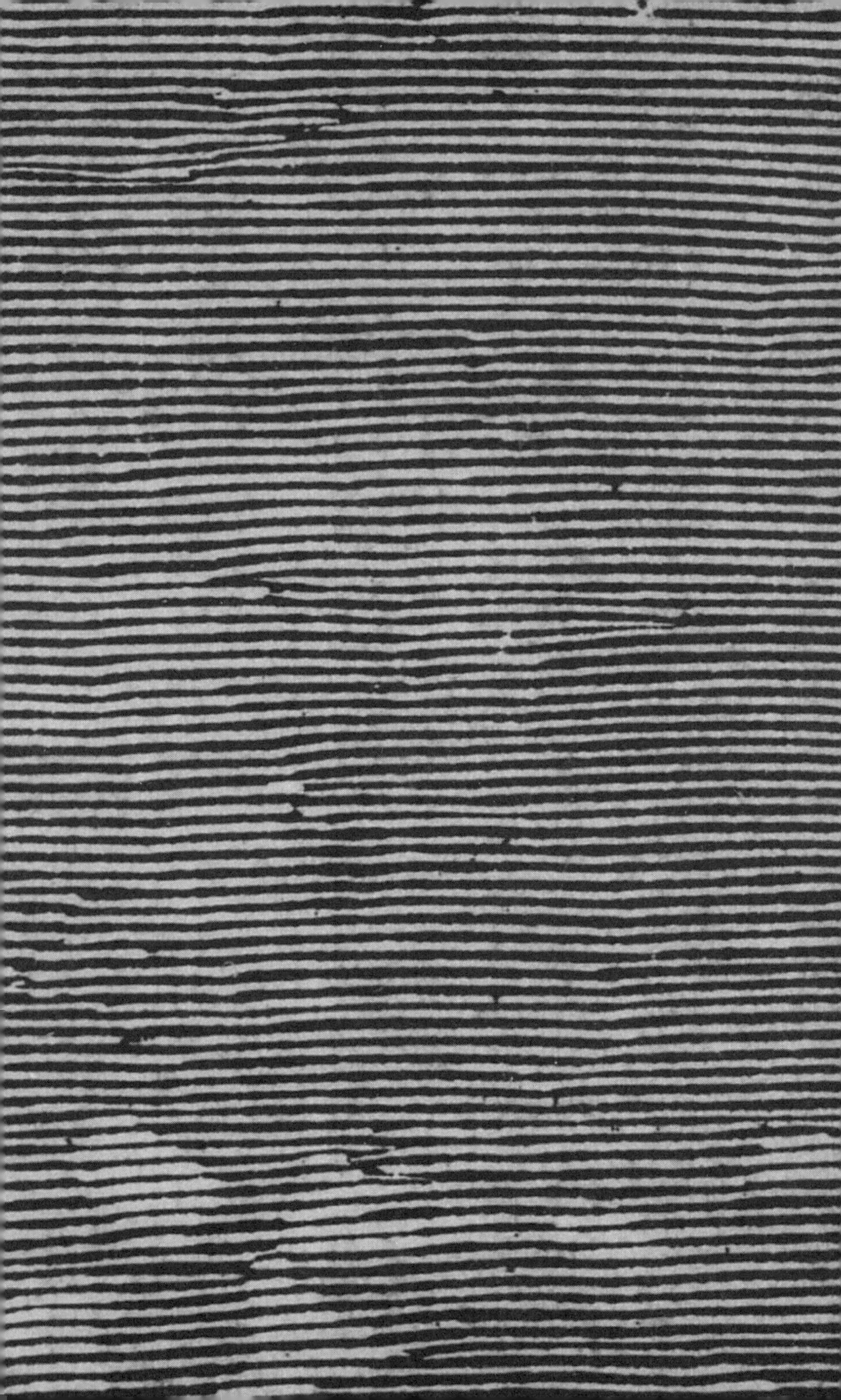

An Analytics of Obligation
On Algorithmically Mediated Labor and the Transference of Racial Value

Ramon Amaro

Recent advances in machine learning have led to increased concern over the impact of algorithms on future labor practices. In fact, machine learning has already begun to rearticulate the ways work is performed—for instance, manual assembly procedures have given way to new assemblages of manual operation, semiautonomous robotics, and algorithmically aided production systems. The algorithmic turn in production aims to better optimize network flows to meet increased demand for multi-product, multi-period, and multi-stage production systems.[1] With "optimize," I refer to the achievement of maximum efficiency, or the skillful avoidance of wasted time and physical or mental energy—effects typically associated with human knowledge, performance, and aptitude. To optimize algorithmically is therefore to yield benefits for companies aiming to maximize worker productivity while minimizing labor costs and human contingencies such as workplace injuries, illness, fatigue, worker apathy, and error. That is, algorithms stand as intermediaries between human acts, or the act of being human, and a network inflated by the demands of growth and profitability.

While extensive thought on the value of work, and its ensuing alienation, is inspired by perspectives on class, gender, and racial hierarchy, its continued appeal is restricted to a universal topography of the world—that is, the predominance of generalizations about labor, alienation, and freedom. It is clear that identifying the distance between the structural components of capitalism and an obligation for change takes priority over critical appraisal of these components, yet the accommodation of economic struggle as that which provokes universal liberation is reductive of the undeniable configuration of the world as foremost colonialist. For instance, Frantz Fanon charted the

1. Akebo Yamarami, Marcia T. Takahashi, and Marcus F. H. Carvalho, "Comparison of Some Algorithms for Manufacturing Production Planning," *IFAC Proceedings Volumes* 33, no. 20 (July 2000): 291–95.

obligation for change as an appeal to the dimensions of social relations—relations that both oblige and organize labor and exploitation. The obligations of labor, as supplemental to the imperatives of the racial order, are entangled with the ideological concept of the Human, whereby the centralizing concept of species excludes Blackness and other bodies of difference. Humanistic possibilities for the world, as set forth by the colonial milieu, emphasize a subjective dimension of labor, though the relation between humans and work remaps and reinforces the primary objects of racial sorting and the self-conscious act of naturalizing the racial order of the world.

In our contemporary milieu, as algorithms take possession of consumer products and the technological processes that bring these objects into being, we are faced with a new, yet stubbornly familiar, obligation of care. These modes of care as mediated by algorithmic possibility explain the oversimplification of the erosive mechanisms of economic systems based on the private ownership of capital. Although Fanon's life was cut short by illness prior to the contemporary algorithmic turn, he made it clear that in order to provoke authentic social change we must estrange ourselves from our routine gestures of racial reification. We are hence encouraged to practice an active *disalienation* by or through which an authentic humanity might be amputated from the multiple varieties of capitalism and racial scripting. Although the link between algorithms and race is not readily conceived of as an act of denial of a positive racial identity, Fanon reminds us that identity itself is of special interest to modes of desire that stimulate the psychic complexities of law, order, and subordination.[2] It is apparent that the algorithmic has altered the topology of global labor and economics. And by algorithmic, I refer to systems organized around a set of procedures specifying problem-based solutions. The algorithmic has summoned forth an alienation that corresponds with the widespread dissemination of the techno-human imagination, an imagination that has situated itself as mediator of curiosity, creativity, and human gesture (dissenting or otherwise).

2. Ramon Amaro, "As If," *e-flux architecture*, no. 97 (February 2019), https://www.e-flux.com/architecture/becoming-digital/248073/as-if.

In this essay, I prioritize algorithmic alienation as the distance from one's desire for unconstrained choice amid the act of economic enforcement. This phenomenon is what I call an *analytics of obligation*, a notion that extends beyond a simple analysis of algorithmic labor by reaching back into the enduring paradigm of economic arrangements as set forth by the historical racial imaginary. To be obliged is to be under a moral directive to do an unspecified thing using one's agency to an unspecified degree. To be obliged is to be bound to a cause of indebtedness by providing a service or favor. An analytics of obligation is therefore a principle of obligation governed by various forms of analysis as enacted in algorithmically aided working environments. I argue that an analytics of obligation is both that which constrains, depriving the human of free movement, and that which catalyzes internal desire to limit the extent to which one is determined as and by the limits of a calculus. Obligation is, in this sense, both internally and externally derivative, connected to an interdependent relation between profound desire and the attempt to recapture that which is prohibited. It is what Fanon called "affective erethism," or a phenomenon that represents the sum of the experiences and observations of one's life. It is "a bilateral process, an attempt at securing—through internalization—the once forbidden values."[3] I return to Fanon to consider what an analytics of obligation might mean with respect to the presence of Blackness, or nonhuman life, as imagined in a racially organized world, including new iterations of algorithmically mediated labor. What I consider is a mode of existence that might, for all its discoveries, amount to a type of human reality where one can regain one's balance despite the complete problem at hand. This mode of existence, as I argue, demands that we "eradicate this narcissism whereby [we think we are] different" from any imposed categorical imperative.[4]

Algorithmic Management

Algorithms are aggregates of mathematical equations, logical tool sets, statistics, pattern recognition, and probability functions,

3. Frantz Fanon, *Black Skin, White Masks*, trans. Richard Philcox (New York: Grove Press, 2008), 45.

4. Fanon, 13.

to name a few of their components. They are thought to provide operational benefits such as decentralized decision-making (as in the case of robotic systems), human assistance (in the performance of tasks that might be too dangerous for humans), information translation (in the application of data in real-world situations), and cross-communication (in the functionality to interact and communicate with humans and other computer systems). Algorithms are proficient at complex problem-solving yet are bound by logical rule sets. Recurrent rule sets infer a sound intelligence and objective judgment in situations considered otherwise uncertain or unknown; they mitigate uncertainty by assigning an optimized, evaluated, and often efficient means of engaging in a task while simultaneously relying on consistent procedural outcomes. The technological manifestation of the Enlightenment cause is characterized broadly by the extinction of desire and individual consciousness.

Considering what has been described as "algorithmic management" in relation to labor, algorithms provide a diverse set of solutions by which emerging problems, such as remote working, are planned, implemented, and managed.[5] Algorithmic management is becoming more common owing to the widespread adoption of gig economies, which are organized around an extensive network of data aggregation and worker-surveillance tools. Work is supervised by the key characteristics of algorithmic management, consumer rating systems, and automated notifications that nudge workers into compliance with both company policies and arbitrary consumer satisfaction ratings. The adoption of these techniques helps companies shift accountability away from human-centered management and toward semiautonomous decision-making processes. Gig workers, characterized by short-term contracts or freelance work as opposed to permanent jobs, are furthermore classified as being "independent" of a company's core team. Whereas company managers have traditionally presided over workers' schedules and well-being, in the gig economy responsibility is transferred to individual workers bound to a series of terms and conditions.

5. Alexandra Mateescu and Aiha Nguyen, "Explainer: Algorithmic Management in the Workplace," Data & Society, February 2019, https://datasociety.net/wp-content/uploads/2019/02/DS_Algorithmic_Management_Explainer.pdf.

These work practices are not limited to the gig economy. They span several industries, from domestic work to streaming platforms, that replace the ordinary infrastructure of work by algorithmic management. The practices raise questions concerning workers' rights, transparency, and accountability, as well as hidden racial biases and discrimination. Failure to adhere to imposed terms and conditions—as set forth by the company without worker input—can result in reprimands, de-incentivization, fines, penalties, and even termination. For those who are racialized, algorithmic management amounts to our surrender to a mechanism of choice that degrades our basic human needs, relegating them to a vault distant from reality.[6] There is a kind of magic in the anticipated consent of our surrender to the absolutism of the algorithmic: shaping the world we want is conditioned by an oracle who specifies the terms of payment or penalty based on one's willful indebtedness to a company for service or favor.

Algorithmic Manumission

We have seen this before. While the owners of the contemporary conditions of servitude are newcomers in the dialectic of basic human need and exploitation, they join (or perhaps were never separated from) the rehearsal of an economy organized under the premises of worker obligation. Our present rehearsal of obligation is reminiscent of chattel slavery—for example, as seen in the British Empire's Slavery Abolition Act of 1833 (formally known as "An Act for the Abolition of Slavery throughout the British Colonies; for promoting the Industry of the manumitted Slaves; and for compensating the Persons hitherto entitled to the Services of such Slaves"). Whereas the act is most widely known for its emancipatory legal framework, the slow act of freedom is largely distanced from the economic benefit British slave owners gained in the making of a so-called new world. The act formally freed some eight hundred thousand Africans who had been the legal property of Britain's slave owners, yet it contained provisions to grant financial compensation to previous British slave owners.

6. I employ the term "racialized" in reference to the embodied act of racialization, which signifies the propagation of racial meaning into group and individual relations as well as social practice. See Michael Omi and Howard Winant, *Racial Formation in the United States: From the 1960s to the 1980s* (New York: Routledge & Kegan Paul, 1986).

In lieu of complete liberation for enslaved Africans, the act facilitated more localized acts of manumission.[7] The historian Verene Shepherd defines manumission as an act of gratuitousness, which is first enacted as a gesture of benevolence, sentimentality, and reward to those in servitude.[8] Manumission facilitated the transfer of value away from direct slave labor and toward less tangible commitments by freed slaves who were asked to pledge their loyalty to former slave owners, even after emancipation. At the same time, manumission was generally viewed as an act of emancipation from formal ownership contracts. The transposition of slave labor, whereby the owner and his *populus* thought manumission was the humane act of reconciliation, distributed the qualities of a grossly pragmatic transaction between forced labor and the affect of freedom. As such, the "new" world of work and emancipation was not completely detached from the chains of subjection, but instead altered labor value from a direct monetary benefit to an implied reserve of debt in the form of the slave's lifelong devotion to the master, the *populus*, and the land. This allowed owners to release enslaved people from their physical binds only to transfer obligation to a systemic circulation of affective erethism. In this sense, the act of obligation, although distanced from the ore and iron of chains, imposes a state of internal attachment between owner and owned, stimulated by an erroneous representation of self-will and self-movement.

Although historical motivations for manumission are varied and complex, the problem of labor draws on the anticipation of release, generated in part by the possession, or the right to organize the possession, of the conditions for one's exposure to obligation. As the terms of contemporary capital depart from the derivation of value as a direct engagement of the body to value as the relinquishment of one's attachment to propriety, the conditions of algorithmic manumission today represent a breach in the organizational structures of labor, which are otherwise consumed by the order of production. Our current social order sees as taboo the forced ownership of corporeal flesh. Nonetheless, the

7. "Center for the Study of the Legacies of British Slavery," UCL, accessed September 2, 2020, https://www.ucl.ac.uk/lbs.

8. Verene A. Shepherd, "Freedom in the Era of Slavery: The Case of the Barclay Brothers in Jamaica," *Jamaica Gleaner*, February 24, 2008, http://old.jamaica-gleaner.com/gleaner/20080224/news/news3.html.

enactment of an economic system that seeks to rearticulate the organization of labor by means of obligation is a recurrent act of servitude. To say that contemporary algorithmic economies are systems of slavery is to reduce the plight of enslaved Africans and their descendants; however, to suggest that racial discrimination within algorithmically aided economies is extraordinary is to simplify the preexistence of this phenomenon in the colonial imaginary.

From Physical Body to Abstract Risk

Although the process of manumission, and its rehearsal on the slave body, might help us understand the ease with which contemporary capital can shift attention toward new obligatory mechanics, the theorist Alessandra Raengo argues that the entire framework of Western economics already presupposed Black alienation. This "ontological scandal perpetrated by slavery," Raengo writes, was as much a recurrent cycle of forced extraction as it was an indispensable measure of Anglo-European identity.[9] In this case, Anglo-European identity was intertwined with marine logistics and the desire for economic expansion. Although dependent on a deep intimacy with material flesh, this expansion effectively dematerialized corporeal survival by abstracting it into new streams of indemnity, speculation, and capital risk.

The forceful emergence of Anglo-European capitalism is illustrated by the *Zong* massacre. In 1781, the British slave ship *Zong*, overcrowded with 470 men, women, and children, departed for Jamaica from Accra. Partway through its journey, the ship was stranded in the area of the Atlantic with little or no wind known as "the Doldrums." While at rest, disease and malnutrition spread throughout the cargo hold, resulting in the death of over fifty of the enslaved and seventeen crew members. Within a week, the captain instructed the remaining crew to jettison an additional 132 enslaved people who were ill; another ten perished by throwing themselves overboard. Upon reaching its destination, the ship's owner, James Gregson, filed an insurance claim against the loss of human cargo. He argued that the massacre was necessary

9. Alessandra Raengo, "Reification, Reanimation, and the Money of the Real," *World Picture*, no. 7 (Autumn 2012), http://www.worldpicturejournal.com/WP_7/Raengo.html. Subsequent quotes by Raengo are from this source.

and demanded compensation since there was not enough food or water onboard to sustain the living cargo. In an unsuccessful attempt to dispute the claim, the insurance underwriter submitted a counterargument stating that the *Zong* still held approximately 420 gallons of water onboard when it arrived at the Jamaican coast.

The massacre aboard the ship and Gregson's subsequent legal battles prompted public outcry and became a principal argument for the abolishment of British slavery. Although the massacre swayed public opinion toward abolition and the right to life, neither the crew nor the captain or owner were ever charged with murder. Judicial and parliamentary debates instead prioritized legal precedent and the economic circumstances surrounding the events. When the insurers refused to pay, the court initially upheld a decision that the murder of enslaved people was legal under British law, and that an insurance settlement for each dead slave should be paid to the ship's owner. Subsequent court decisions ruled against the slave owners, suggesting they were at fault for the loss of life and therefore not entitled to compensation.

The *Zong* massacre is a powerful illustration of the historical relation between slavery, anti-Blackness, the law, and the alteration of economic frameworks. Although there was public outcry over the life and death of the enslaved, the legal and political economies understood the issue of Black life as one of capacity, monetary value, and speculative risk. Seven years later, the British Parliament passed the Slave Trade Act of 1788 to limit the number of enslaved bodies legally allowed for transport, mitigating further risk of death and disease. By 1791, Parliament had prohibited insurance companies from reimbursing shipowners who murdered or lost slaves during passage. According to Raengo, the acts shifted the circulation of monetary value away from corporate responsibility for survival and toward the procedural commodification and abstraction of the Black body, effectively subordinating the physical and spatial presence of the enslaved body to its more lucrative temporal value. Raengo describes: "The body of the slave is also tied to different conceptions of time: it can represent a unit of currency or a commodity in the present, but it can also offer an investment and, therefore, a financial return in the future." This, Raengo writes, is reinforced by "the fact that the slave is at the same time a person and a thing, an object of property but a subject of sentiment, a monetary value (in an insurance contract, for example) and a laboring tool (in a cotton field), immobile (like real estate) but obviously mobile (and potentially fugitive) as well."

As Raengo indicates, the spatiotemporal commodification of Black life is as relevant today as it was during the transatlantic trade, to the extent that contemporary capital would be grossly misrepresented without direct reference to its historical disregard for Black life. As Raengo argues, race *is* the image of capital, "precisely because the slave became a form of money." This reading of the shifting terms of capital as "repeated with each instance of alienated black labor, each time blackness functions as a physical or abstract commodity," demonstrates the continued reification of anti-Black sentiment. The history of anti-Blackness bears witness to the historical misrecognition of alienation as that which can be universalized across all tentacles of capitalism. The chilling effects of anti-Blackness within the emergence of macro- and micro-economies constitute the very fabric of labor and economic expansion. Today, when one arrives at the intersection of technology and human labor, one is also confronted by the failure to account for the realities of race, anti-Blackness, and slavery.

Along with the de-prioritization of Black life by means of capital and the technologies of chattel slavery, contemporary debates on algorithms and labor tend to mute the specificities in favor of the more universal concept of workers' rights. By this, I mean the forced removal of race from the general concept of capital emergence, as if anti-Black sentiment had not already fueled economic expansion. Whether algorithms are likely to displace entire workforces or whether they will succumb to the burdens of continued alienation from human life remains unknown. Equally opaque is any commitment to the reconciliation of the racial histories of emerging labor-related technologies, not to mention their disproportionate impact on racialized laborers. What I suggest is that without a return to the colonial origins of Western economics, concepts of workers' rights will continue to misplace the structures of alienation. In this regard, the characterization of algorithmic labor in the so-called new economy is race-adjacent and cannot be decoupled from the real conditions of its emergence. The significance of this claim is not one of representation, whereby a causal comparison can be established between present circumstances and the technological substances of race. I propose instead an *analytics of obligation* that foregrounds the a priori conditions by which contemporary algorithmic management systems are allowed to unfold. In other words, the algorithmic object is devoid of life without interaction with the human, an interaction in turn devoid of a more palatable understanding in the absence of the conditions of race relations. There are, instead, responses to the misrecognition of obligatory platforms rooted in the contemporary notions of algorithmic imposition. I posit that to show these conditions, particularly in relation to the rehearsal of the dynamics of obligation on freed slaves in the Americas and the Caribbean, obscures the nature of algorithmically mediated work contracts while preconditioning the place of work for racially motivated bias and discrimination.

My argument, while centered on the historically crooked umbrella of slavery, is attentive to the commonalities between forced labor, domestic servitude, domestic and sexual violence, and the logistics of human trafficking in the present day. For instance, discourse on contemporary workers' rights has extended the reach of so-called modern slavery to include additional human and non-human categories such as migrant labor, asylum seekers, modern human trafficking, and labor exploitation.[10] A focus on modern slavery and forced labor reveals a delineation between contemporary forms of labor as free or unfree under the normative approach to global capitalism—foregrounding equality and freedom as key dimensions by which a liberal conception of justice might emerge. Equality, as such, departs from the duality of employer and employee, master and slave, owner and owned. In turn, (in)equality is legitimized through forms of exchange among human agents.

I reignite an analysis of the future of work to consider the merger between algorithmic labor practice and promises of freedom from human-based labor. Together, they form an unprecedented expansion of the issue of equality while illuminating the various complexities imposed on a future of algorithmically mediated working practices. Within this complexity, value is derived from an experiential approach to labor exchange by means of an algorithmic solution. Nonetheless, it is necessary to create new trajectories of thought and new practices within our shared

10. Judy Fudge, "What Makes Labour Free? (And Why This Question Matters)," *Futures of Work*, May 24, 2019, https://futuresofwork.co.uk/2019/05/24/what-makes-labour-free-and-why-this-question-matters.

affective erethism. We are prompted to consider how our existence—racial or otherwise—is underwritten by a calculus of value and deterritorialization through the perpetual disregard for Black life. While we might view "our capacity to go beyond the machine," as Lewis Mumford argued, as resting "upon the power to assimilate the machine,"[11] there are additional capacities with the human–machine relation that provide what W. E. B. Du Bois identified as "second sight"[12]—a visual faculty whereby the act of looking, seeing, and knowing one's lived experience presupposes a range of mental visions that operate within the languages of domination. In other words, the capacity to redirect the activities of erethism is as much an issue of internal perception as it is externally catalyzed. A recognition and re-prioritization of this self-image can activate alternative perspectives of the self and technology.

Algorithmic Manumission as Kindred Spirit

While an explicit divide between self and algorithmic perception might rest on the reconciliation of two seemingly incompatible objects, less considered is the productive potential of shaping the perception of the technological from within the actual multi-product, multi-period, and multi-stage experiences of Black life. Octavia Butler's 1979 novel *Kindred* provides insight into these tensions. The novel follows the protagonist Dana Franklin's reconciliation of her sense of freedom as a contemporary Black woman in Los Angeles with her ancestral history as a descendant of slaves. Early in the narrative, Dana is transported back in time to 1824 Maryland through a portal of unknown origin. There, she saves a young boy from drowning, only to later discover that the child is the son of a slave owner and she—a modern Black woman—is his descendant. Amid a series of violent encounters, she is pulled back and forth through the time portal, oscillating between past and present. She gains a sensitivity to her spatiotemporal surroundings and soon discovers that her

11. Quoted in Joel Dinerstein, *Swinging the Machine: Modernity, Technology and African American Culture between the World Wars* (Amherst: University of Massachusetts Press, 2003), 4.

12. See Julio Cammarota, "The Praxis of Ethnic Studies: Transforming Second Sight into Critical Consciousness," *Race Ethnicity and Education* 19, no. 2 (2016): 233–55.

journeys to the past are connected not only to the life of her white ancestor but to her own survival. Dana is faced with a recurring dilemma each time she is transported back in time: save her white ancestor whose life is in danger, and thereby save herself, or stand by and let him die, effectively ending a cycle of rape, violence, and abuse. The story is further complicated when Dana realizes that her time travel is triggered by the boy's duress as well as her own. Their relationship is aspatial, atemporal, and grotesquely parasitic; their bond exceeds the hard boundaries of causality and oversimplification. Every act is informed by both its motivations and its consequences in Dana's life as well as the boy's. Dana's present is History; History is Dana's present. This includes the shame, guilt, wisdom, courage, disruption, and compassion catalyzed by the conditions of survival itself.

In a 1991 interview with the writer Randall Kenan, Butler disclosed the motivations behind *Kindred*: "I wanted to take a person from today and send that person back to slavery. My mother was born in 1914 and spent her early childhood on a sugar plantation in Louisiana. From what she's told me of it, it wasn't that far from slavery, the only difference was they could leave, which they eventually did."[13] Butler's experiment with space, time, and labor demonstrates the complexity of an existence bound by the scales of History. She suggests that one can gain access to an affective erethism by repositioning the limits of one's proximity to duress. By rearticulating Dana's spatial awareness and sending her back in time, Butler is able to draw upon the transference of her mother's own proximity to slavery to imagine how a compulsory threat might unfold in the present day. It is this act of creation that rebuilds an intelligibility in order to self-represent in observance of the conditions of obligatory agreement. Butler seems to imply that the terms of survival, as a part of obligation, are far more nuanced than a legal or compulsory agreement to leave or remain in one's surroundings. Erethism is also informed by an affective transference of the conditions of duress from parent to child.

Butler recounted in the interview: "My mother did domestic work and I was around sometimes when people talked about her as if she were not there, and I got to watch her going in back

13. Randall Kenan, "An Interview with Octavia E. Butler," *Callaloo* 14, no. 2 (Spring 1991): 496.

doors and generally being treated in a way that made me … I spent a lot of my childhood being ashamed of what she did."[14] These moments manifest as a psychosocial space nurtured by an incomprehensible estrangement between capitalism and Black presence; the intergenerational transference between mother and child, amplified by the nuances of capital production, is consistent. Here, Butler describes the process of making, and making do, as akin to the image of Black being/nonbeing to reconcile the disparities between the enduring line of capitalism and her own self-image. Her testimony is a tension between the self and what Kenan describes as the "visceral immediacy" of slavery.[15] Butler suggests that this immediacy can be called on by virtue of its transformative potential: "I couldn't really let her [Dana] come all the way back. I couldn't let her return to what she was, I couldn't let her come back whole […]. Antebellum slavery didn't leave people quite whole."[16] Although Butler negates the potential for complete self-actualization, there still exists a generative capacity to work through the complications of fragmentation to make real "a sense of proportion of respect for life."[17] By going back, going through the back door, Butler is able to reenact her mother's historicity, even though their proximities to labor differ. Thus she bears witness to the threads that bind past circumstance with the contemporary image of capital. Here, the historical consciousness of slave labor is reinvented as that which brings historical struggle into present value for Black maneuverability. Furthermore, this consciousness diverts from manumission toward a more affirmative image of systems of transgenerational knowledge. Capitalism loses its legitimacy as sole owner of obligation and gives way to the deliberate repositioning of the courses of action that one might take toward a state of being that compels oneself to the transformative knowledge made available in the history of subjection.

Technologies of the Black Self

Butler's overwhelmingly affirmative proposition characterizes what I have argued is an *analytics of obligation*, a space where the Black individual can inhabit a place of self-actualization through

14. Kenan, 496.
15. Kenan, 497.
16. Kenan, 498.
17. Kenan, 497.

and in between the transference of violence and the opacity of capital exploitation. Whether a technological transference can be described as science fiction or time travel is important in Butler's assertion. "With *Kindred*," she states, "there's absolutely no science involved. Not even the time travel. I don't use a time machine or anything like that." Yet a technology of the self does serve as a device for "getting the character back to confront where she came from."[18] Nonetheless, a particular semantics is immaterial to an affective erethism where one might "bring back a sense of proportion of respect for life."[19] Butler's expression of this possibility rests within a speculative future that does not necessarily subvert the operations of capital but instead enacts alternative modes of exchange by means of transference. However, to imagine this new relation is to dislodge self-perception from the structural organization of the world.

On the other hand, this building of newness, a new yet incomplete iteration of the self, is driven by a fundamental rearticulation of the position from which one addresses inter-human and techno-human relations. A centering of domination as catalyst for transference opens the terrain to more affective agreements between one's sense of self in confrontation with one's historical matrix as well as present course of action. This reading of the self directs us toward the tools by which investigations into modified working conditions might signal a psychic modality whereby the technologies of the contemporary are always in relation with technologies of the past. Therefore, we might consider how new iterations of alienating labor practices—even algorithmic labor—might lead to authentic disalienation. Fanon reminds us that disalienation will come into being through the refusal to accept history or the future as definitive. If we are to rearticulate the relationship between present-day work and algorithmic intervention, then we must first bring it into conversation with the transference of historical trauma. As Fanon writes: "As for me, I would know full well how to react. And in one sense, if I had to define myself I would say I am in expectation; I am investigating my surroundings; I am interpreting everything on the basis of my findings. I have become a sensor. At the start of my history that

18. Kenan, 496.
19. Kenan, 497.

others have fabricated for me, the pedestal of cannibalism was given pride of place so that I wouldn't forget."[20] This second sight is, in a sense, already revolutionary.

20. Fanon, *Black Skin, White Masks*, 99.

Biometrics as White Biopolitics

Nitzan Lebovic

The History of the Definition of Biometrics

Biometrics is usually characterized as "the identification of humans by their characteristics or traits," such as using biological data for automatic facial recognition, fingerprint or DNA identification, voice recognition, or iris scans.[1] Computerized recognition systems that translate this data into metrics or algorithms are becoming common in biometric databases around the globe—at border crossings, immigration offices, police archives, military command centers, hospitals, and banks, and increasingly in driver's licenses and passports. The proliferation of such systems adds a new component to everyday life, accelerating the fusion of security, information, and identification systems—the "human-machine assemblage," as theoreticians of surveillance call it.[2] They show that the codification of biological data as a useful paradigm serves the biopolitical creation of a "zone of indifference" between the internal and external, or the private and public, justifying and legitimizing itself in the "urgent need" for a new and total archive that is—supposedly—unique and absolute, impossible to forge or copy.

The history of biometrics is embedded in the history of European colonialism, which demonstrates the inherent link between the rise of the nation-state and its colonial ambition, externally as well as internally. As the statistician D. R. Cox explained in *Biometrika: One Hundred Years*, and the sociologist Armand Mattelart showed in his excellent *The Globalization of Surveillance*, biometrics is rooted in eighteenth-century morphology, specifically the phrenology and physiognomy of Franz Josef Gall and Johann Kaspar Lavater.[3] If the stated purpose of eighteenth-century scientists was to find a way

1. Ganesh Chandra Deka and Sambit Bakshi, *Handbook of Research on Securing Cloud-Based Databases with Biometric Applications* (Hershey, PA: Information Science Reference, 2015), 321.

2. See, for example, Lisa Parks, *Rethinking Media Coverage: Vertical Mediation and the War on Terror* (New York: Routledge, 2018); and Elke Schwarz, *Death Machines: The Ethics of Violent Technologies* (Manchester: Manchester University Press, 2018).

3. D. R. Cox, "*Biometrika*: The First 100 Years," in *Biometrika: One Hundred Years*, ed. D. M. Titterington and D. R. Cox (Oxford: Oxford University Press, 2001); and Armand Mattelart, *The Globalization of Surveillance: The Origin of the Securitarian Order*, trans. Susan Gruenheck Taponier and James A. Cohen (Cambridge: Polity, 2010).

to unite the internal characteristics of an individual with external phenomena and expression, nineteenth-century science brought this approach into the realm of policing and criminalization. In France, the journalist Émile de Girardin talked about shaping physiological markers in "life records" for the sake of "universal politics," and the demographer Alphonse Bertillon invented a card and photography index to create "spoken portraits" based on data taken from prisoners and the mentally ill—for instance, skull measurements, "the valleys and hills that crisscross the ear," and eye pigmentation—in order to overcome the limitations of bodily change during one's lifetime.[4] Developed in the aftermath of the repression of the Paris Commune in 1871, the index system won the full support of the French interior ministry (Bertillon used its archive of photos) and the Parisian police. The system also classified handwriting. Bertillon was called as an expert witness in several court cases to help identify the signature of potential offenders. In the Dreyfus affair, he was the head of the prefecture's Service of Judiciary Identity and "demonstrated great zeal and a desire for personal recognition."[5] He proved his high level of professionalism by identifying Dreyfus's presumed "self-forgery"—he accused Dreyfus of tampering with evidence by changing his own handwriting.

During the 1880s, Juan Vucetich—a Croatian from the Austro-Hungarian empire who emigrated to Argentina and became the director of a police department in La Plata—and Francis Galton—Charles Darwin's cousin and the founder of the study of eugenics and social Darwinism—further developed Bertillon's system, connecting it to the indexical study of fingerprints. Both developed innovative ways of archiving and classifying fingerprints in order to help police departments track criminals and political dissenters. Vucetich explained the need for such databases as "the right to identify." His system spread to Brazil, Chile, Uruguay, Bolivia, Paraguay, and Peru. Galton argued that "biometrics has been dedicated to proving that numbers exist" and "can be found in nature."[6] In a major study published in 1892 and titled simply *Finger Prints*, he explained, "My attention was first

4. Alphonse Bertillon, *La photographie judiciaire*, quoted in Mattelart, 16.

5. Jean-Denis Bredin, *The Affair: The Case of Alfred Dreyfus*, trans. Jeffrey Mehlman (New York: George Braziller, 1986), 52.

6. Quoted in Cox, "*Biometrika*: The First 100 Years," 1.

drawn to the ridges [of fingers] in 1888 when preparing a lecture on Personal Identification for the Royal Institution, which had for its principal object an account of the anthropometric method of Bertillon, then newly introduced into the prison administration of France."[7] In this passage, consciously or not, Galton exposes the link between biometrics and a disciplinary system. As the South African scholar Keith Breckenridge showed in a recent book, Galton's introspections took him in two opposite directions. One extended to southern and southwestern Africa, where he helped create a massive biometric archive that was used to criminalize the population, and that in turn helped the Germans carry out the first recorded genocide, the slaughter of the Herero people.[8] A second, parallel track led to the founding of the Galton Laboratory at the University of London in 1904, which merged the Eugenics Record Office and the Biometric Laboratory.[9] Both tracks, one helping white people oppress Black people, the other helping police identify and surveil criminals and dissenters, were based on the opposition between a norm and a deviation, or the "law of the deviation from an average."[10]

As he reviewed the history of the difference between normality and abnormality, Georges Canguilhem showed—and Michel Foucault later reiterated—that the combination of morphology with other strands of scientific "vitalism" effected "the transplantation of the biological concept of organic totality onto political terrain."[11] Where normality is equated with "life" and "the political," any deviation from it is charged with the power of negation of life, politics, and legitimate existence. It is a genocidal logic, even where the power of oppression is not apparent. Foucault wrote that modern science is put in service of exclusion: "Perhaps for the first time in Western culture, life is escaping from the general laws of being [...]. It becomes a fundamental force, and one that is opposed to being in the same way as movement to immobility, as time to space,

7. Francis Galton, *Finger Prints* (London: Macmillan, 1892), 2.

8. Keith Breckenridge, *Biometric State: The Global Politics of Identification and Surveillance in South Africa, 1850 to the Present* (Cambridge: Cambridge University Press, 2014), 39.

9. Breckenridge, 31.

10. Breckenridge, 50.

11. Georges Canguilhem, *Knowledge of Life*, trans. Stefanos Geroulanos and Daniela Ginsburg (New York: Fordham University Press, 2008), 72.

as the secret wish to the visible expression."[12] Indeed, already in 1892, speakers at the Criminal Anthropology Congress in Brussels explained that the purpose of such systems connecting science and life, politics and population, is "to see the system of anthropometric identification adopted and extended to all countries, not only to identify repeat offenders but also to certify individual identity reliably and quickly" for the sake of "social defense which presupposes an enemy" or "a destructive terrorist, more fearsome and savage than the legendary Furies; the blind fanatic; the bold seditionist; the trade-union agitator who generally takes advantage of the worker's innocence and ignorance."[13]

In short, the purpose of the bio-typological system we recognize today as "biometrics" has been, since its initiation in the mid-nineteenth century, a total political weapon that transcends the limitations of space and time, collective ideology and the individual body, and criminalizes any hint of rivalry. Considering the idea from a slightly different angle, it is possible to think about this biopolitical indexology as an alternative "perfect universal language" (the way Umberto Eco describes it in *The Search for the Perfect Language*)[14] and utopia.

Surveillance Society

The biometric system is an absolute system that is part and parcel of the "surveillance society," to use the title of the sociologist David Lyon's 2001 study.[15] The teleological temporality of biometric surveillance is projected onto the individual body much like the watchful eye of God or a king. Still, if the order and legitimacy are teleological and inductive, it is also "scientific." When the system identifies people by isolating body parts from their natural environment, it moves from the part to the whole, and from human

12. Michel Foucault, *The Order of Things: An Archeology of the Human Sciences* (New York: Vintage Books, 1994), 278.

13. *Actes du troisième Congrès international d'anthropologie* (Brussels: F. Hayez, 1893), 481, quoted in Mattelart, *Globalization of Surveillance*, 19.

14. Eco quotes Delgarno's introduction to his *Ars Signorum* (1661) to depict the striving of an intellectual and international community to find a better and more accurate language: "It was necessary to find a language which reduced redundancies, anomalies, equivocations and ambiguities." Umberto Eco, *The Search for the Perfect Language*, trans. James Fentress (Cambridge, MA: Blackwell, 1995), 92.

15. David Lyon, *Surveillance Society: Monitoring Everyday Life* (Buckingham: Open University Press, 2001).

memory, which is slower and weaker, to the omnipotent computers and networks that store and relay biometric data.[16] Algorithmic fragmentation and reconstitution enable the biometric system to assume two positions simultaneously: it sees a body part as particular and belonging to an organic whole, both the singular and the global. The organ functions within both the semantic framework of an organic *inside* (the body) and the context of an *outside* mechanism (security) that looks at body parts separately from their physical whole. This resembles Gilles Deleuze and Félix Guattari's "abstract machine": it "connects a language to the semantic and pragmatic contents of statements, to collective assemblages of enunciation, to a whole micropolitics of the social field."[17] We individuals are recognized as fingers, irises, crooked noses, and "the valleys and hills that crisscross the ear," data that are attached to an existing digital file. Relying on the organ enables the biometric system to assume its synecdochic relation to the body, assuming the temporal continuity between the part and the whole alongside their spatial separation. The system plays the part of a divine authority whimsically inventing and reinventing the role of body parts.

The system's orientation toward the whole, totality, implies a growing need to coordinate science, politics, technology, and economics: biometrics demands multidisciplinary skills. Combining science and imagery simplifies the use of the system and popularizes it. The alliance of the natural sciences, life sciences, mathematics, and data storage reduces individual control over personal information, prompting Ontario's information and privacy commissioner to offer a dystopian prophecy: "The fear is that each element of 'choice' will ultimately disappear from the sphere of identity."[18] In other words, a system designed to preserve a precise record of vast numbers of bodies beyond the limits of space and time also poses a grave threat to those bodies. As Lyon wrote, the proliferation of biometric systems "bring[s] the 'border' to other

16. Ann Cavoukian, "Consumer Biometric Applications: A Discussion Paper," Legislative Assembly of Toronto, September 1999, 16, http://www.ipc.on.ca/english/pubpres/papers/cons-bio.htm (site discontinued).

17. Gilles Deleuze and Félix Guattari, *A Thousand Plateaus: Capitalism and Schizophrenia*, trans. Brian Massumi (Minneapolis: University of Minnesota Press, 1987), 8.

18. Cavoukian, "Consumer Biometric Applications," 32.

locations than the edges or territory, thus further virtualizing it."[19] Indeed, the biometric system and other high-tech surveillance devices require a new consideration of the very concept of borders. Contemporary borders have gradually been transformed into what the architect and researcher Eyal Weizman has characterized as "a discontinuous and fragmented series of self-enclosed barriers that can be better understood as a prevalent 'condition' of segregation—a shifting frontier—rather than one continuous line neatly cutting the territory in two."[20]

By setting out to overcome the limits of space and time, the biometric system threatens to act as a wave of algorithms that erases our notion of self. To Foucault, the erasure of the human a few decades after the "death of God" signaled the end of an era: "As the archaeology of our thought easily shows, man is an invention of recent date. And one perhaps nearing its end."[21] By the end of the 1970s, Foucault would pursue the question of the imminent end of humanity. In a similar pursuit, Deleuze and Guattari described human faces in *A Thousand Plateaus* as "not basically individual; they define zones of frequency or probability." Starting from the mechanism rather than the human, for Deleuze and Guattari the face is "a suggestive whiteness, a hole that captures. [...] Concrete faces cannot be assumed to come ready-made. They are engendered by an abstract machine of faciality." Now, "the abstract machine [...] produces faces according to the changeable combinations of its cogwheels. Do not expect," they warn us, "the abstract machine to resemble what it produces, or will produce."[22]

Today's biometric technology hardly differs from the white abstract machine Deleuze and Guattari envisaged. Beyond the age of the rhizome, we experience its integration and "interiorization" as an operating system.[23] This biometric heterotopia/heterochronia relies on three elements: one, a vast digital storage space; two,

19. Lyon, *Surveillance Studies*, 121.

20. Eyal Weizman, *Hollow Land: Israel's Architecture of Occupation* (London: Verso, 2007), 177.

21. Foucault, *The Order of Things*, 386–87.

22. Deleuze and Guattari, *A Thousand Plateaus*, 168.

23. Weizman has pointed out how the Israel Defense Forces used Deleuze and Guattari's reading of Kafka to rethink its counterterror strategy. See Eyal Weizman, "Walking through Walls: Soldiers as Architects in the Israeli-Palestinian Conflict," *Radical Philosophy*, no. 136 (March/April 2006): 11.

a cloak of constitutional darkness accompanying manifestations of authority; and three, a great speed of execution.[24] Digital space, concealment, and speed are the three basic elements of the biopolitical age. All three rely on their distance from the actual body, and all three enable the invasion and transformation of the private sphere.

The Case of Israel-Palestine

In October 2018, an in-depth article by two journalist-activists was published in the liberal daily *Haaretz* that traced the sale of biometric and other surveillance technology by the Israeli companies Black Cube and NSO to dictatorial regimes, as well as their collaboration with the Israeli Mossad and secret service, especially in the West Bank.[25] The companies' surveillance technology was involved in well-known political scandals in Brazil and Mexico and was used by the Saudi government to track and murder the journalist Jamal Khashoggi. An investigation revealed that the NSO-developed spying program Pegasus led to the arrest of dissenters and civil-rights activists in Africa, South America, and the Middle East. The program allows NSO to retrieve content on a targeted phone or computer and share it with the client for a high fee. Black Cube was allegedly hired by President Donald Trump's aides to follow senior advisors and government functionaries of

24. Jacques Rancière wrote about such convergences as "heterochronies" following Foucault's analysis of heterotopias as "spaces that don't fit in the normal distribution of territories" and heterochronies as "combinations of times that are normally incompatible." Jacques Rancière, "In What Time Do We Live?," in *The State of Things*, ed. Marta Kuzma, Pablo Lafuente, and Peter Osborne (London: Koenig Books, 2012), 34.

25. The Israeli state hides the level of cooperation with such surveillance tools, but independent investigations have discovered the use of Pegasus by the state, and Israeli officials admitted that the sale and use of the tool won the approval of the security forces. See, for example, Phineas Rueckert, "NSO's Pegasus: The Israeli Cyber Weapon Oppressive Regimes Used against 180 Journalists," *Haaretz*, July 18, 2021, https://www.haaretz.com/israel-news/tech-news/.premium-nso-s-pegasus-the-israeli-cyber-weapon-used-against-180-journalists-1.10010446; Wayne Madsen, "Pegasus and NSO at Center of Sweeping and Dangerous Mossad Surveillance Operation," *Intrepid Report*, July 21, 2021, http://www.intrepidreport.com/archives/33154; Elizabeth Dwoskin, "Israel Escalates Surveillance of Palestinians with Facial Recognition Program in West Bank," *Washington Post*, November 8, 2021, https://www.washingtonpost.com/world/middle_east/israel-palestinians-surveillance-facial-recognition/2021/11/05/3787bf42-26b2-11ec-8739-5cb6aba30a30_story.html.

the Obama administration.[26] Recent reports about the Indian government using WhatsApp Messenger to plant phishing and spying malware on civil-rights activists' phones sounds incredibly similar to what happened in Israel.[27] Veterans of the cyber-spying unit 8200 in the Israeli Defense Forces (IDF) are employed by Black Cube and NSO. The high-profile military unit is known as a "greenhouse," preparing young skilled programmers for the private sector of Israeli security. In fact, such companies copy the military unit's internal structure and vocabulary.

Surveillance is the bread and butter of much of the current high-tech industry in the West. Portions of the collaboration between the US and Israel in such activities became too toxic when the spyware was found to be used against American officials and interests.[28] The US Department of Commerce put four spyware firms based in Israel, Russia, and Singapore on its list of "sanctioned entities," and while it publicly discussed the damage done by the Israeli group, it ignored, for the most part, the direct involvement of American industries and politicians, or areas where the collaboration continued to serve shared interests.[29] The list of sanctioned entities—to which other Israeli firms have since been added—is minimal and ignores gross human-rights violations when they do not counter US interests. As a result of the sanctions, Israeli sources reported a reshuffling of positions inside

26. Mark Townsend and Julian Borger, "Revealed: Trump Team Hired Spy Firm for 'Dirty Ops' on Iran Arms Deal," *Guardian*, May 5, 2018, https://www.theguardian.com/uk-news/2018/may/05/trump-team-hired-spy-firm-dirty-ops-iran-nuclear-deal; Oliver Holmes, "Israel Intel Firm Denies It Was Hired by Trump Aides to Discredit Obama Officials," *Guardian*, May 7, 2018, https://www.theguardian.com/world/2018/may/07/israel-intel-firm-black-cube-trump-obama-iran-nuclear-deal.

27. "Timing of 2019 WhatsApp-NSO Hack in India Validates Leaked Database Accessed by Pegasus Project," *Wire*, September 27, 2021, https://thewire.in/tech/timing-of-2019-whatsapp-nso-hack-in-india-validates-leaked-database-accessed-by-pegasus-project.

28. "Ex-Obama Official Exits Israeli Spyware Firm amid Press Freedom Row," *Guardian*, February 4, 2022, https://www.theguardian.com/world/2020/feb/04/ex-obama-official-juliette-kayyem-quits-israeli-spyware-firm-amid-press-freedom-row; "Israeli Company's Spyware Is Used to Target US Embassy Employees in Africa," *New York Times*, December 3, 2021, https://www.nytimes.com/2021/12/03/us/politics/phone-hack-nso-group-israel-uganda.html.

29. See "Commerce Adds NSO Group and Other Foreign Companies to Entity List for Malicious Cyber Activities," U.S. Department of Commerce, November 3, 2021, https://www.commerce.gov/news/press-releases/2021/11/commerce-adds-nso-group-and-other-foreign-companies-entity-list.

NSO but also increased interest in related firms or collaborators that are already involved in numerous scandals. In turn, reports about the ongoing expansion of surveillance and ensuing scandals have followed. In summer 2023, the US Department of Commerce extended the sanctions to another Israeli spyware firm that was involved in surveilling liberal politicians and human-rights activists in Greece.[30]

The Israeli Case as a Model of White Biopolitics/Biometrics
For many, biometrics and the erasure of privacy sound like a "soft" form of power, or a cost worth paying for technological innovation and crime control. In 2009–10, I wrote a critical policy paper with Avner Pinchuk, lawyer and director of the privacy desk at the Association for Civil Rights in Israel, about the creation of the Israeli biometric database.[31] The paper details not only the motivation of the legislators—most of them centrists, which is worth noting—but also the unconstitutional procedural tricks they pulled to approve the database, which was originally meant to share biometric data among the army, police, major banks, and hospitals. This Big Brother model was eventually pared down after it was twice brought before the Israeli Supreme Court, which forced the government to build a pilot program that it had tried to avoid. However, as an expert explained during a gathering we organized at the Faculty of Law at Tel Aviv University on May 7, 2009, the same people who work with such data during their army service advance to positions in the police or private sector.[32] They bring with them skills and connections that enable the sharing of data among different governmental organs or between the public and

30. AFP, "US Blacklists Israeli-Controlled Firms behind Predator Spyware," *Times of Israel*, July 18, 2023, https://www.timesofisrael.com/us-blacklists-israeli-controlled-firms-behind-predator-spyware/.

31. Nitzan Lebovic and Avner Pinchuk, "The State of Israel and the Biometric Database Law: Political Centrism and the Post-Democratic State," Israel Democracy Institute, June 20, 2010, https://en.idi.org.il/articles/6823. For a wider historical and theoretical interpretation, see Nitzan Lebovic, "Biometrics, or the Power of the Radical Center," *Critical Inquiry* 41, no. 4 (Summer 2015): 841–68.

32. Among the participants at the gathering were representatives of the Knesset Research and Information Center; the director of information technology at the Ministry of Justice; the legal advisor to the Knesset's Constitution, Law and Justice Committee; professors of law; representatives from the secret service and prime minister's office; and a director of Metaform, which oversaw the technology and safety of the database.

private sectors. In one of the unpublished documents we exposed in our paper, at a July 2009 meeting, Minister of the Interior Meir Sheetrit, a liberal Likud party member, explained the logic of the database: "The purpose of the new [biometric] IDs is to know who is truly an Israeli. It isn't really clear in many cases, and endangers the security of the state."[33] According to Article 21 of the Biometric Database Law, the security forces have unlimited access to the biometric database. This access was granted as an exception to the law, and its language of deregulation enabled a hybrid of state organs and private corporations to participate and then sell surveillance technology that was tried out, and proven "reliable," in the Gaza Strip and the West Bank. "The paradox here," as Mattelart explained in a short section in his book about the IDF's use of biometric technology, "is that the specifically Israeli mode of putting the concept of national security into practice developed outside any official ad hoc doctrine."[34] The database became fully operative in 2017.

In his 2006 essay "What Is an Apparatus?," Giorgio Agamben identified "a new European norm [that] imposes biometric apparatuses on all its citizens by developing and perfecting anthropometric technologies invented in the nineteenth century in order to identify recidivist criminals [...] Surveillance by means of video cameras transforms the public space of the city into the interior of an immense prison. In the eyes of authority—and maybe rightly so—nothing looks more like a terrorist than the ordinary man. [... This] is the beginning, and, at the same time, the vanishing point of every politics."[35] For Agamben and other critics, the zero point of politics is also where sovereignty and its biopolitical methods of control are revealed in their most comprehensive form.

My essay has built on the realization that a new form of European or white biopolitics is now operating globally. However, it is impossible to argue theoretically about the case without taking

33. From the minutes of the Joint Committee session, July 23, 2009, quoted in Lebovic and Pinchuk, "Israel and the Biometric Database Law," note 17 (translation by the authors).

34. Mattelart, *Globalization of Surveillance*, 157.

35. Giorgio Agamben, "What Is an Apparatus?," in *What Is an Apparatus? and Other Essays*, trans. David Kishik and Stefan Pedatella (Stanford, CA: Stanford University Press, 2009), 23–24.

into consideration that its political semantics still owe their soul to the colonial-racist system of the nineteenth century. In *Along the Archival Grain*, the anthropologist and historian Ann Laura Stoler explained that colonial archives enabled a "state sovereignty [that] resides in the power to designate arbitrary social facts of the world as matters of security and concerns of the state."[36] She might as well have been writing about biometric archives. This digital storehouse exists, as Foucault said when discussing the potentiality of archives, "outside time and place [...]. Its threshold of existence is established by the discontinuity that separates us from what we can no longer say."[37] But the absolute trust-based aspiration of biometric archives enables the simultaneous colonization of outside and inside because of "archival events [...] that realign the certainties of the probable more than they mark wholesale reversals of direction."[38] More specifically, white biopolitics/biometrics enables the "outlawing" of the Palestinian or Black body as a tool, an "apparatus," for, as the scholar Calvin Warren writes, "outlawing is outside law, since it contravenes the ethical imperative to see the invisible, and also inside law, since it enables and conditions this very imperative—the censure is at the very heart of the law."[39]

36. Ann Laura Stoler, *Along the Archival Grain: Epistemic Anxieties and Colonial Common Sense* (Princeton, NJ: Princeton University Press, 2009), 26.

37. Michel Foucault, *The Archaeology of Knowledge*, trans. A. M. Sheridan Smith (New York: Routledge, 2002), 147.

38. Stoler, *Along the Archival Grain*, 51.

39. Outlawing is a term that serves Warren to overcome the ontological difference at the heart of Western ethics and identify "the physical black body [as] a distortion and an ontic illusion." Calvin L. Warren, *Ontological Terror: Blackness, Nihilism, and Emancipation* (Durham, NC: Duke University Press, 2018), 65, 71.

Digital Colonialism

Felix Stalder

In the following, I want to bring together two perspectives on fascism that belong to very different intellectual traditions. One is poet and politician Aimé Césaire's notion, paraphrased by the editors of this volume, that "what in Europe is called 'fascism' is just colonial violence finding its way back home."[1] The other is economic historian Karl Polanyi's inference that fascism appeals to certain segments of society by appearing as a "protective counter-movement" against the ravages of radical laissez-faire capitalism, which undermines the reproduction of society by treating labor, land, and money as nothing but commodities.[2] At first glance, these two perspectives seem to offer competing explanations for the same phenomenon, but I see them as building on each other. In other words, the rising fascist sentiment in the West today can be seen, at least in part, as a reaction to people revolting against the experience of their own colonization.

This raises a number of questions: What is the structure of colonial violence that is now coming back? What are the contemporary mechanisms by which this structure is being implemented, and what is the shape of the defensive reactions specific to these mechanisms?

Césaire expressed the basic mechanism of colonialism as an equation: "colonization = 'thingification.'"[3] That is, at the heart of the colonial project lies the reduction of people, cultures, and natures to the status of mere objects without inherent dignity, agency, or value; their value rather lies exclusively in their ability to be exploited. Of course, this project never fully succeeded in

1. Kader Attia, Anselm Franke, and Ana Teixeira Pinto, "Curatorial Statement: The White West IV," Haus der Kulturen der Welt, accessed May 18, 2022, https://www.hkw.de/en/programm/projekte/2021/the_white_west_iv/the_white_west_iv_kuratorisches_statement/text.php.

2. Karl Polanyi, *The Great Transformation: The Political and Economic Origins of Our Time* (Boston: Beacon Press, 2012), 144.

3. Aimé Césaire, *Discourse on Colonialism*, ed. Robin D. G. Kelley, trans. Joan Pinkham (New York: Monthly Review Press, 2000), 42.

robbing people of their dignity and agency.[4] Thingification was not only attempted through direct violence; it was rather the consequence of a comprehensive ideological and administrative system of which direct violence was but one expression. The system was characterized by a specific economy based on what one could call, following David Harvey, "appropriation by dispossession"[5]—of labor through slavery or other forms of bondage, of land through legalized theft, of resources through forced labor working the land. The effects of this economic system were an extreme concentration of wealth in the hands of the colonizers and widespread misery on the side of the colonized. Like all economies, this one was also embedded in and supported by a system of governance that treated the colonized not as subjects but as objects. By denying people their subjectivity, it became possible to impose, with no regard to the "non-subject's" own sense of self, descriptive and administrative categories that did not need to be explained and could not be appealed. The administrative system was based on a legal system that created, at least in the eyes of the colonizers, a semblance of justification and lawfulness, shielding it from challenges from within. It supported the imposition of rules, procedures, and contracts to enact appropriation by dispossession. A historically notorious example of such imposition is the Spanish Requirement of 1513, a legal document read to Indigenous peoples in the Americas, who did not understand Spanish, to inform them of their submission to the pope and the king and to justify the crushing of any resistance in the name of God. As the text stressed, the acceptance was "of their own free will," though failing that, "the deaths and losses which shall accrue from this are your fault."[6] Many other similar laws and edicts would follow that gave a veneer of legality to enslavement, theft, and destruction. More indirect but no less consequential was an epistemic form of violence also enacted through the law: a colonial legal system that eradicated

4. Peter Linebaugh and Marcus Rediker, *The Many-Headed Hydra: Sailors, Slaves, Commoners, and the Hidden History of the Revolutionary Atlantic*, 2nd ed. (Boston: Beacon Press, 2013).

5. David Harvey, "The 'New' Imperialism: Accumulation by Dispossession," in *The New Imperial Challenge*, ed. Leo Panitch and Colin Leys, vol. 40 of *Socialist Register* (London: Monthly Review Press, 2003), 63–87.

6. Angela Weiler, "The Requerimiento (1513)," *Open Anthology of Earlier American Literature*, ed. Timothy Robbins, accessed May 18, 2022, https://press.rebus.community/openamlit/chapter/the-requerimiento.

other ways of organizing the social. In his 1956 essay "Colonialism Is a System," Jean-Paul Sartre wrote about the export of the French legal system to Algeria, particularly the Code Civil, often regarded as one of the crowning achievements of the French Enlightenment, which codified theoretical concepts such as private property and the rule of law, enabling the destruction of communal forms of land ownership since only individual ownership was recognized.[7] Applied to Algeria, large swaths of agricultural land that seemed to belong to nobody were there for the taking. Dividing the land furthermore forced peasants onto ever-more fragmented plots of land that could then be bought cheap by the French colonialists.

In practice, legalized dispossession was made operational through the rollout of infrastructure and organizational methods. Under the colonial matrix, newly built infrastructure generally reorganized the land for maximal extraction through the creation of ports, roads, railways, and telegraph systems that supported this agenda rather than serving the local population, which, to the degree that it did, was a secondary or unintended consequence.[8] To make full use of the infrastructure and generate the profit to expand it, new management techniques were invented, most importantly the plantation, which provided the blueprint for the factory, in terms of spatial layout, division of labor, and accounting practices.[9] These techniques were embedded in an ideological system that declared acts of appropriation by dispossession to be something else, namely the application of impersonal law, which justified them in moral terms. This ideology, detailed by Edward Said in *Orientalism*, ran on two levels. One was the devaluation of local cultures, knowledges, and practices—if not simply ignored, they were declared primitive, backward, of no value to the march of progress; if they were valued, it was as a projection screen for exoticized, heavily gendered fantasies. The other level was the colonizers' claim to superiority of their own civilization—its

7. Jean-Paul Sartre, "Colonialism Is a System," *Interventions* 3, no. 1 (2001): 127–40, https://doi.org/10.1080/13698010020027074.

8. Jessica Ackerman, "The Infrastructural Boom of Colonialism," Edges of Empire, April 30, 2015, https://people.smu.edu/knw2399/2015/04/30/the-infrastructural-boom-of-colonialism/.

9. Caitlin Rosenthal, *Accounting for Slavery: Masters and Management* (Cambridge, MA: Harvard University Press, 2018).

cultures, religions, and technologies.[10] Given the postulated chasm between Indigenous and Western culture, the colonizers saw no need to learn anything from the other; rather, their own worldview could be simply imposed on people deemed too primitive to help themselves. There was no need to ask people about their own reasoning, which, as "things," they were not deemed capable of possessing anyway. Acts of resistance were interpreted as yet more signs of backwardness that served to justify more draconian impositions.

Neo-behaviorism

Today, thingification is achieved through the widespread implementation of a digitally supercharged form of behaviorism (often called "social physics"[11]): the understanding of people based exclusively on behavioral acts that can be observed and measured externally. Behaviorism was, in the aftermath of the Second World War, a highly influential branch of psychology that aims to put the field on a "scientific," that is, strictly empiricist, footing by replacing the recounting of one's own mental states, which was deemed subjective and unreliable, with third-party observations, which, in contrast, were deemed objective and reliable. Hence people's self-knowledge was of no value, and there was no need to talk to them. Not only could mental states—reflections, moods, feelings, and interpretations—not be observed, and were thus outside the bounds of science, they were also considered illusions, epiphenomena created by repeatedly experiencing the consequences of one's behavior.

To this approach, radical behaviorism, usually associated with the psychologist B. F. Skinner, added the idea of control through "environmental modification" and "operant conditioning"—if the motivation of behavior lay not in a subject's inner world but only in their experience of external stimuli, then it was logical to use these external factors for control purposes. "Environmental modification" means changing the environment in which the object of study exists so that certain actions become more likely than others. Contemporary theories call this "nudging," small inputs

10. See Edward W. Said, *Orientalism* (New York: Vintage Books, 1979).
11. Alex Pentland, *Social Physics: How Social Networks Can Make Us Smarter* (New York: Penguin Books, 2015).

and design interventions that steer people in the desired direction. As a governance system it is described as "libertarian paternalism"—that is, leaving people formally free to choose their own courses of action while creating a top-down "choice architecture" that favors certain outcomes over others.[12] The other technique proposed by Skinner is "operant conditioning," which rewards desirable behavior and punishes undesirable behavior. Once again, the objects are not directly coerced to do certain actions; rather they simply had to adapt to the predetermined consequences of their agency. With the removal of mental states, the difference disappeared between thinking and nonthinking, subject and object, human and animal, and Skinner studied the "behavior of organisms" rather than of people.[13]

Although Skinner's radical behaviorism had wide appeal deep into the 1970s—some of his books became bestsellers—the theories were always controversial. This was in part because behavior—"action of the organism upon the outside world"[14]—was exceedingly difficult to precisely measure outside the laboratory, and behavioral acts much more ambiguous to code. Hence the idea of gaining comprehensive knowledge of human beings through distanced observation of their actions remained question-able; Noam Chomsky was not the only one who called it a "pseudo-science."[15] But that was only part of its problem. Radical behaviorism was also criticized as fundamentally authoritarian on two levels. First, because there was such an extreme knowledge differential between the observer and the observed: only the observer held valid, that is scientific, knowledge, while the observed held no useful knowledge at all, whether the observed was a pigeon (Skinner's favorite animal)[16] or a person. Thus there was no way to contest the judgment of the observer. Second,

12. Richard H. Thaler and Cass R. Sunstein, *Nudge: Improving Decisions about Health, Wealth, and Happiness* (New Haven, CT: Yale University Press, 2008), 20–21.

13. Burrhus F. Skinner, *The Behavior of Organisms: An Experimental Analysis* (New York: Appleton-Century-Crofts, 1938).

14. Skinner, 6.

15. Noam Chomsky, "The Case Against B. F. Skinner," *New York Review of Books*, December 30, 1971, https://chomsky.info/19711230/.

16. Jérôme Ségal, "The Pigeon and the Predictor: Miscarriage of a Cyborg in Spite of Foundations Supports," in *American Foundations and Large-Scale Research: Construction and Transfer of Knowledge*, ed. G. Gemelli (Bologna: Editions CLUEB, 2001), 131–57, http://jerome-segal.de/Publis/pigeon.html.

behaviorism was never simply about disinterested observation; it was about "improving" the condition of the observed. But it remained unclear what counted as an improvement, who would determine it, and who could set environmental variables and structures of positive and negative reinforcement. In practice, this was simply done by the observers themselves.[17]

Digital Colonialism as a System

The resurgence of behaviorism as the operative method of corporate digital media is driven by three developments. First, all our mediated actions leave traces, and ever-more actions are being mediated in order to leave even more traces, creating opportunities to observe behavior across a wide range of contexts with a degree of detail that first-wave behaviorists could not achieve in the laboratory. Now seemingly everything can be observed all the time, and the minutest conclusions can be drawn. And these observations allow seemingly deep insights. Studies claim that by analyzing about two hundred "likes" on Facebook (about twenty months of average use), a person's psychological profile drawn up by the platform matches the assessment made by the person's spouse.[18] There are, of course, many problems with these kinds of comparisons—not least the category of profiling itself—but they are taken by the tech industry as evidence that the methodological problems of understanding a person through behavioral observation have been solved. Second, environmental modification (changing the input variables) and reinforcement learning (selecting the most promising outputs for further learning) are the two basic artificial intelligence systems driving new models of "intelligence" more generally. In other words, critical reflection or self-awareness is no longer seen as a prerequisite for intelligent behavior. Third, the political problem of how to set the categories for coding observation and the goals for "modification" and "learning" have been

17. Jack W. Johnston, "An Evaluation of the Major Criticisms of the Behaviourist Revolution in the Political Sciences. 21/10/2016," Jack Johnston, July 22, 2017, https://jackwjohnston.wordpress.com/2017/07/22/an-evaluation-of-the-major-criticisms-of-the-behaviourist-revolution-in-the-political-sciences-21102016/.

18. Wu Youyou, Michal Kosinski, and David Stillwell, "Computer-Based Personality Judgments Are More Accurate than Those Made by Humans," *Proceedings of the National Academy of Sciences* 112, no. 4 (2015): 1036–40, https://doi.org/10.1073/pnas.1418680112.

neutered by delegating them to the algorithms that seemingly find correlations within big data that humans cannot as well as by bland talk of "efficiency," "personalization," and "empowerment."

Of course, such instrumental means do not exist in a void but are embedded in a comprehensive system that realizes them in a particular form. In the present case, thingification is part of an extractivist system. It builds on older, (neo)colonial systems of extraction, but is different insofar as the extraction is not directly physical but a process of abstraction through which a myriad of lifeworlds is measured so that they can be translated into proprietary knowledge for the new centers of power. This economic system has been described as "surveillance capitalism"—that is, a system that gathers as much data as possible in order to understand and influence people, and then rents out that capacity to the highest bidder.[19] Deeply intertwined with this economic rationale, sometimes leading it, sometimes following it, are security concerns both within and between nation-states.

This economic system is made possible by a particular technical infrastructure connecting billions of distributed computers (stationary and mobile) and sensors to vast centralized data centers through airwaves reaching to satellites in the sky and through cables lying on the seabed. In these data centers, the "raw" data can be analyzed according to the changing requirements of the owners. This infrastructure not only opens up societies around the world to data extraction but also provides the means of environmental modification and operant conditioning through which behavior modification is effected.[20] Since this economic system as a whole focuses more than ever on manipulating people's behavior—throughout the twentieth century this was mainly the focus of a distinct subsystem of the economy, namely advertising—economic wealth and political power move ever closer together, fueling speculation that a tech CEO such as Mark Zuckerberg might run for the office of president of the United States.

The extraction of data and experience is supported by a legal system that shields it from challenges. The present-day equivalent of the Spanish Requirement is the end-user legal agreement that

19. Shoshana Zuboff, *The Age of Surveillance Capitalism: The Fight for a Human Future at the New Frontier of Power* (New York: PublicAffairs, 2018).

20. Yasha Levine, *Surveillance Valley: The Secret Military History of the Internet* (New York: PublicAffairs, 2018).

all users must adhere to by clicking "accept"—a text that seems purposefully impenetrable to most people and allows for changes without reauthorization. On the international level, policies for the "free flow" of data are championed, a euphemism for the unrestricted centralization of data across borders.[21] Equally important are the various legal mechanisms that ensure that breaking the law when it does not actively support extraction carries only minor consequences that can be factored in as a cost of doing business. Thus far, not even legislation at the European level (most notably the General Data Protection Regulation in place since May 2018) has been able to substantially affect this system of extraction.

The ideological glue that justifies the entire system of thingification is the claim of the superiority of machinic knowledge articulated on both a popular and a scientific level. Big data is assumed to fulfill the promise of revealing the world as it is rather than as it appears to the limited sensory and cognitive capacities of ordinary humans.[22] This claim has two consequences. First, this type of knowledge is concentrated in a small number of institutions that construct themselves as black boxes although its production depends on vast amounts of resources—computing power, data, and algorithms.[23] Second, these knowledge claims, and the actions based on them, cannot be challenged, since machinic knowledge is, by definition, superior to anything outsiders can muster. Thus, the elevation of machine-generated knowledge goes hand in hand with a devaluation of human knowledge based on direct experience and critical reflection. As Zuboff concludes, "A pathological division of learning forged by unprecedented asymmetries of knowledge and power fixes us in a new inequality marked by the tuners and the tuned, the herders and herded, the raw material and its miners, the experimenters and their unwitting subjects, those who will the future and those who are shunted toward others' guaranteed outcomes."[24] Or perhaps more clearly, the colonizer

21. Parminder Jeet Singh and Jai Vipra, "Economic Rights over Data: A Framework for Community Data Ownership," *Development* 62, nos. 1–4 (2019): 53–57, https://doi.org/10.1057/s41301-019-00212-5.

22. Nathan Jurgenson, "View from Nowhere: On the Ideology of Big Data," *New Inquiry*, October 9, 2014, http://thenewinquiry.com/essays/view-from-nowhere/.

23. Frank Pasquale, *The Black Box Society: The Secret Algorithms That Control Money and Information* (Cambridge, MA: Harvard University Press, 2015).

24. Zuboff, *Age of Surveillance Capitalism*, 317.

and the colonized. As this system seems to fall within the space denoted by Césaire's original equation, it can be called yet another form of colonialism—digital colonialism. It operates on both national and geopolitical levels; for instance, the United States (and arguably also China) is pursuing its colonial project both internally and externally.[25] Advanced developing countries pursue policies that are anti-colonial on a geopolitical level (see, for example, India's rejection of Facebook's offer to deliver "free" internet access) while developing a colonial system internally.[26]

Neo-fascism as Countermovement

The authoritarian, far-right, and fascist tendencies within Western tech industries cannot alone explain the rising appeal of far-right politics across the world.[27] In the West, this attraction can be seen as a countermovement against the diffuse effects of digital colonialism. Polanyi's *Great Transformation* (1944) argued that unfettered laissez-faire capitalism undermines the reproduction of life by treating labor (human life), land (nature), and money as commodities, as things that are produced only to be sold in the market and thus subject to radically changing valuation until the point where there is no value to be gained and production is stopped. He called them "fictitious commodities," since neither life nor nature is produced by and for the market; rather they are produced outside it, relying on richer and more complex sets of relations. Neoliberal capitalism, particularly under austerity conditions, once again reduces labor and land, human life and nature, to mere commodity. Additionally, contemporary surveillance capitalism reduces all human communication and behavior to data-generation engines.[28]

25. Nick Couldry and Ulises Ali Mejias, *The Costs of Connection: How Data Is Colonizing Human Life and Appropriating It for Capitalism* (Stanford, CA: Stanford University Press, 2019).

26. Rahul Bhatia, "The Inside Story of Facebook's Biggest Setback," *Guardian*, May 12, 2016, https://www.theguardian.com/technology/2016/may/12/facebook-free-basics-india-zuckerberg; Rajesh Kasturirangan, "Authoritarian Regimes Are Using Algorithms to Control Minds and Power," *Quartz India*, October 3, 2019, https://qz.com/india/1720516/kashmir-to-lgbt-modi-and-bjp-use-algorithms-to-manipulate-minds/.

27. Ana Teixeira Pinto, "Capitalism with a Transhuman Face: The Afterlife of Fascism and the Digital Frontier," *Third Text* 33, no. 3 (2019): 315–36, https://doi.org/10.1080/09528822.2019.1625638.

28. Felix Stalder, "Anti-Kommunikation und Wertschöpfung," *Le Monde Diplomatique*, March 7, 2019, https://monde-diplomatique.de/artikel/!5571198.

And this data has meaning not for the humans who create it but for those who gather and analyze it. As by-products of the process of optimizing data generation, human meaning making is disorganized and human relations devalued. A widespread feeling of being manipulated, of the available narratives not being able to account for what is happening, is driving all kinds of conspiracy theories that provide graphic metaphors for diffuse and confusing experiences. Political elites might not be drinking the blood of children, as the QAnon conspiracy theory claims, but the YouTube algorithm that feeds videos to children does not have their mental well-being at heart, and rather pursues a relentless strategy of data extraction and behavior modification in the pursuit of profit maximization.[29]

The far-right political program is gaining popularity against the background of experiences of sudden thingification. But rather than addressing the underlying dynamic, it offers its followers an easy solution: supremacy at the expense of others, which it fortifies by rooting it in what is constructed as unchangeable and deeply physical, beyond the reach of the system of digital manipulation—that is, race. Taken together, the process of thingification through digital colonialism and the countermovement of constructing an outside through the oppression of others create the coalition of far-right new elites and people finding themselves, to their surprise, in the position of being colonized. This profoundly destructive process can only be countered by fighting against the reduction of people's bodies and experiences to commodities—a rejection not of technology but of the dominant techno-political paradigm of this new internal colonialism.

29. James Bridle, "Something Is Wrong on the Internet," Medium, November 6, 2017, https://medium.com/@jamesbridle/something-is-wrong-on-the-internet-c39c471271d2.

Contributors

Larne Abse Gogarty is a writer and art historian. She works as a lecturer in art history and art theory at the Slade School of Fine Art, University College London. Gogarty is the author of *What We Do Is Secret: Contemporary Art and the Antinomies of Conspiracy* (Sternberg Press, 2023) and *Usable Pasts: Social Practice and State Formation in American Art* (Brill, 2022), and has published in *Art Monthly, New Socialist, Tate Papers,* and *Third Text,* among other publications. In 2020, she and Andrew Hemingway edited a special issue of *Kunst und Politik* on "Keywords for Marxist Art History."

Norman Ajari is a lecturer in Francophone Black studies at the University of Edinburgh. He is the author of *Darkening Blackness: Race, Gender, Class, and Pessimism in 21st-Century Black Thought* (Polity, 2023) and *Dignity or Death: Ethics and Politics of Race* (Polity, 2022). Ajari is a member of the international board of the Frantz Fanon Foundation.

Ramon Amaro is a senior researcher in digital culture at the Nieuwe Instituut, Rotterdam. His writings, research, and artistic practice emerge at the intersections of Black study, digital culture, psychosocial study, and the critique of computational reason. His book *The Black Technical Object: On Machine Learning and the Aspiration of Black Being* (Sternberg Press, 2023) contemplates the abstruse nature of programming and mathematics, and the deep incursion of racial hierarchies, to inspire alternative approaches to contemporary algorithmic practice.

Kader Attia is a multidisciplinary artist who draws upon the lived experiences of two disparate cultural identities: Algerian and French. From this place of cultural intermediacy, Attia's practice interrogates sociopolitical complexities rooted in histories of colonialism and cultural obfuscation. In his practice, Attia employs poetic installations and sculptural assemblages to investigate the far-reaching emotional implications of Western cultural hegemony and colonial systems of power for non-Western subjectivities, focusing particularly on collective trauma and notions of repair.

Sladja Blazan is an interim professor in the English Department at the University of Marburg. She received her PhD from Humboldt-Universität zu Berlin and her habilitation from the University of Würzburg. She has taught at the University of Würzburg, New York University, Freie Universität Berlin, University College Dublin, and Bard College. Her areas of research include speculative fiction, critical posthumanism, environmental humanities, critical refugee studies, and migration as a literary topic. In addition to her academic career, Blazan has worked as a theater director, dramaturge, and translator.

Denise Ferreira da Silva is the Samuel Rudin Professor in the Humanities in the Department of Spanish and Portuguese at New York University. She is the author of *Unpayable Debt* (Sternberg Press, 2022) and *Toward a Global Idea of Race* (University of Minnesota Press, 2007). Her artworks include the films *Soot Breath / Corpus Infinitum* (2020) and *4 Waters: Deep Implicancy* (2018), with Arjuna Neuman; and Poethical Readings and the Sensing Salon, with Valentina Desideri. She has taught at the University of British Columbia,

Queen Mary University of London, University of São Paulo, Université de Paris VIII, and University of California, San Diego.

Anselm Franke is head of the Curatorial Studies program at the Zurich University of the Arts. From 2013 to 2022, he was the head of the visual arts and film department at Haus der Kulturen der Welt, Berlin, where he realized exhibition projects including "Ceremony: Burial of an Undead World" (2022, with Elisa Giuliano, Denise Ryner, Claire Tancons, and Zairong Xiang), "Love and Ethnology: The Colonial Dialectic of Sensitivity" (2019–20, with Diedrich Diederichsen), and "Neolithic Childhood: Art in a False Present, ca. 1930" (2018, with Tom Holert). He curated the 8th Taipei Biennial in 2012 and the 10th Shanghai Biennale in 2014, among others.

Donna V. Jones is an associate professor of English at the University of California, Berkeley. Her research interests include the literature of the Americas and the African diaspora, postcolonial literature, and critical theory. Her publication *The Racial Discourses of Life Philosophy: Négritude, Vitalism and Modernity* (Columbia University Press, 2010) was awarded the Jeanne and Aldo Scaglione Prize for Comparative Literary Studies. She is currently working on the project *The Promise of Decline: Race and Historical Pessimism in the Era of the Great War.*

Nitzan Lebovic is a professor of history and the Apter Chair of Holocaust Studies and Ethical Values at Lehigh University, Bethlehem, PA. He is the author of *Zionism and Melancholy: The Short Life of Israel Zarchi* (Indiana University Press, 2019), *The Philosophy of Life and Death: Ludwig Klages and the Rise of a Nazi Biopolitics* (Palgrave Macmillan, 2013), and the forthcoming *Homo Temporalis: Martin Buber, Walter Benjamin, Hannah Arendt, and Paul Celan about Time.* Lebovic coedited *Catastrophes: The History and Theory of an Operative Concept* (De Gruyter, 2014) and *The Politics of Nihilism: From the Nineteenth Century to Contemporary Israel* (Bloomsbury, 2014).

Olivier Marboeuf is a writer, curator, and film producer. In the 1990s, he and Yvan Alagbé founded Amok (now Frémok), a comic-book publisher, and from 2004 to 2018 he directed Espace Khiasma, a center for visual art and living literature in northeastern Paris. He currently divides his work between transmission, speculative writing, drawing, and film production with Spectre Productions. He recently published the essay *Suites décoloniales: S'enfuir de la plantation* (2022) and the poetry book *Les matières de la nuit* (2022), both with Éditions de Commun. A large part of his writing is available on his blog, *Toujours Debout*, https://olivier-marboeuf.com/.

A. Dirk Moses is the Anne and Bernard Spitzer Professor of International Relations at the City College of New York, CUNY. He is the author and editor of multiple publications on genocide and memory, including *The Problems of Genocide: Permanent Security and the Language of Transgression* (Cambridge University Press, 2021), and the senior editor of the *Journal of Genocide Research.*

Rijin Sahakian uses writing, art making, and teaching to examine the relationship of images and rhetoric to experiences of violence. She founded Sada, an arts-education initiative for Baghdad-based students, which operated from 2011 to 2015. Sahakian has been a visiting professor at the California Institute of the Arts, Santa Clarita, and a Fulbright, Art Matters, and Open Society fellow. Her work has been exhibited at the 22nd Biennial Sesc_Videobrasil (2023) and documenta fifteen (2022), and her writing has been published in *e-flux journal*, *n+1*, *Artforum*, *Al-Mutanabbi Street Starts Here*, *Warscapes*, and *World Records Journal*.

Nikhil Pal Singh is a professor of social and cultural analysis and history at New York University and chair of the Department of Social and Cultural Analysis. He is the author and editor of several books, including *Race and America's Long War* (University of California Press, 2017) and *Black Is a Country: Race and the Unfinished Struggle for Democracy* (Harvard University Press, 2004).

Kerstin Stakemeier is an educator at the Academy of Fine Arts Nuremberg and a writer who mostly works with others. In 2021, "Illiberal Arts," an exhibition she conceived with Anselm Franke, opened at Haus der Kulturen der Welt, Berlin; in 2023, "Illiberal Lives," its second iteration, curated with Eva Birkenstock, Franke, and Holger Otten, opened at Ludwig Forum, Aachen. Stakemeier coauthored *Universal Receptivity* with Bill Dietz (AdBK Nürnberg, 2021) and *Reproducing Autonomy: Work, Money, Crisis and Contemporary Art* with Marina Vishmidt (Mute, 2016). She is the author of *Entgrenzter Formalismus: Verfahren einer antimodernen Ästhetik* (Polypen, 2017).

Felix Stalder is a professor of digital culture at the Zurich University of the Arts. His work focuses on the intersection of culture, politics, and technology, particularly new modes of commons-based production, copyright, datafication, and the transformation of subjectivity. He recently was moderator of the mailing list nettime, a nexus of critical net culture. He is a member of the World-Information Institute and the Technopolitics Working Group, both based in Vienna. Stalder has written and coedited numerous books, including *From Commons to NFTs* (Aksioma, 2022), *Digital Unconscious: Nervous Systems and Uncanny Predictions!* (Autonomedia, 2021), and *Aesthetics of the Commons* (Diaphanes, 2021). http://felix.openflows.com

Ana Teixeira Pinto is a writer and cultural theorist based in Berlin. She is a professor of art theory at the University of Art, Braunschweig, and a theory tutor at the Dutch Art Institute. Her writings have appeared in publications such as *Third Text*, *Afterall*, *e-flux journal*, *Artforum*, and *Texte zur Kunst*. She is the editor of the book series On the Antipolitical published by Sternberg Press and the author of the forthcoming volume *Entropy and Chronopolitical Allegory*.

The White West
Fascism, Unreason, and the Paradox of Modernity

Edited by Kader Attia, Anselm Franke, and Ana Teixeira Pinto

Managing Editor: Max Bach
Proofreading: Danielle N. Carter
Graphic Design: Stuart Bertolotti-Bailey
Printing: Tallinn Book Printers, Estonia

ISBN 978-3-95679-533-6

Reprinted with the kind permission of the authors and publishers: Donna V. Jones, "Inheritance and Finitude: Toward a Literary Phenomenology of Time," *ELH: English Literary History* 85, no. 2 (2018): 289–303. © 2018 Johns Hopkins University Press; Denise Ferreira da Silva, "Fractal Thinking," *aCCeSsions*, no. 2, April 27, 2016, https://accessions.org/article2/fractal-thinking/; parts of Rijin Sahakian's "Anything You Can Imagine Is Here" first appeared on thederivative.org, an online publication of the Beirut Art Center; Larne Abse Gogarty, "The Art Right," *Art Monthly*, no. 405, April 2017.

Cover image: Rajkamal Kahlon, *You've Come a Long Way, Baby!*, 2011, detail. Courtesy of the artist.

Distributed by The MIT Press, Art Data, Les presses du réel, and Idea Books

Published by
Sternberg Press
71–75 Shelton Street
London WC2H 9JQ
www.sternberg-press.com

Realized with funds from Stadt Wien Kunst GmbH / Kunsthalle Wien

Stadt Wien Kunst GmbH
Kunsthalle Wien
Museumsplatz 1
A–1070 Vienna
www.kunsthallewien.at

Kunsthalle Wien is the city of Vienna's institution for international art and discourse.

kunstHalle wien
Stadt Wien | Kultur

Part of the HKW project *Das Neue Alphabet* (2019–22), supported by the Federal Government Commissioner for Culture and the Media due to a ruling of the German Bundestag.

Haus der Kulturen der Welt
John-Foster-Dulles-Allee 10
D-10557 Berlin
www.hkw.de

HKW
Haus der Kulturen der Welt

Haus der Kulturen der Welt is a business division of Kulturveranstaltungen des Bundes in Berlin GmbH (KBB).

Director: Bernd Scherer (until December 31, 2022)
Managing Director: Charlotte Sieben
Chairwoman of the Supervisory Board: Claudia Roth MdB, Federal Government Commissioner for Culture and the Media

Haus der Kulturen der Welt is supported by the Minister of State for Culture and the Media as well as by the Federal Foreign Office.

Minister of State
for Culture and the Media

Federal Foreign Office